OXFORD WORLD'S CLASSICS

THE NATURE OF THE GODS

MARCUS TULLIUS CICERO (106-43 BC) was the son of a Roman knight from Arpinum, some 70 miles,(112 km.) south-east of Rome. He rose to prominence through his eloquence at the bar and in the Senate; but, without hereditary connections or military achievements, he lacked a solid power-base; and so, in spite of strenuous manoeuvres, he failed to reconcile the youthful Pompey and later Octavian (Augustus) to the senate. In the Great Civil War of 49, he could have joined Caesar, but he refused and was eventually murdered at the insistence of Antony, whom he had castigated in his *Philippics*. But although Cicero was ultimately a political failure, he became for long periods of Europe's history not only a symbol of constitutional government but also a model of literary style. More important still, he is recognized as the main vehicle for the transmission of Hellenistic philosophy to the West. As a historian of thought, his discussions of philosophical systems were judicious. But in political theory, where he purported to be describing a constitution or framing laws, his conservatism tended to outweigh his intellectual open-mindedness. Hence, in his vision of political life, he remained above all an old-fashioned Roman.

P. G. WALSH was Emeritus Professor of Humanity at the University of Glasgow. His translations for Oxford World's Classics include Cicero's *On Obligations* and *Selected Letters*, Apuleius, *The Golden Ass*, Boethius, *The Consolation of Philosophy*, Petronius, *The Satyricon*, and Pliny, *Complete Letters*. He also published extensively on Livy, on the Roman novel, and on patristic and medieval Latin.

OXFORD WORLD'S CLASSICS

*For over 100 years Oxford World's Classics have brought
readers closer to the world's great literature. Now with over 700
titles—from the 4,000-year-old myths of Mesopotamia to the
twentieth century's greatest novels—the series makes available
lesser-known as well as celebrated writing.*

*The pocket-sized hardbacks of the early years contained
introductions by Virginia Woolf, T. S. Eliot, Graham Greene,
and other literary figures which enriched the experience of reading.
Today the series is recognized for its fine scholarship and
reliability in texts that span world literature, drama and poetry,
religion, philosophy and politics. Each edition includes perceptive
commentary and essential background information to meet the
changing needs of readers.*

OXFORD WORLD'S CLASSICS

━━

CICERO

The Nature of the Gods

━━

Translated with an Introduction and Notes by
P. G. WALSH

OXFORD
UNIVERSITY PRESS

OXFORD

UNIVERSITY PRESS

Great Clarendon Street, Oxford OX2 6DP

Oxford University Press is a department of the University of Oxford.
It furthers the University's objective of excellence in research, scholarship,
and education by publishing worldwide in

Oxford New York

Auckland Bangkok Buenos Aires Cape Town Chennai
Dar es Salaam Delhi Hong Kong Istanbul Karachi Kolkata
Kuala Lumpur Madrid Melbourne Mexico City Mumbai Nairobi
São Paulo Shanghai Taipei Tokyo Toronto

Oxford is a registered trade mark of Oxford University Press
in the UK and in certain other countries

Published in the United States
by Oxford University Press Inc., New York

First published as an Oxford World's Classics paperback 1998
Reissued 2008

British Library Cataloguing in Publication Data

Data available

Library of Congress Cataloging in Publication Data

Cicero, Marcus Tullius.
[De natura deorum. English]
The nature of the gods / Cicero; translated with an introduction
and notes by P. G. Walsh.
(Oxford world's classics)
Includes bibliographical references and index.
1. Gods, Roman. 2. Philosophy, Ancient. 3. Gods, Greek.
I. Walsh, P. G. (Patrick Gerard). II. Title. III. Series: Oxford
world's classics (Oxford University Press)
[PA6308.D4W35 1998] 292.07—dc21 97–38753

ISBN 978–0–19–954006–8

20

Printed in Great Britain by
Clays Ltd, Elcograf S.p.A.

For
David and Winifred

Acknowledgements

This translation is based on the text of Plasberg–Ax. I have checked my rendering regularly against the reliable version of H. Rackham in the Loeb series, and occasionally against the Penguin translation of H. C. P. McGregor. The annotations owe much to the learned edition of J. B. Mayor, and to a lesser degree to that of A. S. Pease. Details of these works are listed in the bibliography.

I am especially indebted to Professor Jonathan Powell, who has read the whole typescript, and has notably improved both the translation and the annotations. Professor Michael Winterbottom read a preliminary draft of the first sections of the translations and notes, and offered helpful criticisms, as did the anonymous reader who scrutinized the specimen on behalf of the Press. To all three I offer my grateful thanks.

P.G.W.

Contents

Abbreviations   x

Introduction   xi

Summary of the Text   xlvi

Note on the Text and Translation   xlix

Select Bibliography   lii

THE NATURE OF THE GODS   1

Explanatory Notes   147

Index and Glossary of Names   216

Abbreviations

ACW	*Ancient Christian Writers*
ANRW	*Aufstieg und Niedergang der römischen Welt*
BICS	*Bulletin of the Institute of Classical Studies*
CAH	*Cambridge Ancient History*
G&R	*Greece and Rome*
JRS	*Journal of Roman Studies*
Kirk–Raven–Schofield	G. S. Kirk, J. E. Raven, and M. Schofield, *The Presocratic Philosophers*[2] (Cambridge, 1983)
Latte	K. Latte, *Römische Religionsgeschichte* (Munich, 1960)
MRR	T. R. S. Broughton, *The Magistrates of the Roman Republic*
OCD	*Oxford Classical Dictionary*
REL	*Revue des Études Latines*
Warmington	E. H. Warmington, *Remains of Old Latin*[2], 3 vols. (Loeb edn., London, 1956)

Introduction

In recent years Cicero's philosophical works have enjoyed a modest rehabilitation; the respect they earned in western Europe during the Patristic era, in the medieval period (more patchily), and above all in the years from the Renaissance to the eighteenth century, has been partially restored. Our more indulgent and balanced climate once more recognizes him as an amateur philosopher of high culture and intelligence, for whom academic research and publication was always subordinated to political activity, but who returned with enthusiasm to his reading and writing when precluded from participation in affairs of state. The low esteem into which his philosophical writings fell in the nineteenth century was attributable to several factors: first, the general eclipse of his reputation at the hands of Theodore Mommsen, the great nineteenth-century historian of Rome, whose preference was for men 'of blood and iron'; second, the more rigorous approaches of the scientific historians of that era, who perused the treatises not so much to evaluate them for their intrinsic worth as to reconstruct the Greek sources on which Cicero naturally relied so heavily; and, above all, the nineteenth-century enthusiasm for the Greek genius as manifested in every branch of literature and art, so generously acknowledged by literate Romans, which encouraged a patronizing and dismissive judgement of the humbler Roman achievements. Cicero's own self-deprecating assessment of his studies in 45 BC ('These writings are mere copies, produced with no heavy labour; I supply only the words, of which I have a rich store') was often quoted in such condemnations, which tended to drown the temperate judgements of such outstanding scholars as J. S. Reid and J. B. Mayor.[1]

[1] For Mommsen's withering condemnation ('With equal peevishness and precipitation, he composed in a couple of months a philosophical library', exhibiting 'that sort

Cicero had no ambition to be an original thinker. The Roman society in which he lived was one to which philosophy had come late; treatises in Latin were virtually confined to recommendations of Epicureanism. His aim was to broaden the horizons of his contemporaries by introducing them to the wide-ranging ideas of the various Greek schools, and to accommodate their thinking within the different cultural framework of Roman tradition. He is therefore to be judged primarily as a Roman transmitter of Hellenistic philosophy, and since so much of the Greek originals has been lost, his work assumes a particular importance on this ground alone. Secondly, in setting these discussions within a Roman frame, he offers valuable insights into traditional Roman modes of thought when they are challenged by these Greek doctrines; as we shall note, this factor assumes particular importance for *The Nature of the Gods*.[2]

I

While still in his 'teens, and doubtless encouraged by a studious middle-class father at Arpinum, the precocious young Cicero sought instruction at Rome from eminent philosophers. He gained acquaintance with the Epicurean Phaedrus, who thereafter remained a cherished friend; he attended the lectures of the Stoic Diodotus, who became so close an associate that he resided in Cicero's house until his death in 59; and above all, Philo, the celebrated head of the Academic school, who had

of bungling which a man of letters who has not attained to philosophic thinking, or even to philosophic knowledge, and who works rapidly and boldly, shows in the reproduction of dialectic trains of thought'), see *History of Rome* (Everyman edn.). iv. 578 f. Cicero's (uncharacteristic) modesty is at *Att.* 12. 52. 3. For the more generous modern assessments, see e.g. A. E. Douglas in T. A. Dorey (ed.), *Cicero* (London, 1964), ch. 6; Elizabeth Rawson, *Cicero* (London, 1975), ch. 13; Paul MacKendrick, *The Philosophical Books of Cicero* (London, 1989); French scholars like André, Boyancé, Marrou, and Doignon have shown similar appreciation.

[2] For the Epicurean C. Amafinius and his successors, see *Acad.* 1. 6; *Fam.* 15. 16. 1. For their widespread influence, *Tusc.* 4. 6 f., in spite of their being *mali verborum interpretes* (*Fam.* 15. 19. 2). Lucretius is of course another matter; Cicero praises both his *ars* and his *ingenium*, and may even have edited his poem (*Ad Q. fratrem* 2. 10; Jerome, *Ad Euseb. Chron. ad ann. Abr. 94* (?93)).

come to Rome from Athens as a fugitive from the Mithridatic War about 87 BC, swept Cicero off his feet with his formidable combination of philosophical and rhetorical learning. This early acquaintance with prominent figures from the Greek world made him the most highly educated of emergent orators when he embarked on a forensic career in his mid-twenties; by this time he had already published a treatise on rhetoric, the *De inventione*, and a verse-rendering of the *Phaenomena* of Aratus; this translation of Hellenistic astronomical lore he was to exploit extensively in the second book of *The Nature of the Gods*.[3]

In the year 79, by which time Cicero had already made a name for himself in the courts, he decided to travel abroad to undertake further study. Plutarch suggests that this was a prudent departure to escape the wrath of the dictator Sulla, which Cicero had aroused by his defence of Roscius of Ameria, whose property Sulla's henchman Chrysogonus hoped to acquire; but Cicero himself states that his lungs were under strain through over-enthusiastic delivery in the courts, a condition which demanded rest and a revision of his pleading techniques. He remained abroad for two years, the first six months being spent in Athens. The new head of the Academy there was Antiochus of Ascalon, with whom Cicero struck up a close friendship; we shall note that Antiochus sought to establish a closer entente between the doctrines of Academics and Stoics, a position towards which Cicero appears to incline in the present treatise. Unfortunately there were no outstanding Stoic teachers in Athens at this time, so that we have little evidence of how Antiochus' ecumenical advances were received. Cicero seems to have spent much of his time in discussion with Epicureans; the leading figure of that school was Zeno of Sidon, whose lectures Cicero may have attended on the recommendation of Philo. Phaedrus, too, was back in Athens by this time, and Cicero with his friend Atticus attended his presentations. Another companion of his in

---

[3] For his early acquaintance with the Epicurean Phaedrus, see *Fam.* 13. 1. 2; as auditor of the Stoic Diodotus, *Acad.* 2. 115 (for Diodotus' death in 59, *Att.* 2. 20. 6); for his devotion to Philo at the age of 18, *Brutus* 306. For the *De inventione*, see G. Kennedy, *The Art of Rhetoric in the Roman World* (Princeton, 1972), 106 ff. For the translation of the *Phaenomena* of Aratus, see below 2. 104 ff., with nn.

Athens was Marcus Pupius Piso, whose allegiance was to the
Peripatetic school, and whose absence from this imaginary dialogue is regretted in the prologue; this friendship with Pupius
ensured that Cicero furthered his knowledge of the teachings of
Aristotle and his successors.[4]

From Athens Cicero journeyed to the Asian coastal cities; at
Smyrna he had conversations with the exiled Rutilius Rufus, a
committed Stoic who obtains a mention in this dialogue. He
then proceeded to Rhodes, with the main intention of deepening
his knowledge of rhetorical theory through meetings with his
former teacher Molon. But in Rhodes he also met the leading
Stoic of the age, Posidonius; through his works more than those
of any other Stoic he absorbed the main tenets of the school, and
he is cited in the dialogues more than any other single philosopher. Like Diodotus, Posidonius had earlier visited Rome, and
had doubtless met Cicero then.[5]

Thus as early as 77 BC Cicero had acquired a firm grasp of the
tenets of the Hellenistic schools, acquired through extended discussion with their leading scholars. The next fifteen years witnessed his meteoric rise to forensic and political eminence, from
his quaestorship in Sicily in 75, through his praetorship in 67 (in
which he emerged at the top of the poll), to his turbulent consulship in 63, in which he repressed the Catilinarian conspiracy.
Though he had little opportunity for protracted study during
this time, his surviving correspondence from 68 BC onwards indicates a continuing enthusiasm for the purchase and perusal of
scholarly works. Once he had stepped down from the consulship,
he set aside for study all the time he could spare from his forensic
activities. Thus in May 60 he informs Atticus of the gift of a collection of books from his friend Paetus, and he adds: 'Every day
I seek further relaxation in these studies, in the time I can spare

[4] Plutarch's allegation that Cicero left Rome through fear of Sulla is at Plut. *Cic.* 3; for
Cicero's own explanation, *Brutus* 313 ff. For his contacts with Antiochus, *Brutus*, 315,
Fin. 5. 1; with Zeno of Sidon, *Acad.* 1. 46; *Fin.* 1. 16 (and see 1. 59 below; does Cotta's
claim to have heard Zeno's lectures on Philo's recommendation actually represent
Cicero's experience?); with Phaedrus, in Atticus' company, *Fin.* 1. 16; with Pupius
Piso, *Fin.* 5. 1 ff.

[5] Conversations with Rutilius Rufus, *Rep.* 1. 13 (see also 3. 80 and 86 below); with
Posidonius in Rhodes, Plut. *Cic.* 4. 5; in Rome in 87, Plut. *Marius* 45. 4.

from my activities at law.' Other letters during this period reveal him studying the writings of the Peripatetics Dicaearchus and Theophrastus.[6]

But in early 58 his public and private activities alike were halted by Clodius' bill denying fire and water to anyone who had executed citizens without trial as Cicero had done with the Catilinarian conspirators; the hostile tribune followed this with a further bill in March which outlawed Cicero by name and confiscated his goods. Cicero anticipated condemnation by retiring to Macedonia, where he spent an unhappy eighteen months until a combination of Pompey's influence and popular support brought the repeal of his banishment. Following his return to Italy in August 57, his political impotence afforded him abundant leisure for study; between 55 and 52 he composed not only the three books of *De oratore*, with its extended discussion of the relationship between oratory and philosophy, but also *De republica* and *De legibus*, works of political philosophy which deliberately evoke by their titles the masterpieces of Plato, to which he repeatedly refers.[7]

On being appointed to the governorship of Cilicia, the largest Roman province in the East, Cicero left Rome in the spring of 51, and took the opportunity to revisit Athens en route. He expresses some disappointment at the decline of the city as a philosophical centre, remarking that Aristus, the brother of Antiochus, was the only outstanding figure in evidence. In the course of his journey from Athens to his province, he spent some time at Mitylene in the company of Cratippus, the Peripatetic who was later to become head of the Lyceum; Cicero praises him as the most considerable of all the Peripatetics he had heard. The various activities of a governor, military as well as administrative and judicial, diverted him from serious study in Cilicia, but on his journey home in late 50 he again visited

---

[6] For Paetus' gift, *Att.* 1. 20. 7; study of Dicaearchus and Theophrastus, *Att.* 2. 2. 2; 2. 3. 4 (late 60–early 59).

[7] For these studies between 57 and 52 see *Att.* 4. 10 f.; 4. 16. 3 'I followed the example of our divine Plato in his *Republic*'; 4. 18. 2 'I return to my books and studies, the life most suited to my nature'. For his reflections on the relationship between oratory and philosophy, see *De or.*, esp. 3. 56 ff.

Athens and resided with Aristus, renewing his acquaintance with other philosophers in the city. It is astonishing, and a reflection of his continuing engagement with philosophy, that he should be so eager to renew these links at a time when the dramatic conflict between the senate and Julius Caesar was about to explode into the Great Civil War.[8]

Cicero's career as an ardent senatorial, and more fundamentally his studies in political philosophy, made it inevitable that he would support Pompey and the senate against Caesar in 49–48 BC, in spite of his closer attraction to Caesar as an individual. Pompey is repeatedly criticized in the letters of this period for his arrogance and his uninspiring leadership. This disillusionment with his leadership continued after Cicero joined his camp in Macedonia. He did not participate in the decisive battle of Pharsalus in August 48, but remained at Dyrrhachium pleading poor health, and thereafter he remained conspicuously aloof from the continuing struggle. Caesar after his victory treated him generously as always, and he was allowed to return to Italy in October 48, but he deemed it prudent to remain in Brundisium until Caesar returned from the East in September 47.[9]

On his return to Rome, he had determined that if Caesar restored the republican constitution he would again involve himself in politics, but that otherwise he would serve the state in private with his scholarship. Of his two great scholarly enthusiasms, the theory and practice of oratory took immediate preference over philosophy; at this time in late 47 and early 46 he composed his history of Roman oratory, the *Brutus* (in which he claims that the Roman achievement stands comparison with that of the Greeks), and the *Orator*, an analysis of the ideal form of oratory based on consideration of the appropriate styles. Of lesser importance were the treatises *De optimo genere oratorum*, intended to serve as preface to translations of speeches by

[8] Disappointment in Athens, *Att.* 5. 10. 5. Meeting with Cratippus, *Timaeus* 1 ('parem summis Peripateticis', *Div.* 1. 5). His return visit to Athens, *Att.* 5. 20. 3, *Tusc.* 5. 22; meeting with other philosophers, *Att.* 7. 1. 1.

[9] Criticism of Pompey, *Att.* 7. 21. 1 'Our Gnaeus has . . . no spirit, no plan, no resources, no energy'; *Att.* 8. 2. 2 'I consider no statesman or general of any nation has ever behaved more disgracefully than our friend'.

Demosthenes and Aeschines, and *De partitione oratoria*, a technical discussion of the principles of speech-composition. But it is clear that at this date in early 46 he was already formulating his plan to embrace in a series of treatises a comprehensive history of contemporary philosophy for the benefit of fellow-countrymen too timid to tackle the Greek authors in the original.[10]

II

This rapid survey of the first sixty years of Cicero's life amply confirms his claim that philosophy from his earliest days had been the focus of his intellectual life. In his preface to *The Nature of the Gods*, he draws attention to the personal grief caused by the death of his daughter Tullia in childbirth as a contributory reason for his decision to seek the consolations of philosophy, but truth to tell he had already decided on his programme of writing before her death; it was his conviction that Rome needed a philosophical literature to enhance its culture which was his primary motive, as the prefaces of other treatises indicate. Perhaps more fundamentally he hoped by his writing to provide the ordinary Roman with a code of living to enable him to make responsible moral decisions, for ethics was at the centre of his philosophical concerns.[11]

The demanding programme which he determined to carry through between late 46 and December 44 he summarized at the outset of Book 2 of the *De divinatione*. Following the *Consolatio* (now lost) which he addressed to himself on the loss of his daughter, he planned and executed the sequence of works as follows (the dates can only be tentative):

Introduction: *Hortensius* (fragmentary): Exhortation to Philosophy (late 46)

---

[10] For Cicero's thoughts on the alternatives of politics or private study and publication, see *Fam.* 7. 3. 3 f. For his decision to concentrate on philosophy, *Fam.* 9. 2. 5.

[11] For philosophy as the focus of his intellectual life, see *Tusc.* 5. 5; *Rep. 1.* 7. For the death of Tullia, see 1. 9 n. below. For his basic aim of providing Rome with a history of philosophy, see the prefaces to *Tusculans* and *De finibus*. For his desire to educate Romans in moral decisions, see H. A. K. Hunt, *The Humanism of Cicero* (Melbourne, 1954), ch. 1.

1. *Academica*: the theory of knowledge (first version completed April–May, second version by June 45)
2. *De finibus*: ethics—the highest good (first half of 45)
3. *Tusculans*: ethics—the means to happiness (June–July 45)
4. *De natura deorum*: physics and theology (August 45–early 44)
5. *De divinatione*: physics and theology (February–April 44)
   [*De senectute, De gloria, De amicitia*: Ethical treatises (early–late summer 44)]
6. *De fato*: physics and theology (mid-44)
7. *De officiis*: ethics: principles of social conduct (Sept.–Dec. 44)[12]

Though many of Cicero's contemporaries were steeped in Greek culture, in public life they were slow to abandon suspicion and even contempt for things Greek; philosophy in particular was considered to be an undesirable pursuit. Cicero decided to meet this attitude head-on in his preliminary work the *Hortensius*, an exhortation to philosophy in the tradition of Aristotle's *Protrepticus*. Cicero's dialogue is set in the late 60s; three participants, Catulus, Lucullus, and Hortensius, are spokesmen for poetry, historiography, and oratory respectively. In the course of his presentation, Hortensius delivers a sharp attack on philosophy, and Cicero as the fourth contributor rejoins with a spirited defence of the discipline. He appeals to the doctrine of Aristotle central to the *Nicomachean Ethics*, that the highest pursuit by which to attain human happiness is the intellectual contemplation which seeks a knowledge of the truth, for all men have an innate desire to know. In response to Hortensius' attack on philosophy, he claims that the validity of the argument can be assessed only by philosophers. The celebrated encomium of Augustine, proclaiming that this work set him on the path to Christian conversion by implanting in him a longing for 'the immortality of wisdom',

---

[12] For *Hortensius* (composed) and *Academica* (begun) at Puteoli in 46, see Pliny, *NH* 31. 6, and T. N. Mitchell, *Cicero, the Senior Statesman* (Yale, 1991), 283 n. 160. The first version of the *Academica* was finished in May 45 (*Att.* 12. 44. 4). For the dating of the later treatises, see Mitchell, 283 ff., refining on Hunt's discussion in *Humanism*, ch. 1.

has made the *Hortensius* one of the most famous lost treatises in world literature.[13]

Following this introductory volume, Cicero commenced the series proper with the *Academica*, a work devoted to epistemology. He started it at his villa at Puteoli, which as a self-styled adherent to the Academic school he called his Academy. A first version (*Academica Priora*) was composed in two books, entitled *Catulus* and *Lucullus*; he later brought out an expanded version (*Academica Posteriora*) in four books. A single book from each version has survived, and they together form the modern text of the work. The purpose of the book is to refute the views of rival schools that the evidence of the senses is infallible (so the Epicureans), or at any rate mostly reliable (so the Stoics). Cicero adheres to the older standpoint of the Academic school as represented by Carneades, who argues that we can establish only probabilities, not certainties, as against the later doctrine of Cicero's contemporary Antiochus, who accepts at least the possibility of the truth of some sensations. Book 1 (the first book of the *Posteriora*) is devoted to the notion of the probable (see 1. 11 f. of this treatise), while Book 2 (*Lucullus*, the second book of the *Priora*) reviews the general problem of scepticism as discussed by successive Academics, and is chiefly concerned with the differing approaches of Carneades and Antiochus.[14]

After the *Academica*, Cicero turned his attention to the subject of ethics, which since the time of Socrates, and more intensively in the Hellenistic period, had become the central preoccupation of philosophers. In the five books of *De finibus*, he surveys the main Hellenistic theories about the chief end of life at which we should aim. The first two books are devoted to the Epicurean view; Torquatus presents the thesis that pleasure is the chief good to be sought, and Cicero responds in his own name with an extended critique. Books 3 and 4 analyse the Stoic thesis that virtue is the only good; the younger Cato presents the Stoic arguments, and

---

[13] For Roman 1st-cent. attitudes to Greek culture, see J. P. V. D. Balsdon, *Romans and Aliens* (London, 1979), ch. 3. For suspicion of philosophy, see e.g. Tacitus, *Agr.* 4. 4. For Augustine's tribute to the *Hortensius*, see *Conf.* 3. 7.

[14] On the *Academica*, see J. S. Reid's Introduction to his edn, 36 ff.: Hunt, *Humanism*, ch. 2; MacKendrick, *Philosophical Books*, ch. 10.

Cicero again performs the role of devil's advocate. In the final book, the position of the Academy as represented by Antiochus is reviewed; Piso as Peripatetic spokesman praises Antiochus for returning to the outlook of the Old Academy that virtue is the chief good, but that 'externals' such as health, wealth, and beauty are subsidiary goods; the Peripatetic notion that intellectual discovery is pre-eminent is happily incorporated into the concept of virtue. In this instance Cicero does not offer full-blooded objections to the thesis, but assumes the Socratic role of obtaining elucidation by questioning.[15]

A second ethical treatise follows, the *Tusculan Disputations*, again in five books. Granted that all human persons seek *eudaimonia* ('well-being' more precisely than 'happiness'), how is this to be attained? In the throes of his personal worries and depression, Cicero heroically seeks some justification for the human condition. In the first book he parades the arguments for accepting death with equanimity; in the second, he argues that pain is not a major evil, and can be overcome by constancy and fortitude. The third book turns to the problem of mental disturbance, to argue that anxiety in its various manifestations is not only futile but also unnatural. Book 4 pursues the topic further by condemning other irrational emotions, fear, overweening joy, and lust. In the final book Cicero essays a more positive note. He proclaims that virtue is sufficient for happiness, arguing that in this respect the standpoint of the Stoics and the Academic–Peripatetic viewpoint proposed by Antiochus are essentially identical, and the differences merely verbal.[16]

These two interconnected discussions of ethics are followed by three treatises which can loosely be described as theological, though since the time of Aristotle (who coined the word theology) and earlier, discussion of the gods was inseparable from that of the natural world. The first of these three, *The Nature of the Gods*, we must analyse at length later; the two which Cicero composed next, *De divinatione* and *De fato*, are a continuation of his survey of Stoic natural theology treated in *The Nature of the Gods*.

[15] See Hunt, *Humanism*, ch. 3; MacKendrick, *Philosophical Books*, ch. 11.
[16] See the edn. of *Tusculans* by T. W. Dougan and R. M. Henry (Cambridge, 1905–34): Hunt, *Humanism*, ch. 4; MacKendrick, *Philosophical Books*, ch. 12.

On Divination is a dialogue in two books conducted between Cicero and his brother Quintus, who lays the foundation for the argument by suggesting that divination had not received the detailed discussion in *The Nature of the Gods* which it merited. Quintus then lists the various 'artificial' and 'natural' indications of the future, including dreams, and then subjoins the Stoic arguments which justify credence in them; these arguments stem probably from Posidonius. In his response in the second book, Marcus treats these phenomena systematically, and probably with the help of the observations of Clitomachus, mouthpiece of Carneades, denies that these are reliable prophecies. He himself in the spirit of a true Academic, prefers to suspend judgement about them.[17]

In the fragmentary treatise *On Fate*, a dialogue between Cicero and Hirtius, Cicero adopts the Aristotelian thesis in the *Nicomachean Ethics*, that we have the freedom to make choices and are responsible for the choices we make. He naturally accepts the laws of causality, but denies that they have the finally determining influence on action. A free act can be determined and predictable by reason of such external causes, but need not be necessary. In this treatise Cicero shows a sophisticated grasp of logic, and rises above the conventional assessment that he is a philosophical amateur. For this reason it is to be regretted that this work has not survived complete.[18]

This close concentration on the technicalities of Stoic theology must have been a monotonous task, and it seems that while working on *De divinatione* and *De fato*, Cicero sought recreation from them by composing three shorter discussions on topics more closely related to real life. The first of these, *On Old Age*, is dedicated to Atticus, and is an exhortation to his friend and to himself (both now in their sixties) to look positively at this stage of life.

[17] There is an exhaustive edition of *De divinatione* by A. S. Pease (2 vols, Urbana, 1920–3). See also Hunt, *Humanism*, 142 ff.; MacKendrick, *Philosophical Books*, ch. 14. On divination in general, see R. M. Ogilvie, *The Romans and their Gods* (London, 1969), ch. 4; J. H. W. G. Liebeschuetz, *Continuity and Change in Roman Religion* (Oxford, 1979), 7 ff.

[18] The Tusculum edn. (1980) with German trans. (ed. K. Bayer) is the most serviceable for the professional philosopher. H. Rackham's useful Loeb translation curiously appears in vol. ii of *De oratore* (1942). There are good discussions in Hunt, *Humanism*, 149 ff.; MacKendrick, *Philosophical Books*, ch. 15.

Old Cato is given the role of apologist, an ideal choice in view of
his vigorous life as an octogenarian. The secret of a happy old
age is practice of the cardinal virtues, and a continuing busy life
until the end; senility is not inevitable, and the loss of physical
pleasures is easily borne.[19] This treatise evokes the early discussions in Plato's *Republic*; the second of the three treatises, *On
Friendship*, recalls the prominence lent to this theme at the close
of Aristotle's *Nicomachean Ethics*. Gaius Laelius is chosen as spokesman because of his proverbially unselfish friendship with the
more distinguished Scipio Aemilianus, and additionally because
of his reputation as a virtuous Stoic. The Aristotelian categories
of friendship—utilitarian, pleasurable, virtuous—are here presented in Roman dress, with Aristotle's judgement that true
friendship is that which is bonded between men good and alike
in virtue.[20] The third treatise, *On Glory*, is unfortunately lost; it
would have been instructive, composed as it was shortly after the
assassination of Caesar, to observe how Cicero handled the traditional notion of *gloria* (embodied, for example, in Scipio Africanus) as a noble aim sought in the service of the state, as
contrasted with the self-advancement of a Caesar, who had
brought the senatorial government to its knees and established
the domination of a single man. Certainly in his next work the
De officiis, composed after the tyrant's death, he waxes indignant
about Caesar's depraved ambition, comparing him with the
most vicious autocrats in history. This work *On Duties* contains a
long section on *gloria* which probably provides a general outline
of the lost treatise.[21]

In the *De officiis*, the final discourse of the series, Cicero returns
to his central concern of ethics. This work on social obligation,
composed in three books, is not, like the earlier treatises, written

[19] See now J. G. F. Powell's edn, (Cambridge, 1988); earlier, that of J. S. Reid (rev.
Kelsey, Cambridge, 1882). See also MacKendrick, *Philosophical Books*, ch. 16.

[20] The fullest edn. of *De amicitia* is that of M. Seyffert and C. F. W. Müller, *Laelius: De
amicitia dialogus* (Hildesheim, 1965); earlier that of J. S. Reid (Cambridge, 1882).
Recent discussion in MacKendrick, *Philosophical Books*, ch. 17.

[21] For earlier indications of Cicero's attitude to *gloria*, see *Pro Sestio* 139: 'Praise given
to right actions and reputation for great merits *in the service of the republic*' (my italics).
Also *Philippics* 1. 29, *Tusc.* 3. 3. For his condemnations of Caesar in *De officiis*, see 1. 26,
2. 24 ff. For the section on *gloria*, 2. 31 ff.

as an imaginary dialogue, but in the form of a letter of advice written to his son Marcus, who was currently studying under the Peripatetic Cratippus at Athens. The first book outlines a general theory of duty by separate discussion of each of the cardinal virtues: wisdom is pre-eminent considered as a virtue, but justice ranks first in its guiding role in action. In addition to analysis of justice, courage and temperance, the virtue of liberality, so prominent in Aristotle's treatise, is also detailed and exemplified. The second book is devoted to the concept of the *utile* or expedient, treated in its more positive aspect as a spur to public duty. But in the final book Cicero underlines the areas of potential conflict between such personal advantage and moral obligation.[22]

III

Before examining in detail Cicero's survey of Greek philosophical ideas about the gods, and in particular the theories of the Hellenistic schools, we may briefly consider the traditional Roman notions of the gods which he inherited, for this inevitably coloured his interpretation of Greek thought. In contrast to the Greek literary depiction of gods as fallible human beings writ large, the Roman deities are impersonal and remote. They do, however, keep a watchful eye on the activities of the Roman state; though private households maintained their own shrines and made modest offerings to their household gods, Roman religion was predominantly the province of the state, conducted scrupulously by ritual and cult. Departure from the prescribed norms was to invite divine displeasure. By Cicero's day such piety towards the gods had to be allied to the practice of other Roman virtues, notably justice and good faith (*iustitia* and *fides*) in upholding treaties and solemn promises struck with other communities, harmonious collaboration in domestic relationships, with due deference to authority (*concordia* and *disciplina*), prudent foresight and courage in war (*prudentia* and *virtus*),

---

[22] H. Holden's annotated edn. (Cambridge, 1854) has never been superseded. Michael Winterbottom has now published an Oxford Classical Text (1994). For discussion, see Hunt, *Humanism*, ch. 6; MacKendrick, *Philosophical Books*, ch. 19.

chastity and modest living in domestic life (*pudicitia* and *frugali-tas*). The belief was pervasive that observance of these and con-comitant virtues had in the past won divine benevolence for the Roman state; indeed, many such impersonal qualities had been deified and awarded public shrines. Contrariwise, reverses in war and disorder in the state were attributed to the increasing prevalence of the opposing vices. In short, many leading Romans regarded their nation as a chosen people, earlier guided to world-dominion because they had espoused upright behaviour, but now suffering divine vengeance for having abro-gated the Roman virtues.[23]

The conduct of Roman religion was managed by the politi-cians. The senate was endowed with supreme authority in all matters religious. They delegated decisions to the four main priesthoods, the *pontifices* (the advisory board of priests who assisted the magistrates in their sacral functions), the augurs, the *quindecimviri sacris faciundis* ('the fifteen men in charge of the ritual' who were custodians of the Sibylline books), and the *septemviri epulonum* (the seven in charge of the feasts), but the indi-viduals appointed to these offices were not a priestly caste, but men active in public affairs. Apart from the priest of Jupiter (*flamen Dialis*), who could not quit Rome for extended periods and whose political advancement was therefore restricted, sacral officials were usually magistrates or ex-magistrates. The criticisms levelled at religious practice by Cotta in the third book of this treatise are muted precisely because he was a *pontifex* as well as politician, simultaneously maintaining his attachment to the Roman gods and sceptical of arguments for their existence. Cicero himself, augur as well as active statesman, exhibits a sim-ilar ambivalence. At the conclusion of this dialogue he guardedly inclines towards the Stoic theology which Balbus reconciles with the traditional Roman religion. In short, Roman philosophers of the Academic persuasion differed from their Greek counterparts

---

[23] For useful summaries of Roman religious practices, see Mary Beard, *CAH* ix[2] (Cambridge, 1994), ch. 19; Liebeschuetz, *Continuity and Change*; Ogilvie, *Romans and their Gods*. With Cicero, Livy offers the fullest evidence of Roman piety; see my *Livy* (now Bristol Classical Press, 1989), ch. 3; D. S. Levene, *Religion in Livy* (Leiden, 1993). For the interconnection between *pietas* and the other Roman virtues, see 2. 153 below.

in their reverence for their religious traditions, an attitude of mind which fundamentally affects the course of the debate.

Since the *pax deorum* ('the gods' benevolence') had pervaded every aspect of public life, religious ritual accompanied every political or military initiative. Before the magistrates departed to their provinces, they offered sacrifice; before armed forces went into battle, they were ritually purified. Prodigies were regularly reported and interpreted as signs of divine disfavour; the deities were duly appeased by sacrifices or periods of public prayer. Treaties were signed and sealed with the appropriate ceremony. When enemy cities were levelled, the deities were solemnly invited to withdraw. Behind all this ceremonial lies the fundamental fact that Roman religion was a bargaining religion. Roman commanders in the field vowed public thanksgivings and shrines provided that victory was granted them. The characteristic formula in ceremonial prayer is: 'If you deities duly lend your aid, we in return will reward you.' It is therefore hardly surprising to find Cicero claiming that humans will acknowledge the presence of gods only if some response is granted to them.[24]

These traditional attitudes, idealized as characteristic of the early and middle Republics, were by Cicero's day being increasingly called into question. Ritual practices began to fall into disuse. The office of the *flamen Dialis* remained unfilled between 87 and 11 BC. Balbus in this treatise laments the abandonment of the practice of taking the auspices before battle. Livy senses that he is out of step with other historians when he records the yearly prodigies; he speaks of 'the religious indifference inspiring the general belief that the gods foretell nothing'. Religious practices were discredited when politicians blatantly exploited religious taboos, as when Bibulus, the consular colleague of Julius Caesar, sought to block his legislation by watching the sky for omens, thereby invalidating meetings of the assembly.[25]

[24] For the bargaining element in such ceremonial, see e.g. Macrobius, *Sat.* 3. 9. 7, the formula of evocation used before the destruction of Carthage, urging the deities to quit the city for Rome; 'si ita feceritis, voveo vobis templa ludosque facturum'. Likewise Livy 1. 24. 8 in the formula for a solemn treaty. For Cicero's insistence on some rapport between gods and men, see 1. 3 below.

[25] No appointment as *flamen Dialis*, Tacitus, *Ann.* 3. 58; Dio 54. 36. 1. The lament of Balbus, see below, 2. 9. Livy's isolation, 43. 13. 1. Bibulus observing the sky, Dio 38. 6. 1.

The challenge for Romans with a strong and apologetic sense of religious tradition was to defend that tradition while conceding that it was often a breeding-ground for superstition, incorporating procedures and assumptions which were unworthy of thinking minds. Marcus Terentius Varro, friend of Cicero and like him a devotee of the Academic school, is a key witness in this respect. His *Antiquitates rerum divinarum* has not survived, but citations from it in Augustine's *City of God* indicate its general approach. Varro, like Livy later, regarded religion as a human institution, but one which it was important to preserve for the good of society. He therefore devoted rigorous study to the origins of religious cults. The *Antiquitates* had been issued only two or three years before Cicero began work on *The Nature of the Gods*, and it is clear that it provided a useful quarry for Cotta's survey of the multiple origins of the Roman deities in Book 3. Cicero pays tribute to this devoted research at the outset of his *Academica*, which was dedicated to Varro: 'Your books led us home, when we were wandering like strangers in our own city ... You have revealed to us the names, types, duties and origins of all things divine as well as human.'[26]

In these researches Varro sought to expel superstitious fears from the minds of his fellow-citizens, just as Lucretius had sought to do with his widely differing Epicurean message; Augustine quotes Varro as saying that whereas the superstitious man fears the gods, the truly religious person venerates them as parents. This observation is closely mirrored in Cicero's celebrated distinction between *religio* and *superstitio* in his work *On Divination*:

We must perpetuate religious belief, which is closely associated with the knowledge of nature, but we must likewise eradicate superstition root and branch. Superstition breathes down your neck, following you at every turn. You may be listening to a seer or an omen; you may be offering a sacrifice or observing a bird's flight; you may be confronting an astrologer or a soothsayer. It may be lightning or thunder or a bolt from heaven; it may be the birth or creation of some prodigy.

---

[26] For Varro as Academic, see Cicero, *Acad.* 1. 4; For Augustine's observations on his work, *Civ. Dei* 6. 4. Cicero's tribute, *Acad.* 1. 9, and in general M. Griffin, *CAH* ix² 701 ff.

Something of this sort must necessarily occur almost every day, so that our minds can never be at rest.[27]

No clearer indication could be given of why Cicero incorporated this philosophical survey of the nature of the gods into the series of treatises composed for the education of his fellow-citizens.

IV

Cicero devoted the first of the three books of this treatise to a brief outline of Epicurean theology and its defects. Velleius prefaces his explanation of the doctrine of the school with a withering survey of earlier and other contemporary systems in order to demonstrate the distinctive differences of Epicurus' teaching. Books 2–3 are devoted to Stoic theology; Balbus offers his eloquent rationale in Book 2, and Cotta in Book 3 makes his response in a more deferential spirit than he showed in confronting the Epicureans. A crude comparison of the relative lengths of the discussions of the two schools indicates where Cicero's attention is chiefly focussed. Velleius' presentation of the Epicurean theology covers only fourteen pages of the Teubner text, and this includes the substantial resumé of other theological views; Cotta's counter-attack is accorded 26 pages. Discussion of the Stoic theology is on a much larger scale; Balbus is given 69 pages to present his case, and Cotta's response in Book 3, from which considerable sections have been lost, still fills over 40 pages, as much as is given to the entire discussion of the Epicurean theology.

Though Cicero, as we have seen, possessed an intimate knowledge of the main tenets of the Hellenistic schools throughout his adult life, he could not have composed this technical treatise so rapidly without the aid of books at his elbow. His description of his writings as 'copies' confirms this impression that *The Nature of the Gods* is largely, though not wholly, derivative.[28]

---

[27] For Varro's distinction between the superstitious man and the religious person, see Augustine, *CD* 6. 9; Cicero's criticism of superstition, *Div.* 2. 149.

[28] See above, p. xi and n. 1.

For the first book devoted to Epicurean theology three can-
didates present themselves as likely sources. The first is Phaedrus,
who was head of the Epicurean school before dying in 70 BC.
Cotta's account of his encounters with the irascible old gentleman may be a description of Cicero's own experiences. In a
letter to Atticus dated August 45 (the date of the commencement
of work on *The Nature of the Gods*), Cicero writes: 'Please send me
the books about which I wrote to you earlier, especially Phaedrus
On the Gods.' A second possible source is Zeno of Sidon; at 1. 59
Cotta (as Cicero's *porte-parole*) speaks appreciatively of Zeno's
style, thereby showing Cicero's acquaintance with his work.
Zeno was the teacher of the third candidate Philodemus, the
most intriguing of the three. In the eighteenth century a library
was uncovered in a villa at Herculaneum, subsequently given
the names *Domus Pisonis* and *Villa dei Papiri*; among the discoveries was a long fragment of a treatise *On Piety* by Philodemus, a
Greek friend of Calpurnius Piso, father-in-law of Julius Caesar.
The fragment contains an extended account of older views of
the gods followed by an exposition of Epicurus' own teaching, a
structured account similar to that of Velleius in this treatise.
There are clear parallels in the two accounts of the Epicurean
theology, but differences in the summary accounts of earlier
views. These differences, however, do not necessarily disqualify
Philodemus as the possible source; either he or his teacher Zeno
could have been Cicero's main quarry for 1. 18–56, perhaps sup-
plemented by information obtained from the treatise of Phaedrus.[29]

Cotta's rebuttal of the Epicurean doctrines derives in part from
Academic spokesmen, and probably in part from the Stoic Posidonius. In offering an Academic's critique, Cicero was here on
his home ground. The Epicureans had for long been a target for
criticism from the Academics, to whom Cicero claims allegiance,
and his writings in the previous year had repeatedly addressed
Epicurean issues, so that his school's objections to Epicurean

---

[29] For Cotta's encounter with Phaedrus, see 1. 93. For Cicero's letter requesting
Phaedrus' treatise, see *Att.* 13. 39. For Cicero's knowledge of Philodemus' writings, see
In Pisonem 1. 70, 'non philosophia solum sed etiam litteris perpolitus'. For Zeno rather
than Philodemus as possible source, Mayor's edn. of *ND* i, pp. xliii ff.

tenets were fresh in his mind. It is reasonable to suggest that Cicero composed this section (1. 61–124) more freely, drawing on his knowledge of the sayings of Carneades (mediated through his pupil Clitomachus), of Arcesilaus, and of Philo of Larissa. Criticisms of the Epicurean theology by Stoic spokesmen were also grist to his mill; it is worth noting that at the close of the book Cicero incorporates a criticism of Epicurus from Posidonius' 'fifth book of *The Nature of the Gods*', and Stoic arguments appear unobtrusively at other points. Such a free treatment by Cicero, incorporating citations (perhaps from memory) of both Academic and Stoic authorities, may account for certain inaccurate observations; note also the wide range of Roman allusions.[30]

There is general agreement among scholars that the systematic structure of Book 2 under its four main headings points to consultation of a single source. Since Cicero cites Cleanthes, the second head of the Porch, as the originator of the four arguments, and he is repeatedly quoted throughout the book, his claims at first sight are strong. But Chrysippus, the third and most famous president of the school, is likewise cited repeatedly, and in one place Zeno, Cleanthes, and Chrysippus are cited collectively. It is a reasonable assumption that Cicero found such quotations gathered in a single work, and Posidonius is the obvious candidate. It is true that Cicero wrote to Atticus in June 45 requesting a copy of Panaetius, *On Providence*; but Book 2 contains much technical detail of astronomy, meteorology, geography, and animal life, all areas of study handled by the versatile Posidonius. This Stoic's treatise *On the Gods* was composed in five books, the last of which was devoted to refutation of Epicurean theology; it is reasonable to suppose that the earlier four corresponded with the four divisions of the topic as announced by Balbus at the outset of his discourse. Cicero may well have expanded the section on the heavenly bodies as marvels of nature (2. 104–15) in order to advertise his prowess as a youthful translator of Aratus;

---

[30] For detailed scrutiny of the sources of 1. 61–124, see Pease's edn. of *ND* i, 36 ff. (arguing for Carneades); Mayor, *ND* i, pp. lii ff. (arguing for Posidonius). Numerous criticisms of Epicurean tenets appear in *Academica*, *De finibus*, and *Tusculans*. For Stoic arguments, see e.g. 1. 80, 97, 121. Inaccuracies, 1. 66, 72, 121. Roman allusions, 1. 63, 71, 79, 82, 97, 106, 113, 119.

the section on the wonders of animal life may likewise have been
extended by incorporation of material from Aristotle's various
treatises on animals.[31]

Cotta's response in Book 3 to the discourse of Balbus draws
heavily on the arguments of Carneades as preserved by Clitomachus. Carneades, the head of the Middle Academy who died in
129, was the Academic whom Cicero admired most; in the
second book of the *Academica* he is cited no less than ten times. In
this book there are extended quotations of his argumentation at
3. 29 ff. and 44 ff.; the reference to Carthage at 3. 91 may be a
further indication of the influence of Clitomachus, since that
was his native city. The learned excursus on the multiple origins
of Roman deities (3. 53 ff.) must lean heavily on Varro's recently
published work on Roman religious antiquities. Like Cotta's
response to Velleius in Book 1, this third book is lent a strongly
Roman flavour, to accommodate Cotta's persona as a Roman
priest; in this book too we must visualize Cicero not as a scissors-
and-paste composer, but as one who freely adapts the arguments
of his Greek authorities to harmonize with the widely different
Roman religious culture of his time.[32]

V

It will be useful at this point to present an outline of the philosophies of the three main Hellenistic schools towards the existence
and nature of the Roman gods, in order to understand the main
lines of the discussion.

Epicurus had founded his school at Athens about 306. At his
death in 270 he bequeathed a garden to his adherents, so that

---

[31] Citation of Cleanthes, 2. 13; also 2. 24, 40, 63 (P. Boyancé, *Hermes* (1962), 45 ff.
espouses his claim). For Chrysippus, see 2. 16, 37, 63, 160; collective citation of Zeno,
Cleanthes, Chrysippus, 2. 63. The letter requesting the treatise of Panaetius, *Att.* 13. 8.
For Posidonius as source, see the compelling arguments of Mayor, *ND* ii, pp. xvi ff.
Close correspondences with Aristotle on animals are detailed in the notes to 2. 123 ff;
they may have been obtained directly, or indirectly through Posidonius, who rivals
Aristotle in the breadth of his scientific interests.

[32] Cotta cites Carneades even where the argument is irrelevant to Balbus' thesis (3.
45 n.). For Varro's contribution, see p. xxvi above. For the additional Roman flavour,
introduced by Cicero, see 3. 5 f., 11, 43, 52, 63, 74, 80.

the school became commonly known as 'The Garden'. The founder-figure and his doctrines became objects of veneration; his writings, carefully preserved, were an unchanging canon constantly cited by his followers, in a manner similar to those Christian sects which baldly quote chapter and verse from the bible to address every problem. We possess his *Letter to Herodotus* on physics, his *Letter to Menoeceus* on ethics, and his *Kuriai Doxai*, a catechism of forty principal maxims. Our knowledge of the teachings of the school is further enhanced by surviving fragments of Philodemus, and by the third-century account of Diogenes Laertius. But the chief supplementary sources enabling us to understand the Epicurean philosophy in the round are in Latin; they are Lucretius' poem *De rerum natura*, and the writings of Cicero, the present treatise in particular. [33]

Velleius' outline of the Epicurean theology can be filled out by recourse to these additional sources. He deals first with epistemology or the theory of knowledge. Following Aristotle, Epicurus argued that the senses are the source of all knowledge, and that they are infallible; if we are deceived by them, this is attributable to our faulty interpretation of the evidence which they provide (see Lucretius 4. 377 ff.). According to Epicurus, every object constantly gives off a film of atoms, described as 'images' or *eidola*, which retain the shape of the object. These *eidola* strike the senses, which is why the senses cannot err, unless the images are attenuated or damaged en route. Some images are so fine that they bypass the organs of sense and strike the mind directly; this is how dreams and mental pictures are formed in our consciousness. (Velleius does not explain this adequately with his exposition of *prolepsis* at 1. 43; see the note there.)

Since we obtain these mental pictures of the gods, they must objectively exist. What are they like? They are like humans writ large, because this is how they strike our minds; moreover, since humans have the most beautiful shape and are endowed with

---

[33] The texts are gathered in A. A. Long and D. N. Sedley, *The Hellenistic Philosophers* (2 vols. Cambridge, 1987). Vol. i contains translations and commentary; vol. ii, the texts with notes and bibliography. For God, the main texts cited are Lucretius 5. 1161 ff.; 6. 68 ff.; 5. 146 ff.; *Letter to Menoeceus* 123 f.; *Letter to Herodotus* 76 f.; Sextus Empiricus, *Against the Professors* 9. 43 ff.

reason, the gods must be similarly formed. Epicurean physics insists that all things are formed of atoms, so the gods too must be atomic compounds; but their bodies are quasi-bodies, and their blood quasi-blood (§49); in other words, the atoms which compose them are of a finer texture than those which make up the material objects of the world. As a result, their bodies do not decompose like all other compound creations; they are immortal (§45). Velleius does not devote sufficient discussion to the problem raised by this paradox.

How many deities are there? Since the Epicureans argue that the number of atoms is infinite, the number of gods too is potentially infinite. There is a balance (*isonomia*) of opposing objects in the universe to maintain its harmony; since the number of mortals is potentially infinite, so too is the number of immortals.

What do the deities do? They live a happy life of self-absorption and tranquillity remote from this world, delighting in their wisdom and virtue, and taking no part in the creation or maintenance of the world. From Philodemus we learn that they converse philosophically in Greek 'or in something not much different'; he also tells us that they require food and drink and periods of rest as we do. Friendship (with each other, not with mortals) is the greatest blessing which they enjoy.

How should we regard them? Since they are both eternal and blessed (§45), they are worthy of our reverence. We must worship them for the beneficent effect such worship exercises upon ourselves. We are to use reverent names for them, as Epicurus tells us in *The Letter to Herodotus*. As Philodemus explains, 'The wise man regards with wonder the nature of the gods and their disposition; he endeavours to draw near and yearns to touch it, and to be in its company.'

Velleius' brief account does not discuss the habitation of the gods. Lucretius describes it as 'similar to their tenuous bodies', and Cicero locates it in what he calls the *intermundia*, the 'space between the worlds'.[34]

The account of the Epicurean theology mediated through the mouth of Velleius is cursory; it is a system profoundly alien to a

---

[34] See Lucretius 5. 146 ff.; Cicero, *Fin.* 2. 75, and below 1. 18.

traditionalist Roman like Cicero, who accordingly devotes less attention to a positive projection of it than to the objections raised by Cotta which follow.[35]

VI

The Stoics derived their name from the Stoa Poikilē, the painted colonnade on the north side of the Athenian agora which was the site of the school. Stoicism was a more dynamic philosophy than Epicureanism, in the sense that its doctrines evolved radically during the two and a half centuries between its foundation about 300 BC and the time of Cicero. The Early Stoa was dominated by its first three heads: the first was the Cypriot Zeno of Citium, who laid the foundations of the system; his successor Cleanthes lent a more religious dimension to the doctrines of the school, in the face of the increasingly sceptical stance of the Academics; and the third President Chrysippus is credited with a systematic development of the doctrines of the school, though with the loss of his voluminous writings it is difficult to pin-point these advances. Major shifts, or at least modifications, of those early doctrines were introduced by Panaetius of Rhodes, head of the school (by now 'The Middle Stoa') between 129 and 109, a strong admirer of Plato and Aristotle, who built bridges with the Peripatetics. His pupil Posidonius of Apamea, scientist and historian as well as philosopher, and a scholar of almost Aristotelian stature, gave the doctrines of the school a more scientific edge. These two later Stoics were responsible for popularizing Stoic doctrines at Rome; Panaetius was the first to teach them there, and Posidonius was the chief philosopher through whom Cicero gained his knowledge of the system. Unfortunately, none of the writings of these five formative figures have survived in substance, and knowledge of their contributions rests on the citations of later commentators.[36]

---

[35] For general accounts of Epicurean philosophy, see J. M. Rist, *Epicurus: An Introduction* (Cambridge, 1972); A. A. Long, *Hellenistic Philosophy* (London, 1974), ch. 2.

[36] For the personalities of the early Stoa, see F. H. Sandbach, *The Stoics* (London, 1975), ch. 7. The religious orientation of Cleanthes is documented by his surviving

Like the Epicureans, the Stoics accepted the Aristotelian doctrine that all knowledge comes through the senses, from which all our perceptions (*phantasiai*) are said to derive. The first Stoics speak of impressions made on the soul by objects as if on wax (*tuposis*); Chrysippus prefers the term *heteroiosis* to describe the effect registered on the soul ('making other'). This may be compared in modern terms to the effect on the brain-cells of light-waves and sound-waves. These sensations are stored in our memories, and by combining them we form 'primary conceptions' (*koinai ennoiai*). These give us certainty in some matters, but in others our sense-impressions may be inaccurate, causing us in these instances to apply 'suspension of judgement' (*epoche*).

Observation of the nature of the universe led the Stoics to espouse the theory earlier promulgated by the pre-Socratic thinker Heraclitus of Ephesus, that the universe originated from fiery breath (*pneuma*), which continues to animate all matter, thus creating a dynamic continuum. In describing this atmospheric current of fire which pervades the world, the Stoics alternate between scientific and religious language; at one time they call it fiery breath, and at another the divine element, or Providence, or Reason, or Destiny, or Necessity. The *pneuma* is creative, initiating the process by which air, water, and earth are successively formed; the reverse process then ensues, by which there is gradual decomposition back into the *pneuma*. Once more it commences to create, thus continuing a cyclic pattern of creation and destruction. (Panaetius, influenced by the Aristotelian doctrine of the eternity of matter, dissented from this earlier teaching.)

The universe, then, is animated by the *pneuma*, the world-soul which is the Stoic conception of God. Every human person in the world is likewise animated by a soul which is a part of this world-soul, and which at the death of the body is absorbed back into it.

Hymn to Zeus (translation in Long and Sedley, i. 326 f.). For 'the innovations of Panaetius' and 'the imprint of Posidonius', see J. M. Rist, *Stoic Philosophy* (Cambridge, 1969), chs. 10–11. For the fragments relating to Stoic theology, see H. Von Arnim, *Stoicorum Veterum Fragmenta* (Leipzig, 1903–5); Long and Sedley, i. 323 ff.

Because the fiery *pneuma* controls the universe and guides it on its predestined course, everything in the world is predetermined. Hence Fate (*heimarmene* or *fatum*) is a key concept in Stoicism, in radical opposition to the Epicurean doctrine which claims that since the world and all within it are formed and destroyed by the fortuitous collision and separation of atoms, the future is always unpredictable.

The Stoic vision of an immanent and dynamic force in nature, guiding the world on its predestined course, obtained a hospitable reception at Rome, where it could be readily accommodated with the traditional religion. The Roman deities presiding over their prescribed provinces (Jupiter as sky-god, Neptune as sea-lord, Ceres as corn-goddess, and the rest; the animistic *numina* immanent in every sphere of nature and every area of human life) could be visualized as symbols of the fiery *pneuma* at work throughout the creation. In addition, the Stoic concept of necessity or fate accorded well with assumptions inherent in Roman religious prophecy. The arts of haruspicy and augury rest on the assumption of a predetermined pattern of events; and the reports of prodigies assembled year by year presuppose a harmony in nature in which disorder in the microcosm (whether a thunderbolt striking a temple or a mule born with three legs) connotes similar disorder in the world at large.[37]

VII

The Academics claimed descent from the Academy of Plato, maintaining that they remained true to the Socratic technique of cross-questioning to elicit the validity of the doctrines of other schools; but their true forebears were the Sceptics (whose name means 'examiners'), founded by Pyrrho of Elis, who had accompanied Alexander the Great on his eastern expedition. In the tradition of the sophist Protagoras, the third-century Academics argued that no objective certainty could be established about

---

[37] For Stoic physics, see especially S. Sambursky, *Physics of the Stoics* (London, 1959). There is a full bibliography in Long and Sedley, ii. 501 ff.

the gods as about all else, and that the only sane attitude was that
suspension of belief which induced mental tranquillity. This was
the doctrine preached by Arcesilaus (315–240), founder of the
so-called Second Academy.

A similar stance was maintained by Carneades (214–129),
who established the Third Academy in the mid-second century.
He presented a more systematic and effective justification of the
scepticism of the school. His views were mediated through his
pupil and successor Clitomachus of Carthage, and continued by
Clitomachus' successor Philo of Larissa, who on his visit to
Rome won Cicero over to the philosophy of the school. Cicero
thereafter became a committed adherent to the sceptical views
of Carneades and Philo in the areas of epistemology and physics
(which included theology), to the extent of supporting the relent-
less agnosticism of those Academics towards gods, Providence,
prophecy, and fate. But their views on ethics were another
matter; the doctrine of Carneades on the highest good, 'voluptas
cum honestate' (Cicero, *Brutus* 306), an attempt to reconcile the
dissonant views of Epicureans and Stoics, was too close to the
Epicurean position for Cicero's taste.

Antiochus of Ascalon (*c.*125–*c.*68), the founder of the so-called
Fifth Academy, introduced a decisive shift in the position of the
school by abandoning the scepticism of Arcesilaus and Carneades, and by reverting to the more traditional approaches of
the Old Academy. Antiochus felt that the time was ripe for a
more ecumenical relationship with the Stoics, who by this time
had absorbed many of the doctrines of the Peripatetics. As
Cicero put it, 'The Stoics had taken over everything from the
Peripatetics and (Old) Academics, adopting the same doctrines
under different names', and Antiochus 'was called an Academic,
but if he had changed a few things, he would have been the
truest of Stoics'. Cicero's affection for Antiochus did not seduce
him from his allegiance to the views of Carneades; this makes it
all the more surprising that at the close of this dialogue he
inclines towards support for the Stoic position. The solution
must be that at the time of composition, when his mind was con-
centrated on the traditional practices of Roman religion, his
judgement of what was probable (the characteristic criterion of

Carneades, who argued that this could vary according to time
and place) was swayed by his sense of Roman piety.[38]

VIII

Though Cicero trod consciously in the footsteps of Plato in composing his philosophical works in dialogue-form, there are clear
differences in his presentation. In part, this is attributable to the
differing cultural circumstances. In Plato's dialogues, Socrates
holds the ring; he stands out among the bevy of youthful
enquirers and disputatious opponents offering personal opinions,
which Socrates probes and corrects by his favoured technique of
question and answer. But in Cicero, the spokesmen are usually
representatives of established schools of philosophy whose views
he wishes to present in an ordered and coherent way. There is
accordingly a combination of dialogue (often peremptory) and
extended discourse. The presentations made by the spokesmen
are cast in a highly rhetorical form; for Cicero, as for Aristotle,
there are close connections between philosophy and rhetoric,
the orderly and persuasive art by which we can reach valid conclusions.[39]

The autobiographical prologue, in which Cicero explains the
circumstances of composition and the motives impelling him to
offer philosophical treatises to the Roman public, is another original feature, evocative of the comic dramatist Terence, who
exploits his prologues in self-defence and to mount attacks on his
adversaries.[40]

Cicero next sets the scene for the discussion in a manner not
unlike that of Plato and Xenophon. Plato's *Republic*, for example,

[38] For the complex shifts in the doctrines of the Academic school, see the passages in
Long and Sedley, i. 438 ff., and Long, *Hellenistic Philosophy*, 75 ff., 223 ff. Cicero's claim
that the Stoics had absorbed Peripatetic doctrines is in the area of physics an oversimpli-
fication; see Long, *Hellenistic Philosophy*, 146 f. For Cicero's claim that Antiochus drew
close to Stoicism, see *Acad.* 2. 132.

[39] On the rhetorical form of the dialogues, see MacKendrick, *Philosophical Books*,
25 ff.

[40] For Terence's apologias, see G. E. Duckworth, *The Nature of Roman Comedy* (Princeton, 1952), 62.

begins with Socrates making his way back from the Piraeus, when he encounters Polemarchus and a group of friends who shanghai him and bear him off to the house of Polemarchus, where the discussion ensues. Xenophon's *Symposium* begins by describing how on the feast of Minerva Callias invites Socrates and a group of friends to his house for dinner. Similarly, Cicero's *Academica* set at Cumae begins when Cicero and Atticus encounter Varro on the road, and escort him back to his house, where the conversation then follows. The occasion for *The Nature of the Gods* is a holiday, as in Xenophon, and the discussion takes place in the house of a friend (Cotta), as in both Plato and Xenophon.

The dramatic date of the dialogue can be assigned to 76 BC. Cotta is designated as *pontifex* but not as consul; he gained the priesthood in 82 and the consulship in 75. Cicero himself appears at Cotta's house as auditor; he had been in Greece and Rhodes between 79 and 77, and he was out of Rome again as quaestor in Sicily in 75. Hence the occasion of the imagined debate is during the *Feriae Latinae* (which took place some time in April–July), of the year 76.[41]

Cicero selects his characters differently from the practice of Plato and Xenophon. There is no dominant figure like Socrates in the Greek dialogues; Cicero chooses leading figures from three of the four established schools, each with a history of more than 200 years behind them. Gaius Velleius, the Epicurean spokesman, is not well known to us as a leading figure in Roman life; he is a senator (1.15), rather surprisingly for an Epicurean, since his school preached a doctrine of tranquil retirement from affairs, and he is said to be a leading member of it at Rome (this may indicate that his attention to philosophy is an intellectual pose rather than integral to his way of life). More curiously, we have no better knowledge of the Stoic spokesman Quintus Lucilius Balbus; the Stoics stressed the obligation to public service, but Balbus, a philosopher of international eminence (see 1. 15), had clearly rejected politics in favour of the intellectual life. Gaius Aurelius Cotta, the Academic spokesman, was the most prominent figure of the three; earlier he had been a youthful

---

[41] For the occasion of the *Feriae Latinae*, see W. Warde Fowler, *The Roman Festivals of the Republic* (London, 1916), 95 ff.

friend of the leading orator at Rome, Licinius Crassus, and a supporter of the ambitious plebeian tribune of 91, Livius Drusus; after suffering exile for his support of Drusus's encouragement of the insurrection of the Italian allies, he returned in 82, and proved to be a moderating influence in the tense years that ensued. In the year following the dramatic date of this treatise, he became consul and was subsequently appointed governor of Cisalpine Gaul, where he won a triumph. He died, however, before he could celebrate it. Cicero's role in the discussion, as befitted a youthful figure in the presence of distinguished elders, was that of mute auditor.[42]

IX

The later history of *The Nature of the Gods* offers a fascinating example of how a magisterial text can be acclaimed and exploited by spokesmen of widely differing ideologies. Christian apologists were the first to adopt it in the early centuries after Christ to direct withering attacks on the fatuities of the pagan religion, and to buttress the Christian arguments for monotheism. By contrast, sceptical figures in the age of the Enlightenment eagerly seized upon it to demonstrate the philosophical uncertainties lying behind orthodox belief. The striking conclusion to be drawn from study of the *Nachleben* of the treatise is that it has proved to be a seminal text throughout the history of Western philosophy.[43]

When Christianity began to acquire educated and articulate spokesmen in the West from the late second century onwards, they were naturally men thoroughly schooled in the masterpieces of Roman literature. The leading figures of Christian

---

[42] Velleius may have been plebeian tribune in 90 (Broughton, *MRR* ii. 474). Balbus is known chiefly for his friendship with Posidonius and Antiochus (see further, *De or.* 3. 78). For Cotta's later career, see *MRR* ii. 96 and 111.

[43] The classic study of Cicero's later influence is Th. Zielinski, *Cicero im Wandel der Jahrhunderte* (Leipzig and Berlin, 1908). The most recent survey is that of MacKendrick, *Philosophical Books*, ch. 20. There are accounts of the *Nachleben* of *The Nature of the Gods* in the edn of Pease, 54 ff., and in the Penguin trans. (Harmondsworth, 1972) by J. M. Ross.

humanism, from Ambrose and Jerome in the fourth century to
the time of Isidore of Seville (in his *Etymologies*) reveal their
acquaintance with Cicero's treatise by occasional citation or
artistic imitation. But the work was exploited predominantly by
Christian apologists endeavouring to convert pagan associates
by calling in the leading figure of the golden age of Latin literature to support the Christian claims.[44]

The first notable work to exploit *The Nature of the Gods* in this
way was the *Octavius* of Minucius Felix (*c.*220 AD). North
Africa, the provenance of a large proportion of extant second-
century Latin literature, had recently heard the triumphal
boast of Tertullian in his *Apology* (197 AD) that Christianity was
sweeping through the province. Like this predecessor, Minucius
Felix was well grounded in Classical literature, and in both
form and content his work is closely modelled on *The Nature of
the Gods*. This is the sole Christian apologetic in Latin known to
us which is written in the form of a dialogue. The author
describes how he strolled with two friends, one Christian and
one pagan, on the beach at Ostia. The pagan, Caecilius Natalis
(perhaps a historical figure, since his name is found in early
third-century inscriptions from Cirta), presents arguments
based in part on those of Cotta; in reply, Octavius is allowed to
make the Christian case at much greater length, harnessing
some of the Stoic arguments for monotheism, and he succeeds
in converting Caecilius.[45]

Arnobius, another African convert to Christianity, wrote his
seven books *Adversus Nationes* (*c.*295 AD) in disillusionment with
the Roman religion, and to defend Christianity against the
charge that it had brought the civilized world to ruin. Though
inspired chiefly by Plato among pre-Christian authors, he cites
The Nature of the Gods at several points; and he provides a brief
fragment of our text in Book 3 where the original has been lost
(see 3. 65 n.). But the pupil of Arnobius, Lactantius, yet another

---

[44] For the citations of Classical authors in general in the works of the Western Fathers,
see H. Hagendahl, *Latin Fathers and the Classics* (Göteborg, 1958).

[45] Text and French trans. by J. Beaujeu (Paris, 1964); Loeb text and trans. by J. H.
Rendall (London, 1931). For a general survey, see P. De Labriolle, *Histoire de la littérature
latine chrétienne*, i[3] (Paris, 1947), 163 ff.

African convert, is the most notable of these Christian apologists to make use of Cicero's treatise. 'The Christian Cicero', as he has often been called, quotes from it no fewer than eighteen times in his *Divine Institutes* (composed 303–13 in reply to attacks on Christianity made by Hierocles, state-official and philosopher), and there are further citations in his *De ira Dei* and *De opificio Dei*. Like Arnobius, Lactantius has provided fragments of the text of Book 3 of *The Nature of the Gods*, which help to fill out Cotta's rebuttal of the Stoic case.[46]

Augustine, yet another African who like these predecessors sought to defend Christianity against the charge that it was bringing low the Roman civilization, likewise attacked the pagan gods in his monumental work *The City of God* (413—26 AD). As befitted a former teacher of rhetoric at Rome and Milan, he knew his Cicero intimately, and there are traces of the influence of *The Nature of the Gods* in various works composed from the time he abandoned his secular profession 'to take refuge in philosophy'. But the presence of Cicero's treatise is most pervasive in *The City of God*, where it is cited fifteen times. In an extended passage, he takes issue with Cotta for denying the possibility of God's foreknowledge (he draws also here on the treatises *On Divination* and *On Fate*). Earlier, he has quoted Balbus at some length in support of the view that the Roman religion was racked by superstition. Elsewhere in the same strain he echoed Cotta's surprise that Romulus was deified, in order to pour further scorn on the pagan theology.[47]

With the rapid Christianization of Europe, the magisterial influence of Cicero declined; no longer was there the need to fight off the rival ideology of pagan Rome with his help. Cicero's philosophical works were collected and read in the Carolingian age, but in a scholarly and educational sense rather than for apologetic purposes. Servatus Lupus, abbot of

[46] For citations in Arnobius (Eng. trans. by G. E. McCracken in *ACW* 7–8, 1949), see Pease i. 54 f. For Lactantius, see R. M. Ogilvie, *The Library of Lactantius* (Oxford, 1978), 66 ff. For the fragments of this treatise supplied by Lactantius, see 3. 65 nn.

[47] On Augustine's knowledge of Cicero, see M. Testard, *S. Augustin et Cicéron* (Paris, 1958), esp. 2. 36 ff. For Augustine's 'taking refuge in philosophy', see *De ordine* 1. 5. Defence of divine foreknowledge, Augustine, *CD* 5. 9 against *ND* 3. 14; Roman superstition, *CD* 4. 30 and *ND* 2. 28; Romulus, *CD* 22. 5 and *ND* 3. 39.

Ferrières (*c.*805–62 AD), is a signal exemplar of this intellectual attitude. He borrowed manuscripts from a wide range of monasteries in order to copy them and to correct those already lying in the monastic library. The famous Vienna codex, which included *De natura deorum* with seven other philosophical works of Cicero, was summoned by him from Corbie, one of the religious houses which were offshoots of Columbanus' Irish foundation at Luxeuil.[48]

The circulation and copying of these manuscripts made them widely available to the humanistic scholars of the twelfth and thirteenth centuries; whereas in the Carolingian age they had remained in religious houses in the Frankish lands, they were now dispersed in other parts of Europe. Monte Cassino, for example, possessed a copy of *De natura deorum* among its proud collection of seventy manuscripts in the Beneventan script. But France, and notably Paris and Chartres, remained the centre of philosophical instruction; Peter Abelard and his pupil John of Salisbury both reveal acquaintance with *The Nature of the Gods*. The leading figures of the emergent religious orders in the thirteenth century, Albertus Magnus and Thomas Aquinas among the Dominicans and Bonaventure and Roger Bacon among the Franciscans, were all naturally acquainted with the work, but by this date the focus of theological speculation had switched to the rediscovered Aristotle and his conflict with the Christian Neoplatonist tradition represented by Augustine, so that Cicero is accorded less prominence.[49]

The birth of the Italian Renaissance brought Cicero's philosophical writings back into greater prominence and esteem; his philosophical authority 'seemed as compelling to the humanists as that of Plato or Aristotle'. Petrarch, regarded by humanists as their first master, included *The Nature of the Gods* in the list of his favourite books. Between 1390 and 1420 the

---

[48] For the diffusion of Ciceronian MSS throughout northern France in the Carolingian age, see p. xlix below. For Lupus' acquisition of MSS, see M. L. W. Laistner, *Thought and Letters in Western Europe, 500–900²* (Ithaca, 1957), 255 f.

[49] For *De natura deorum* at Monte Cassino, see C. H. Haskins, *The Renaissance of the Twelfth Century* (Cambridge, Mass, 1927), 17. For citations of the treatise by Abelard, John of Salisbury, Aquinas, and Roger Bacon, see Pease's edn. i. 52 ff.

range of philosophy written in Latin was gathered into orderly collections by Poggio Bracciolini, Coluccio Salutati, and Niccolò Niccoli. Lorenzo Valla's *De voluptate* (1431) presents a dialogue between spokesmen of the Epicurean, Stoic and Christian persuasions in imitation of the Ciceronian dialogues. The sceptical arguments adduced by Cotta in *The Nature of the Gods* were exploited by scholars like Agricola, Vives and Peter Ramus to illustrate the difficulty of attaining objective truth. The most significant figure in the development of Renaissance scepticism was Montaigne (1533–92), an exponent of the *nouveau Pyrrhonisme*; in the course of his writings, he cites *The Nature of the Gods* no fewer than forty-five times. In short, 'Cicero provided the Renaissance . . . with its prime models of philosophical dialogue, and its fullest knowledge about the ancient philosophical schools.'[50]

In Britain, *The Nature of the Gods* was slow to gain a wide currency; no English translation appeared until 1683, whereas in France a rendering by Lefèvre had appeared a century earlier in 1581. But Thomas Hobbes, author of *The Leviathan* (1588–1679), was resident in France when he wrote that classic work, so that he was more closely in touch with continental currents of philosophical thought. He exploited *The Nature of the Gods* to reject the unworthy attributes imposed on God by Epicureanism, and he argued passionately that philosophical discussion of God's nature is not merely pointless but also sacrilegious; our attitude should be one of piety—a view similar to that adopted by Cicero through his mouthpiece Cotta. Hobbes accepts the Stoic arguments for the existence of God *ex consensu gentium* and from the evidence of design in the universe. The other eminent English philosopher of the seventeenth century, John Locke (1632–1704), had likewise spent some years in France before he wrote his *Essay concerning Human Understanding*, a work set up in the Ciceronian dialogue-form. Locke assumes the traditional stance of the Roman Academic, a modified scepticism which echoes the view of Carneades and of Cicero, that our actions

---

[50] *The Cambridge History of Renaissance Philosophy* (1988) has provided the substance of this paragraph; the first quotation is by B. P. Copenhaver, and the closing one by Anthony Grafton.

must be based on probabilities rather than on the assumption of moral absolutes.[51]

Perhaps the most famous essay in the history of Western philosophy which derives from *The Nature of the Gods* appeared in the age of the Enlightenment, in the shape of David Hume's *Dialogues concerning Natural Religion*, composed in the 1750s. This treatise adopts the structure, the characters, and the arguments of Cicero. The participants are Philo (a latter-day Cotta, given the name of the sceptical head of the Academy who had converted Cicero to his school), who represents Hume's own sceptical standpoint; Cleanthes, who presents arguments on Stoic lines in favour of a natural religion based on reason (his name is that of the second president of the Stoic school); and Demea, who is the orthodox theologian of the day (ironically he is given the name of the irascible old gentleman in Terence's *Adelphi*). At the close of the dialogue, Pamphilus ('Mr Friendly-All-Round', playing the role of Cicero in *The Nature of the Gods*) sums up: 'I cannot but think that Philo's principles are more probable than Demea's; but that those of Cleanthes approach still nearer to the truth'—a nice example of artistic imitation, for this is a conflation of the views of Velleius and of Cicero himself at the close of his treatise.[52]

While Hume's *Dialogues* were exercising their influence on contemporary philosophic thought (not least on Immanuel Kant), France greeted the appearance of the *Encyclopédie* (1751–80), a compendium of the rational thought of the age assembled by Diderot, with contributors including Montesquieu, Rousseau, and Voltaire; the work is a veritable mosaic of Ciceronian thought and expression. It was Voltaire who paid *The Nature of the Gods* the most fulsome tribute which the treatise had received in the eighteen hundred years of its existence. He brackets it with the *Tusculan Disputations* as the supreme manifestations of human wisdom: 'les deux plus beaux ouvrages qui ont jamais

---

[51] See further J. M. Ross's survey in the Penguin trans. of *The Nature of the Gods*, 58 f.

[52] See MacKendrick, *Philosophical Books*, 280 ff. for further detail. Other 18th-cent. writers who attest their debt include Edward Gibbon: 'I read with application and pleasure the most important treatises . . . and imbibed from his precepts and examples the public and private sense of a man' (*Autobiography*, World's Classics edn., 69).

écrits la sagesse qui n'est qu' humaine'. Of the two, *The Nature of the Gods* rises higher: it is 'le meilleur livre peut-être de toute l'antiquité'.[53]

The eighteenth century was the high point in the esteem accorded to Cicero the philosopher. Thereafter, for reasons earlier outlined, his reputation sank lower, suffering disparagement from historians and philosophers alike. But the omens are now favourable for a more balanced assessment; this is a good time for *The Nature of the Gods* to claim a place in the mainstream of undergraduate studies in philosophy.[54]

[53] On the *Encyclopédie*, see further MacKendrick, *Philosophical Books*, 278 ff. I take the citations of Voltaire from Pease's survey, i. 52 ff.

[54] For a brief account of such 19th-cent. attitudes, including the criticisms of Hegel, see MacKendrick, *Philosophical Books*, 286 ff., who also provides an interesting appendix on 'Cicero in America', but without specific reference to *The Nature of the Gods*.

Summary of the Text

The structure of the work is as follows:

Book 1.

A. *Introduction* (1–17): Cicero explains his motives in writing the work, and his general standpoint as a philosopher of the Academic school.

B. *The Epicurean case, in three parts* (18–56):
- (i) 18–24: Attacks on the immediate opponents, Stoics and Academics.
- (ii) 25–43: Criticisms of other views of deity; the philosophers, from Thales onwards, the poets, the non-Greek religions.
- (iii) 43–56: The Epicurean system, a condensed account, but the most systematic presentation which we possess:
  - (*a*) How do we know gods exist? Epistemology (43–5)
  - (*b*) What are they made of? (46–9)
  - (*c*) How many are there? (50)
  - (*d*) What do they do? (51–3)

  [No discussion of their habitat, the vexed question of their immortality; and the account of their activity is spare]

C. *Cotta's criticisms* (57–124):
- (i) 57–61: Praise of Velleius's eloquence, but not of his content.
- (ii) 62–4: Inadequacy of the argument *ex consensu gentium*.
- (iii) 65–74: Refutation of gods as atomic compounds.
- (iv) 75–102: Anthropomorphism of gods ridiculed.
- (v) 103–10: Where do they live? How are their images produced?
- (vi) 111–14: In what does their happiness consists?
- (vii) 115–24: Why should we reverence such deities?

Book 2.

The Stoic case in four parts:

(i) 1–44: The gods exist:
  (*a*) Proof from design in the world.
  (*b*) Proof from divine epiphanies.
  (*c*) Proof from the consensus of mankind.
  (*d*) Proof from divination and prophecy.

  The arguments of Cleanthes (13–15):
  (*a*) Our foreknowledge of future events.
  (*b*) Our temperate and beneficial climate; the earth's fertility.
  (*c*) The awe induced by natural phenomena.
  (*d*) Regular motions and beauty of the heavenly bodies.

  The arguments of Chrysippus (16–44):
  (*a*) The ontological argument: God is that than which there is nothing better.
  (*b*) Human reason as part of the world-intelligence; cosmic harmony (Zeno's syllogisms).
  (*c*) All matter sustained by the self-moving world-heat (*hegemonikon*).
  (*d*) The world superior to its parts and therefore divine.
  (*e*) The hierarchy of being: vegetable, animal, human, ascending logically to the divine.

(ii) 45–72: The nature of the divine:
  (*a*) The divine form is spherical.
  (*b*) Its activity (sun, moon, planets, fixed stars) is rotatory.
  (*c*) Nature as craftsman.
  (*d*) Gods of popular worship symbolizing gifts or aspects of nature.

(iii) 73–153: Providential government of the world:
  (*a*) Nature's activity as controlling agent of a cohesive universe cannot be fortuitous.
  (*b*) Marvels of nature: heavenly bodies; vegetable and animal life; organic structure of sovereign man, his reason and creative talent.

   (iv) 154–68: The world ordered for the benefit of mankind:
       (*a*) The heavens as spectacle.
       (*b*) The vegetables, lower animals, and the inanimate world provided for human use.
       (*c*) Divination, which allows men to foretell the future.

Book 3.
Cotta's criticisms of the Stoic thesis
   (i) 1–9: Acceptance of the existence of gods on ancestral authority, but rebuttal of Stoic arguments seeking to prove it.
   (ii) 10–19: Precariousness of arguments for the existence of gods:
       (*a*) *ex consensu gentium*.
       (*b*) from divine epiphanies.
       (*c*) from divination.
       (*d*) from meteorological disturbances.
   (iii) 20–64: Attack on the Stoic conception of the divine nature:
       (*a*) How can the world be God? The objections of Carneades.
       (*b*) The dubious origins of some gods. The objection to abstract deities.
   (iv) 65: Attack on the notion of providential government of the universe
      [This section wholly lost]
      66–93: Attack on the notion of providential care for mankind:
       (*a*) The gift of reason to men a disaster.
       (*b*) Blessings and reverses, virtues and vices are not divine gifts, but bestowed on humans by humans.
Conclusion of the debate:
   (v) 95: Cotta's criticisms persuade Velleius, but Cicero thinks the Stoic thesis closer to the truth.

Note on the Text and Translation

Though no manuscripts of *De natura deorum* prior to the ninth century have been uncovered, the popularity of the treatise throughout the patristic period in the West ensured its survival into the Carolingian era. All existing manuscripts descend from three copies made in France in that age, *A*, *B*, and *F*, or from an eleventh-century codex copied at Monte Cassino. These manuscripts contained in whole or in part not only *De natura deorum* but also seven other treatises: *De divinatione*, *Timaeus*, *De fato*, *Topica*, *Paradoxa Stoicorum*, *Academica Priora*, and *De legibus*. The manuscripts ABH are housed in the Rijksuniversiteit at Leiden; the works contained in them are familiarly known as the Leiden corpus.

The head of the first of these, Voss. Lat. F 86 (*B*), came from Corbie. From it was copied the late ninth-century codex *F*, which later made its way to Strasbourg, from where Poggio took it to Italy; it now lies in the library of S. Marco at Florence (Laur. S. Marco 257). From it are descended several fifteenth-century Florentine manuscripts.

One of the manuscripts of the second family, Voss. Lat. F 84 (*A*), also came from Corbie. Another member of the same family is the famous Vienna codex, Vindob. 189 (*V*), which was corrected at Ferrières by Servatus Lupus against a Corbie copy. Most late medieval and Renaissance manuscripts are descended from it. The third member of the family, Leiden BPL 118 (*H*), was copied at Monte Cassino in the eleventh century, the first extant copy to be made south of the Alps.

Editions of *De natura deorum* must base themselves on the secure foundations of *ABFH*. The Plasberg–Ax Teubner text (Leipzig, 1933), on which this translation is based, has in addition used other manuscripts from the same families, especially where there are lacunae in one or other of them.[1]

[1] I abstract these details from R. H. Rouse's account in *Texts and Transmission* (ed. L. D. Reynolds, Oxford, 1983), 124 ff.

In contrast to the large number of Italian, German, and especially French vernacular versions, *The Nature of the Gods* has
received little attention from translators in English. The first
rendering was composed in 1683 by an unknown hand (perhaps
the Robert Baker who annotated the volume). It is headed:
'Cicero's three books touching the nature of the gods done into
English . . . setting forth (from all antiquity) what perceptions
man, by the only light of reason, may entertain concerning a
deity.' J. B. Mayor's edition (i, p. lxxiii) comments indulgently
that 'it is written from the ordinary point of view, and contains
copious explanatory notes of an elementary kind.' A second
translation appeared in 1741 from the pen of Thomas Francklin,
Fellow of Trinity College Cambridge, 'with critical, philosophical, and explanatory notes. To which is added an enquiry into
the astronomy and anatomy of the ancients.' On this volume,
which was reprinted several times, Mayor comments: 'It is
what the Germans call a *Tendenz-schrift*, by a follower of Shaftesbury.' (Shaftesbury was a religious sceptic whose views influenced Diderot and other continental philosophers.) The
version of C. D. Yonge (London, 1853) first appeared in the
Bohn's Library series; thereafter it was regularly reprinted, especially in America, enjoying the absence of more learned compe-
tition. Apart from H. Owgan's version in the pedestrian Kelly's
Keys series (1884), there were two other nineteenth-century
translations, by Austin Stickney (Boston, 1889) and by Francis
Brooks (London, 1896, raising the standard by following
Mayor's text).

Recent versions have been more distinguished. Rackham's
Loeb translation (1933), which relies heavily on Mayor's edition, is accurate and elegant. I have not seen H. M. Poteat's rendering (combined with *Brutus*, *De divinatione*, and *De officiis*,
Chicago, 1950). H. C. P. McGregor's Penguin (Harmondsworth, 1972) is well-turned and rather free, but without forsak-
ing the essential sense of the original. It contains an
entertaining 'Imaginary Continuation of the Dialogue' by J. M.
Ross, who sets the scene in the Elysian Fields for a discussion
with Lactantius and an Englishman called Thomas Godless.
Ross borrowed the idea from H. H. Cludius, who published *De*

natura deorum liber quartus: e pervetusto codice' under the pseudonym P. Seraphinus, OFM (Oxford, 1813), in order to guide the discussion towards a need for a teaching authority centred in Church Councils and the Roman Pontiff.[2]

---

[2] For a list of translations into the vernaculars, inevitably incomplete, see Pease, i. 103 ff.

Select Bibliography

Entries marked with an asterisk contain fuller bibliographies relevant to that section.

1. *Modern Editions and Commentaries*

    M. VAN DER BRUWAENE, 3 vols. (*Coll. Latomus 107, 154, 175*; Brussels, 1970–81).
    W. GERLACH and K. BAYER (*Tusculum*; Munich, 1978).
    J. B. MAYOR, 3 vols. (Cambridge, 1880–5).
    A. S. PEASE, 2 vols. (Cambridge, Mass., 1955–8).
    O. PLASBERG and W. AX (Teubner 2nd edn.; Stuttgart, 1933).
    H. RACKHAM (*Loeb*; London, 1933).

2. *Translations in English*

    Anon., with annotations by Robert Baker (London, 1683).
    F. BROOKS (London, 1896).
    T. FRANCKLIN (London, 1741).
    H. C. P. McGREGOR (Penguin; Harmondsworth, 1972).
    H. OWGAN (London, 1884).
    H. RACKHAM (see §1 above).
    A. STICKNEY (Boston, 1889).
    (Translations into other vernaculars are listed in Pease, i. 103–6).

3. *General Studies of* The Nature of the Gods

    P. BOYANCÉ, 'Les preuves stoïciennes de l'existence des dieux d'après Cicéron', *Hermes* (1962), 46 ff.
    D. J. FURLEY, 'Aristotelian Material in Cicero, *De natura deorum*', in Fontenbaugh and Steinmetz (see §4 below), 201 ff.
    B. F. HARRIS, *Cicero as an Academic: A study of the* De natura deorum (Auckland, 1961)
    H. A. K. HUNT, ch. 5 (see under §4 below).

A. J. KLEYWEGT, *Ciceros Arbeitsweise in zweiten und dritten Buch der Schrift* De natura deorum, (Gröningen 1961).

P. MACKENDRICK, ch. 13 (see under §4 below).

L. REINHARDT, *Die Quellen von Ciceros Schrift* de deorum natura, (Breslau, 1888).

4. *Cicero as Philosopher*

E. BECKER, *Technik und Szenerie des Ciceronisches Dialogs* (Osnabrück, 1938).

P. BOYANCÉ, 'Les méthodes de l'histoire littéraire: Cicéron et son œuvre philosophique', *REL* (1936), 288 ff.

K. BRINGMANN, *Untersuchungen zum späten Cicero* (Göttingen, 1971).

K. BÜCHNER (ed.), *Das neue Cicerobild* (Darmstadt, 1971).

M. L. CLARKE, *The Roman Mind* (London, 1956).

A. E .DOUGLAS, 'Platonis Aemulus?', *G&R* (1962), 45 ff.

—— 'Cicero the philosopher', in T. A. Dorey (ed.), *Cicero* (London, 1964), ch. 6.

—— *Cicero* (*G&R New Surveys No. 2*, Oxford, 1968), ch. 5.

W. W. FORTENHAUGH and P. STEINMETZ (eds.), *Cicero's Knowledge of the Peripatos* (New Brunswick and London, 1989).

O. GIGON, 'Cicero und die griechische Philosophie', in *ANRW* i. 4 (Berlin, 1972), 226 ff.

J. P. GLUCKER, 'Cicero's Philosophical Affiliations', in J. Dillon and A. A. Long (eds.), *The Question of Eclecticism* (Berkeley, 1988), 34 ff.

W. GÖRLER, *Untersuchungen zu Ciceros Philosophie* (Heidelberg, 1979).

M. GRIFFIN, 'Cicero and Roman Philosophy', *CAH* ix[2] (Cambridge, 1994), 721 ff.

R. HIRTZEL, *Untersuchungen zu Ciceros philosophischen Schriften*, 3 vols. (Leipzig, 1877–83).

H. A. K. HUNT, *The Humanism of Cicero* (Melbourne, 1954).

D. M. JONES, 'Cicero as a Translator', *BICS* (1959), 22 ff.

G. B. KERFERD, 'Cicero and Stoic Ethics', in J. R. C. Martyn (ed.), *Cicero and Virgil: Studies in Honour of Harold Hunt* (Amsterdam, 1972), 60 ff.

U. KNOCHE, 'Cicero, ein Mittler griechischer Geisteskultur', *Hermes* (1959), 57 ff.

*P. MACKENDRICK, *The Philosophical Books of Cicero* (London, 1989).

P. PONCELET, *Cicéron, traducteur de Platon* (Paris, 1957).

J. S. REID, edition of *Academica* (London, 1885), Introduction.

M. RUCH, *La Préambule dans les œuvres philosophiques de Cicéron* (Paris, 1958).

M. SCHOFIELD, 'Cicero for and against divination', *JRS* (1986), 47 ff.

W. SÜSS, *Cicero: eine Einführung in seine philosophischen Schriften* (Wiesbaden, 1966).

A. WEISCHE, *Cicero und die Neue Akademie* (Münster, 1961).

5. *The Hellenistic Schools*

*A. A. LONG and D. N. SEDLEY, *The Hellenistic Philosophers*, 2 vols. (i, Translations and Commentary: ii, Texts, Notes, and Bibliography, Cambridge, 1987).

General Surveys

J. M. ANDRÉ, *La philosophie à Rome* (Paris, 1977).

A. H. ARMSTRONG (ed.), *The Cambridge History of Late Greek and Early Medieval Philosophy*[2] (Cambridge, 1970).

E. BEVAN, *Stoics and Sceptics* (Oxord, 1913).

R. D. HICKS, *Stoic and Epicurean* (London, 1910).

G. E. R. LLOYD, *Greek Science after Aristotle* (London, 1973).

A. A. LONG, *Hellenistic Philosophy*[2] (London, 1986).

The Academics

V. BROCHARD, *Les Sceptiques grecs*[2] (Paris, 1932).

M. F. BURNYEAT (ed.), *The Skeptical Tradition* (Berkeley, 1983).

J. P. GLUCKER, *Antiochus and the Late Academy* (Göttingen, 1978).

G. LUCK, *Der Akademiker Antiochus* (Bern and Stuttgart, 1953).

C. L. STOUGH, *Greek Skepticism* (Berkeley, 1969).

The Peripatetics

J. P. LYNCH, *Aristotle's School* (Berkeley, 1972).

The Epicureans

E. ASMIS, *Epicurus' Scientific Method* (Ithaca, 1984).

C. BAILEY, *The Greek Atomists and Epicurus* (Oxford, 1928).

—— edition of Lucretius, 3 vols. (Oxford, 1947).

A. J. FESTUGIÈRE, *Epicurus and his Gods* (Oxford, 1955; rev. Paris, 1968).

J. M. RIST, *Epicurus: An Introduction* (Cambridge, 1972).

N. W. DE WITT, *Epicurus and his Philosophy* (Minneapolis, 1954).

The Stoics

H. VON ARNIM, *Stoicorum Veterum Fragmenta*, 3 vols. (Leipzig, 1903–5).

E. V. ARNOLD, *Roman Stoicism* (Cambridge, 1911).

M. DRAGONA-MONACHOU, *The Stoic Arguments for the Existence and the Providence of the Gods* (Athens, 1976).

L. EDELSTEIN, *The Meaning of Stoicism* (Cambridge, Mass., 1966).

D. E. HALM, *The Origins of Stoic Cosmology* (Columbus, Ohio, 1977).

M. LAFFRANQUE, *Poseidonius d'Apamée* (Paris, 1964).

A. D. NOCK, 'Posidonius', *JRS* (1959), 1 ff.

M. POHLENZ, *Die Stoa*², 2 vols. (Göttingen, 1969).

J. M. RIST, *Stoic Philosophy* (Cambridge, 1969).

S. SAMBURSKY, *Physics of the Stoics* (London, 1959).

F. H. SANDBACH, *The Stoics* (London, 1975).

G. WATSON, *The Stoic Theory of Knowledge* (Belfast, 1966).

6. *Roman Religion*

*M. BEARD, 'Religion', in *CAH* ix² (Cambridge, 1995), ch. 19.

R. J. GOAR, *Cicero and the State Religion* (Amsterdam, 1972).

K. LATTE, *Römische Religionsgeschichte* (Munich, 1960).

J. H. W. G. LIEBESCHUETZ, *Continuity and Change in Roman Religion* (Oxford, 1979).

*J. A. NORTH, 'Religion in Republican Rome', in *CAH* vii.2² (Cambridge, 1989), ch. 12.

R. M. OGILVIE, *The Romans and their Gods* (London, 1969).

H. J. ROSE, *Ancient Roman Religion* (London, 1949).

H. H. SCULLARD, *Festivals and Ceremonies of the Roman Republic* (London, 1981).

W. WARDE FOWLER, *The Roman Festivals in the Period of the Republic* (London, 1899).

G. WISSOWA, *Religion und Kultus der Römer* (Munich, 1912).

Cicero

The Nature of the Gods

Book One

1   There are many issues in philosophy which to this day have by no
    means been adequately resolved. But there is one enquiry,
    Brutus,* which is particularly difficult and obscure, as you are
    well aware. This concerns the nature of the gods, the noblest of
    studies for the human mind to grasp, and one vital for the regula-
    tion of religious observance. On this question, the pronounce-
    ments of highly learned men are so varied and so much at odds
    with each other that inevitably they strongly suggest that the
    explanation is human ignorance, and that the Academics have
    been wise to withhold assent on matters of such uncertainty; for
    what can be more degrading than rash judgement, and what
    can be so rash and unworthy of the serious and sustained atten-
    tion of a philosopher, as either to hold a false opinion or to
    defend without hesitation propositions inadequately examined
    and grasped?

2   Take our subject as an example. Most philosophers have
    stated that gods exist, the most likely view to which almost all
    of us* are led by nature's guidance. But Protagoras* expressed
    his doubts about it, and Diagoras of Melos and Theodorus* of
    Cyrene believed that gods do not exist at all. As for those who
    have claimed that they do exist, their views are so varied and at
    loggerheads with each other that to list their opinions would be
    an endless task. Many views are presented about the forms that
    gods take, where they are to be found and reside, and their
    manner of life; and there is total disagreement and conflict
    among philosophers concerning them. There is particularly
    wide disagreement on the most important element in the case:
    are the gods inactive and idle, absenting themselves totally
    from the supervision and government of the universe, or is the
    opposite true, that they created and established all things from
    the beginning, and that they continue to control the world and

keep it in motion eternally? Unless a judgement is made between these views, we must inevitably labour under grievous misap-
3   prehension, in ignorance of the supreme issues. For there are and have been philosophers* who maintain that the gods exer-cise absolutely no supervision over human affairs. If their opin-ion is true, how can we show devotion to the gods, or have a sense of the holy or of religious obligation? All such chaste and scrupulous acknowledgement of the divine power is pointless unless the gods take notice of it, and unless the immortal gods make some acknowledgement to the human race. But if the gods have neither the power nor the desire to help us, if they have no interest whatever and they pay no attention to our activities, if there is nothing which can percolate from them to affect our human lives, what reason have we for addressing any acts of worship or honours or prayers to the immortal gods? If such activities are a mere façade of feigned pretence, they can contain no true devotion, nor indeed any other virtue, and with-out devotion to the gods all sense of the holy and of religious obligation is also lost. Once these disappear, our lives become
4   fraught with disturbance and great chaos. It is conceivable that, if reverence for the gods is removed, trust and the social bond between men and the uniquely pre-eminent virtue of justice will disappear.

But there are other philosophers of high and notable stature who hold that the entire universe is ordered and governed by the intelligence and reason of the gods. They go further, and claim that the gods take counsel and forethought for our lives as men. They believe that harvests and all that the earth bears, the atmospheric changes, the alternation of the seasons, the vari-ations in weather, by which all the produce of the earth ripens and matures, are bestowed by the gods on the human race. They adduce many features (and these will be mentioned in the present work*) such as seem to have been fashioned, so to speak, by the immortal gods for human use. In opposition to these thinkers, Carneades* mounted so many arguments against them as to stimulate even the lowest intelligence with a desire to
5   probe the truth. Indeed, there is no topic on which not merely the unlearned but even educated people disagree so much, and

since their beliefs range so widely and are so much at odds with each other, two possibilities exist: it may be that none of them is true, or at any rate no more than one of them can be.

In my discussion of this question, I can both appease my well-disposed critics and refute malicious backbiters,* forcing the second group to regret their censure, and the first to have the pleasure of being instructed; for those who offer friendly admonition need to be enlightened, while those who make hostile attacks need to be refuted.

6   I see that there has been a wide and varying reaction to the several books which I have published within a short period. Some people have wondered at the reason for my sudden enthusiasm for the study of philosophy, and others have been eager to know what positive beliefs I held on each issue. I became aware, too, that many found it surprising that I approved particularly of the philosophy which in their view doused the light and plunged the issues, so to say, in darkness, and that I had unexpectedly undertaken the defence of a school of thought which men had quitted and long left behind.* But my interest in philosophy is no sudden impulse, for I have devoted no little attention and enthusiasm to studying it, and I was philosophizing when I least appeared to be doing so. This is attested by my speeches, which are chock-full of philosophers' maxims, and by my intimate contact with highly educated men, for my household was regularly honoured by their presence. Then too I was educated by philosophers outstanding in their field,* Diodotus and Philo,
7   Antiochus and Posidonius. Moreover, if the injunctions of philosophy all have a bearing on how we live, I believe that in both public and private spheres I have put into practice the precepts recommended by reason and by learning. But if anyone wishes to know why I have come so late in setting these thoughts to paper, there is nothing which is easier for me to explain. I was at a loose end with nothing to do, for the political situation* demanded that the state be governed by the strategy and supervision of a single man. So my first thought was that I should explain philosophy to my fellow-citizens as a public duty, for I believed that the glory and reputation of the

state would be greatly enhanced if such weighty and celebrated issues were discussed in Latin works as well as in Greek.

8   I am all the more pleased to have embarked upon this plan because it is immediately clear to me that I have stirred the enthusiasm of many not merely to learn but also to write.* Several people schooled by Greek teaching could not share their learning with their fellow-citizens because they were not confident that what they had learnt from the Greeks could be expressed in Latin. But we have already, I think, made such progress in this sphere that the Greeks are not superior to us even in richness of expression.

9   A further incentive to embark on these studies was provided by the mental depression induced by the savage and crippling blow* inflicted by Fortune. Had I been able to devise some more effective alleviation, I should not have taken refuge in this. But I could find no better means of exploiting this plan of action than by devoting myself not merely to a course of reading, but also to grappling with the whole of philosophy. The easiest way to gain acquaintance with all its constituent parts and branches is to deal with the topics fully in writing, for the arguments follow an ordered sequence in a remarkable way, each being clearly linked to its predecessor and all of them fitting closely in association with each other.

10   Those who seek my personal views on each issue are being unnecessarily inquisitive, for when we engage in argument we must look to the weight of reason rather than authority. Indeed, students who are keen to learn often find the authority of those who claim to be teachers to be an obstacle, for they cease to apply their own judgement and regard as definitive the solution offered by the mentor of whom they approve. I myself tend to disapprove of the alleged practice of the Pythagoreans: the story goes that if they were maintaining some position in argument, and were asked why, they would reply: 'The master said so',* the master being Pythagoras. Prior judgement exercised such sway that authority prevailed even when unsupported by reason.

11   As for those who express surprise that I have adopted the Academic system in preference to all others, I think that the four books of my *Academica** offer them a clear enough answer. It is

quite untrue that I have undertaken the defence of positions now abandoned and outmoded. Maxims of individual philosophers do not perish with them, though they perhaps suffer from the absence of the light which an expositor would cast on them. For example, the philosophical method of arguing against every statement, and of refusing to offer positive judgements about anything (an approach inaugurated by Socrates, revived by Arcesilaus, and reinforced by Carneades), has flourished up to our own day, though I understand that it is now left with virtually no exponent in Greece itself. But I put this down not to any deficiency in the Academy, but to general obtuseness; for if mastery of each individual system is a daunting task, how much more difficult it is to master all of them! Yet this is what we must do if in the interests of discovering the truth we decide both to criticize and to support the views of each individual philosopher.

12   I do not claim to have developed practised ease in this great and difficult enterprise, but I can boast that I have made the attempt. I stress, however, that it cannot be the case that those who follow this line of philosophy have no guiding principles. Mark you, I have discussed this matter more rigorously elsewhere,* but certain people are such slow learners that they clearly need to be instructed more than once. We Academics are not the type of philosophers who think that nothing is true. Our claim is that certain falsehoods impinge on all true statements, and that these bear so close a resemblance to the truth that they contain no criterion by which to judge them or to lend assent to them. The outcome of this is our view that many things are *probable*, and that though these are not demonstrably true they guide the life of the wise man, because they are so significant and clear-cut.

13   But my present intention is to clear myself of any suspicion of partiality by presenting the views of the generality of philosophers concerning the nature of the gods. On this issue we are to assemble all of them to pass judgement on which of their views is true. Only if they are all agreed, or if one of them is seen to have ascertained the truth, will I grant that the Academy has been too dismissive. So I am disposed to adopt the rallying-cry of *The Youthful Comrades*:*

> Ye gods, and all ye citizens and youths, I pray,
> I beg, demand, implore, beseech your aid today,

not on some trifling matter, such as the complaint made in that
play that offences deserving the death-penalty were being committed in the city:

> A courtesan spurns money from her love-sick swain!

14   My request instead is that all should attend, investigate, and pass
judgement on the views we are to hold on religion, divine observance, holiness, and religious ceremonial; on good faith and
oath-taking; on temples and shrines and solemn sacrifices, as
well as on the very auspices over which I myself preside.* For
each and every one of these things relates to the issue of the
immortal gods, and certainly the widespread disagreement on
this important matter amongst highly learned men must occasion doubts in the minds of those who believe that they have
attained a measure of certainty concerning it.

15   My thoughts have often turned to this controversy, but never
more so than when we held a most rigorous and careful discussion* on the immortal gods at the home of my friend Gaius
Cotta. At his request and invitation we gathered there during
the Latin festival. When I arrived, I found him sitting in an
alcove arguing with the senator Gaius Velleius, whom Epicureans regarded as their leading light among Romans at that
time. Also present was Quintus Lucilius Balbus,* whose studies
among the Stoics were so advanced that he bore comparison
with the outstanding Greeks of the school.

When Cotta caught sight of me, he said: 'Your arrival is
timely, for I am just getting involved in an argument with Velleius on an important topic. In view of your interests, you will
not be reluctant to join us.'

16   'As you say, it does look as if I have arrived at a good moment',
I replied, 'for here you are, leading figures of three schools of
philosophy, gathered together. If only Marcus Piso* were here,
no school of thought—at least of the respectable ones—would
go unrepresented.'

Cotta then commented: 'But there is no need to regret the

absence of your friend Piso, if the book of our good friend Antiochus which he recently sent to Balbus here tells the truth. He maintains that Stoics are at one with Peripatetics* in substance, and that they differ merely in the terms they use. I am keen to have your views on the book, Balbus.'

'My personal reaction', Balbus observed, 'is surprise that such an outstandingly sharp mind as Antiochus has not noted the world of difference between Stoics, who distinguish the honourable from the expedient not merely in name but as fundamentally different in kind, and Peripatetics, who associate the two and suggest that the difference between them is one of degree or level of meaning, you might say, rather than of kind. This disagreement is no trivial one of words, but an important

17 issue of content. However, this is a topic for another time; let us concentrate at present, if you are agreeable, on the subject on which we have already embarked.'

'That suits me', said Cotta, 'but we mustn't keep our new arrival in the dark about the topic.' He looked over at me. 'We were discussing the nature of the gods, a question which as always I find extremely opaque; so I was sounding out Velleius on the views of Epicurus. So, Velleius, if it is not too much trouble, recapitulate your initial remarks.'

'I'll do that', he replied. 'Mind you, his arrival is a reinforcement for you rather than for me, since both of you' (this he added with a grin) 'have been taught by the same teacher Philo to know nothing.'*

Then I interposed. 'That teaching I leave to Cotta to explain; please don't think that I'm here as his second; I shall listen impartially and without prejudice. No compulsion binds me to defend any particular view willy-nilly.'

18 Then Velleius, with the breezy confidence* customary with Epicureans, and fearing nothing so much as to give the impression of doubt about anything, spoke as if he had just come down from attending the gods' assembly up in the Epicurean *intermundia.**

'What you are going to hear are no airy-fairy, fanciful opinions, like the craftsman-god in Plato's *Timaeus** who constructs the world, or the prophetic old lady whom the Stoics call Pronoia,

and whom in Latin we can term Providentia. I am not going to speak of the universe itself as a round, blazing, revolving deity endowed with mind and feelings. These are the prodigies and
19 wonders of philosophers who prefer dreaming to reasoning. I ask you, what sort of mental vision enabled your teacher Plato to envisage the construction of so massive a work, the assembling and building of the universe by the god in the way which he describes? What was his technique of building? What were his tools and levers and scaffolding?* Who were his helpers in so vast an enterprise? How could the elements of air and fire, water and earth knuckle under and obey the will of the architect? How did those solids of five shapes* from which all other things were fashioned originate, and conveniently station themselves to strike the mind and to produce sensations?* It would be a tedious business to recount all the particulars which appear as castles in
20 the air rather than as genuine discoveries; what takes the palm is that though he represented the world as not merely born but virtually manufactured, he claimed that it would be eternal.

'Do you maintain that Plato had the slightest acquaintance with natural philosophy, when he believes that anything which had a beginning can last for ever? What compound is there which does not break up? What thing has some sort of beginning but has no end?* Now if your Stoic Pronoia, Lucullus, is identical with this,* my question remains the same as before: what agents were there, what scaffolding? What were the planning and arrangement? But if your deity is different, why did Pronoia make the universe mortal rather than eternal as Plato's god did?

21 'The question I put to both of you is this: why did these world-builders suddenly emerge after lying asleep for countless generations? For the non-existence of the universe does not necessarily imply absence of periods of time; by 'periods of time' I do not mean those fixed by the yearly courses of the stars numbered in days and nights, for I grant that such eras would not have come into being without the circular movement of the universe. What I do mean is eternity, so to say, from the boundless past; one cannot measure it by any definite period of time, but one can understand what it must have been in extent,* for one cannot

even envisage that there may have been a time when no time existed.

22   'So what I am asking, Balbus, is this: why did your Pronoia remain idle throughout that boundless length of time? Was she avoiding hard work? But hard work does not impinge upon a god, and in any case there was no such labour, for all the elements of sky, stars, lands, and seas obeyed the divine will. Why should the god have sought, like some aedile, to adorn the world with decorative figures* and illuminations? If his motive was to improve his own living-quarters, then presumably he had earlier been dwelling for an infinite time in darkness, enclosed, so to say, in a windowless hovel. And what happened next? Do we assume that he took pleasure in the varied adornment which we behold in the heavens and on earth? What pleasure can a god take in such things? And if he did derive such pleasure, he could not have foregone it for so long.

23   'Alternatively, did God make this provision for the benefit of humans, as you Stoics usually claim?* If it was for humans, was it merely for the wise? In that case, the massive construction of the world was for the benefit of the few.* Or was it for fools? The first objection to this is that God had no cause to gain the gratitude of worthless people. In any case, what did he achieve for them, in view of the fact that unquestionably all fools are utterly miserable precisely because they are fools? Is there anything which we can mention more wretched than the state of foolishness? The second objection is that life holds so many inconveniences that though the wise alleviate them by weighing the benefits against them, the fools can neither avoid imminent hardships nor endure them when they are present.

   'As for those who have maintained that the world itself possesses life and wisdom, they have totally failed to see into what
24 shape the nature of intelligent mind could be installed.* I shall treat this matter* myself in a moment; for the present I shall merely express surprise at the slow-wittedness of those who would have it that a living creature endowed with both immortality and blessedness is spherical in shape, merely because Plato maintains that no shape is more beautiful than the sphere. In my view, the cylinder, the cube, the cone, the pyramid are more

beautiful. And what sort of life is assigned to this rotund god? Why, to be spun round at speed the like of which cannot even be imagined; I cannot envisage mental stability or a life of happiness resident in that! If an experience were to manifest itself as troublesome even in the slightest degree in our own bodies, it should surely be regarded as troublesome also in the god; now clearly the earth as a constituent part of the universe is also a part of your god, yet we observe that massive tracts of the earth cannot be populated and cultivated, because some of them are scorched by the impact of the sun, and others are in the hard grip of snow and frost owing to the sun's prolonged departure. So if the universe is god, since these lands are a part of the universe, we are to posit that some of god's limbs are ablaze, while others are frozen stiff!

25   'So these are your Stoic tenets, Lucilius. Now I shall recount the older views,* beginning with the most distant of previous philosophers. Thales* of Miletus was the first to investigate such matters. He said that water was the first principle, and that god was the mind that fashioned all things from water. But can gods exist without feelings? And why did he associate mind with water, if the mind can exist independently without a body? Anaximander* holds that gods are worlds beyond counting, which are born and over long periods emerge and disappear. But how can we envisage a god if he is not eternal?

26   'Next, Anaximenes* proposed that god was air, that it is created, unbounded, infinite and always in motion—as if air which is without shape could be a god (whereas most importantly a god should have not merely some shape, but the most handsome shape of all!), and as if everything which has had a beginning can be immortal! Anaxagoras* follows, having received his training from Anaximenes; he was the first to posit that the disposition and due order of all things is delineated and brought to completion by the power and reason of an infinite Mind. In arguing this case, Anaxagoras failed to perceive that no infinite being can be endowed with motion attached to and linked with sensation, and that sensation does not exist at all unless nature herself experiences its impact. Secondly, if he wished this Mind of his to be in some sense a living creature, it will have some

inner force to justify its being called alive; yet nothing can claim such an inner status in preference to the mind itself. It follows 27 that it must be clothed in an outer body. But since he will not have this, the notion of Mind uncovered and simple, not endowed with any organ of sense, clearly eludes the impact and grasp of our understanding.

'Alcmaeon of Croton* attributed divinity to the sun, moon, and stars in general, and also to the soul; he did not realize that he was bestowing immortality on mortal objects. As for Pythagoras,* who posited a soul pervading and passing through the whole of nature, a soul from which our own individual souls are detached, he did not perceive that the god was being rent asunder, torn apart by this forcible separation of human souls; nor that when our souls are wretched, which is an experience shared by many, a segment of the god is wretched, an impossible supposition.

28 'Then again, if the human mind were god, why would it remain in ignorance of anything? And further, if this supposed god were nothing but soul, how could he be implanted or infused into the universe?

'Next in order, Xenophanes* argued that the whole world had a mind attached to it, and was god because it was "unbounded". On this concept of mind as god, he will be subject to the same censure as his predecessors; on the god's infinity, the criticism will be even more severe, for what is infinite can have neither sensation nor connection with anything outside itself. As for Parmenides, he proposes a false solution; he constructs an unbroken circle of fiery light which encircles the sky like a crown (indeed, he labels it a "*stephane*" or "crown"), and this he calls god. No one could ever imagine that this circle has a divine shape or feeling. Parmenides* has in addition many monstrous tenets, for he makes deities out of war, disharmony, desire, and the like, things destructible by disease, sleep, forgetfulness, or old age; he does the same with the heavenly bodies, but as we have censured this in another philosopher,* we can pass over it in his case.

29 'Empedocles* is guilty of many other errors, but his notion of gods is his most distasteful lapse. He would have it that the four elements, from which he maintains that all things originate, are

divine, though it is obvious that the elements come into existence and are destroyed, and lack all sensation.

'Protagoras* likewise appears to have no inkling of the gods' nature; he says that he has no clear notion whatsoever of gods— of their existence or non-existence, or their nature.

'As for Democritus,* who at one moment peoples the company of the gods with his wandering images, at another with the world of nature which emits and dispatches them, at another with our perception and understanding, he is surely in the toils of grievous error. Since he also maintains that there is absolutely nothing which endures, because nothing maintains its own condition for ever, he surely disposed of god so completely as to leave no possible belief in him.

'As for air, which Diogenes of Apollonia* regards as god, what feeling, what divine shape can it possess?

30   'It would take too long to recount the self-contradictions in Plato.* In the *Timaeus*, he states that the father of the universe cannot be named; and in the books of the *Laws*, that we should not investigate the nature of god at all. As for his claim that god is wholly incorporeal (as the Greeks say, *asomaton*), what such a nature could possibly be is inconceivable, for it would inevitably lack sensation as well as practical wisdom and pleasure, all of which we associate with our conception of gods. Plato further states both in the *Timaeus* and in the *Laws* that the universe is god, and that so are the sky, the stars, the earth, our souls, and the deities we inherit from ancestral tradition. Such views are clearly false in themselves, and wildly self-contradictory.

31   'Xenophon,* too, makes much the same mistake in fewer words; for in his account of Socrates' sayings, he presents him as claiming on the one hand that we must not investigate the shape of god, but on the other as calling both the sun and the soul as god, and as saying at one moment that there is one god, and at another a plurality of them. These statements amount to much the same misconceptions as those which we cited from Plato.

32   'Moreover Antisthenes,* in his book called *The Physicist*, in saying that there is one god in nature as opposed to the many in popular belief, deprives the gods of their impact and nature. Speusippus* is not very different, for he follows in the footsteps

of his uncle Plato in positing a kind of vital force by which all things are controlled. He thus seeks to eradicate awareness of the gods from men's minds.

33   'Aristotle,* in the third book of his work *On Philosophy*, creates a hotch-potch of many ideas in dissenting from his master Plato. At one time he assigns divinity solely to Mind; at another he says that the world itself is god; at another, he appoints some other person as controller of the world, and gives him the role of guiding and maintaining the motion of the universe by a kind of counter-rotation. The heat of the heavens he also calls god, not realizing that the sky is a part of the universe which he himself elsewhere denoted as god. Yet how could the heavens maintain divine consciousness when whirling round at such speed? And again, where are we to site all the gods of popular belief, if we regard the heavens themselves as god? And when Aristotle argues that god is incorporeal, he robs him of all feeling and practical wisdom; further, if he is incorporeal, how can he be set in motion, and if he is in incessant movement, how can he be untroubled and blissful?

34   'Xenocrates* his fellow-pupil shows no greater wisdom in this matter, for in his books entitled *The Nature of the Gods*, there is no description of any divine shape. He states that there are eight gods. The planets bear the names of five of them; the sixth comprises all the stars implanted in the sky, to be envisaged as an uncompounded deity whose limbs are, so to say, scattered about; he appends the sun as the seventh, and the moon as the eighth. It is beyond understanding what sensations can impart blessedness to these.

'Heraclides* of Pontus, also a product of Plato's school, stuffed his books with infantile stories. But he too regards as divine at one time the universe, and, at another, Mind. He assigns divinity to the planets as well; he deprives the god of all feeling; he suggests that his shape is changeable; and again, in the course of the same book, he numbers earth and sky among the gods.

35   'Equally intolerable is the inconsistency of Theophrastus,* for at one moment he allots the divine primacy to Mind, at another to the heavens, and at yet another to the signs of the heavenly stars.

'Another figure unworthy of attention is Theophrastus' disciple Strato,* the one they call the Physicist, for he proposes that all divine power lies in nature, which bears within it the causes of birth, growth, and diminution, but which lacks all sensation and shape.

36   'I come now, Balbus, to the philosophers of your school.* Zeno* proposes that the law of nature is divine, with the power of enjoining what is right and of forbidding the opposite. How he lends life to this law—and we certainly require a god to be a living creature—we fail to understand. He also says elsewhere that the upper air is god; but can we fathom a god which is without feeling, a god which never confronts us in our prayers, aspirations, or vows?

'In other books he states his belief that there is a kind of reason which pervades the whole of nature and is endowed with divine power. This same power he assigns also to the stars, and to the years and months and changing complexion of the years. In interpreting Hesiod's *Theogony** (which means 'The Birth of the Gods'), he dispenses totally with customary notions of the gods. He does not regard Jupiter, Juno, Vesta, or deities similarly named as among the company of the gods, but teaches that these names by a sort of symbolism have been pinned on things without life and speech.

37   'His pupil Aristo* proposes an equally misguided thesis; for he argues that it is impossible to comprehend the shape of the deity, he denies that the gods possess feeling, and he is wholly uncertain whether there is a living god or not.

'As for Cleanthes,* who with the last-named was a fellow-disciple of Zeno, he at one point states that the universe itself is god, at another confers this title on the mind and soul of the whole of nature, but at a third decrees that the furthest, highest band of heat which envelops all round and girds and embraces the whole of creation on the outside, is god beyond the shadow of a doubt. Again, in the books which he composed *Against Pleasure*, he writes as if he is off his head, imagining at one moment that gods have a particular shape and appearance, but at another investing the stars with total divinity, and at another decreeing that nothing is more divine than reason. The outcome is that the god which our minds identify, and which we seek to memorize as having left its mental imprint on us,* nowhere makes any appearance at all.

38   'Persaeus,* also a disciple of Zeno, claims that those men have been considered gods who have devised some great and useful contribution to civilized life, and further, that such useful and beneficial contributions have themselves been accorded the status of gods. He did not even qualify this by calling them discoveries by the gods, but maintained that they were themselves divine. What could be more stupid than to attach the dignity of gods to mean and ugly objects, or to grant a place in the company of gods to men already obliterated in death, so that worship of them would consist of nothing but lamentation?

39   'As for Chrysippus,* who is regarded as the craftiest interpreter of the Stoic dreams, he assembles a massive crowd of unknown gods, gods so much beyond our knowing, indeed, that we cannot even hazard a guess at their shape, despite the fact that our minds to all appearances are capable of imagining any conceivable thing. He states that divine power lies in reason, and in the soul and mind of the natural world as a whole; that the universe itself is god, together with its soul which pervades everything; that its guiding principle, at work in the intellect and the reason, is also god; so is the general, all-embracing nature of things, and predetermined fate, and the ineluctable course of future events; and beyond these, fire and the aether which I have mentioned already; also things naturally in flux and flow, like water, earth, the lower air, the sun and moon and stars, and the all-embracing creation; and even those human persons who have attained immortality.

40   'Chrysippus also claims that the one whom men call Jupiter is the aether, that the air pervading the seas is Neptune, that the earth is the one they call Ceres;* and he runs through the names of the other gods similarly. He also states that the power of the enduring and eternal law, which he calls the guide of life and mentor in our duties, is Jupiter, and he calls that law the necessity of fate, the enduring truth of future events. Yet not one of these formulations is of such a kind that divine power seems to reside in it.

41   'These views are set down in the first book of his *Nature of the Gods*. In the second book, he seeks to reconcile the fairy-stories of Orpheus, Musaeus,* Hesiod, and Homer with his own account of the immortal gods in the first book, with the result that even the remotest poets appear to have been Stoics, even though they had never dreamt of such doctrines.

'He is followed in this by Diogenes of Babylon,* who in his book entitled *On Minerva* detaches from the myth the origin of that maiden by childbirth from Jupiter, and rationalizes it in terms of natural science.

42   'These approximate views which I have outlined are not considered judgements by philosophers, but dreams of madmen; indeed, the utterances of poets* are not much more ridiculous, though the very charm they exercise is harmful, with their portrayal of the gods as fired with anger and maddened with lust; they have set before our eyes their wars and battles, their conflicts and wounds, their hatreds and divisions and disagreements, their births and deaths, their plaints and outbursts of grief, their uncontrolled lusts, their adulteries and the bonds confining them, their sexual intercourse with humans, and their begetting of mortals from their immortal seed.

43   'With these untruths of the poets we can associate the monstrosities of the Magi, and the similar lunacy of the Egyptians,* and also the beliefs of the common herd, which their ignorance of the truth renders wholly inconsistent.

'If anyone were to contemplate the thoughtless and random nature of all these claims, he would be bound to revere Epicurus, and to consign him to the company of those very gods who are the focus of our enquiry. He was the only person to realize first, that gods exist because nature herself has imprinted the conception of them in the minds of all—for what nation or category of men does not have some anticipation of gods, without being indoctrinated? Epicurus terms this *prolepsis*,* in other words the conception of an object previously grasped by the mind, without which nothing can be understood, investigated, or discussed. We have come to appreciate the force and usefulness of this reasoning as a result of the divine treatise of Epicurus* entitled *Rule and Judgement*.

44   'So you see that the foundations of this enquiry have been
impressively laid: this belief of ours is not based on any prescrip-
tion, custom, or law, but it abides as the strong, unanimous conviction of the whole world. We must therefore come to the
realization that gods must exist because we have an implanted,
or rather an innate, awareness of them. Now when all people
naturally agree on something, that belief must be true; so we are
to acknowledge that gods exist. Since this is agreed by virtually
everyone—not just philosophers, but also the unlearned—we
further acknowledge that we possess what I earlier called an
'anticipation' or prior notion of gods (we must use neologisms*
for new concepts, just as Epicurus himself adopted *prolepsis* in a
sense which no previous philosopher had employed).

45   'As I was saying, then, we have this prior notion causing us to
believe that the gods are blessed and immortal; for just as
nature has bestowed on us the concept of the gods themselves, so
also she has etched the notion on our minds to make us believe
that they are eternal and blessed. If this is the case, the dictum
expounded by Epicurus* is true: "What is blessed and immortal
neither is troubled itself, nor causes trouble to its neighbour;
thus it is gripped by neither anger nor partiality, for all such attitudes are a mark of weakness."

'If our aim was merely to worship the gods devotedly and to
free ourselves from superstition, we would need to say nothing
more; the pre-eminent nature of the gods would be venerated
by the devotion of mankind because it is both eternal and truly
blessed, for reverence is rightly accorded to all that is supreme.
Moreover, all fear of the gods would have been excised, through
our awareness that anger and partiality are remote from the
gods' blessed and immortal nature. Once these misapprehensions are banished, no fears of the gods loom over us.

'But our minds seek to strengthen these convictions by investi-
gating the shape, the manner of life, the mental activity, and the
mode of operation of the god.

46   'So far as the divine appearance is concerned, we are
prompted partly by nature, and instructed partly by reason.
Each one of us from every nation has a natural conviction that
the gods have no other than human shape, for what other

appearance do they present to us at any of our waking or sleeping hours? But we need not base our entire judgement on such primary concepts,* for reason itself pronounces the same judgement.

47 It seems fitting that the most outstanding nature, in virtue of its blessedness and its immortality, should also be the most beautiful; and what arrangement of limbs, what fashioning of features, what shape or appearance can be more beautiful than the human form? You Stoics, Lucilius (I call you to witness rather than my friend Cotta here, whose views differ according to the moment*), when depicting the divine skill and workmanship, frequently point out how everything in the human form is

48 designed not merely with utility in mind, but also for beauty. So if the human shape is superior to the beauty of all living creatures, and god is a living creature, he certainly possesses that shape which is the most beautiful of all. Since it is certain that the gods are the most blessed of creatures, and no one can be blessed without possessing virtue, and virtue cannot exist without reason, and reason can subsist only in the human form, we must accordingly acknowledge that the gods have human

49 shape. Yet this form of theirs is not corporeal but quasi–corporeal,* containing not blood, but quasi-blood.

'Epicurus' researches were too penetrating, and his explanations too subtle, to be grasped by any Tom, Dick, or Harry, but I rely on the intelligence of my audience here in offering this explanation, which is more succinct than the theme demands. By virtue of his mental outlook and practical handling of things hidden and deeply buried, Epicurus teaches that the vital nature of the gods is such that it is first perceptible not to the senses, but to the mind;* and not in substance or in measurable identity,* like the things which he calls solid bodies because they are substantial. Rather, an infinite appearance of very similar images formed out of innumerable atoms arises, and flows towards the gods. Our minds focus and latch on to these images with the greatest sensations of pleasure; thus they obtain an understanding of what a blessed and eternal being is.

50 'The significance of the infinity just mentioned is supremely important, and repays close and careful scrutiny. We must grasp that its nature is such that there is an exact balance in all

creation—what Epicurus calls *isonomia** or equal distribution. What follows from this principle is that if there is a specific quantity of mortal creatures, the tally of immortals is no fewer; and again, if the destructive elements in the world are countless, the forces of conservation must likewise be infinite.

'Another enquiry, Balbus, which you Stoics often make, concerns the nature of the gods' life, how they spend their days.

51 Well, their life is such that nothing imaginable is more blessed, more abounding in all good things. The god is wholly inactive; he has no round of tasks to perform, and no structures to set up. He takes pleasure in his own wisdom and virtue,* utterly certain that he will be perennially surrounded by the greatest and most abiding pleasures.

52 'This god we can truly call blessed, whereas that Stoic god of yours is plagued with hard work. If the world itself is god, what can be less restful than to circle the vault of heaven at breakneck speed, without stopping for a single moment? Yet nothing is blessed if it is not restful. Or if there is some god resident as governor or guide within the world itself, maintaining the courses of the stars, the changes of the seasons, and the varying economy of creation, surveying lands and seas, protecting the interests and lives of the human race, he is certainly caught up in troublesome and laborious operations.

53 'But we Epicureans define the life of blessedness as residing in the possession of untroubled minds and relaxation from all duties. Our mentor who has schooled us in all else has also taught us that the world was created naturally, without the need for a craftsman's role, and the process which in your view cannot be put in train without the skilful touches of a god is so straightforward that nature has created, is now creating, and will continue to create innumerable worlds. Because you Stoics do not see how nature can achieve this without being endowed with mind, you behave like poets of tragedy, unable to draw the plot to its close, and having recourse to a *deus ex machina*.*

54 'You would surely have no need of the activity of such a figure if you would only observe how unlimited, unbounded tracts of space* extend in all directions. When the mind strains and stretches itself to observe these distances, it journeys abroad so

far that it can observe no ultimate limit at which to halt. It is in
this boundless extent of breadth, length, and height, then, that
innumerable atoms in infinite quantity flit around. There is
space between them, yet they latch on to each other. In gripping
each other they form a chain, as a result of which are fashioned
the shapes and forms of things which you Stoics believe cannot
be created without bellows and anvils. So you have implanted
in our heads the notion of an external lord whom we are to fear
day and night; for who would not stand in awe of a god who is a
prying busybody, who foresees and reflects upon and observes
all things, believing that everything is his business?

55   'The first consequence of this theology is your doctrine of the
necessity of fate, which you call *Heimarmene*. This impels you to
claim that every chance event is the outcome of an eternal
verity and a chain of causation.* How much respect can be
accorded to this school of philosophy, which like a pack of ignorant old women regards all that happens as the course of fate?

'Next follows your doctrine of *mantike*,* the Latin for which is
divinatio (divination). If we were disposed to take any notice of
you, this would overwhelm us with superstition, impelling us to
cultivate soothsayers, augurs,* fortune-tellers, seers, and
56   dream-interpreters. Epicurus has delivered us from these terrors.
Now that we are liberated, we have no fear of the gods, for we
realize that they neither create trouble for themselves, nor seek
to impose it on another. We venerate with devoted reverence
their pre-eminent and outstanding nature.

'But I fear that my enthusiasm has swept me along and made
me too long-winded. But I found it difficult, once I had
embarked upon so important and splendid a subject, to abandon
it, though my role here was to act as listener rather than as
speaker.'

57   Cotta at once responded with his customary bonhomie.* 'But
if you had not had something to say, Velleius, you could certainly
not have heard anything from me, for usually my mind more
readily apprehends the reasons for the falsehood of a statement
rather than its truth. This has often struck me before, as it did
just now as I was listening to you. If you were to ask me my view
of the nature of the gods, I should perhaps have nothing to

reply; but if you were to enquire whether I think their nature is such as you have just outlined, I would say that nothing seems to me less likely.

58 'But before turning to the substance of your argument, I would first like to offer my reflections on you personally. I have often, I suppose, heard that friend of yours Lucius Crassus* assessing you as undoubtedly the most learned of all Roman Epicureans, and saying that few Greeks of the school were a match for you. But my awareness of his remarkable affection for you led me to imagine that he was exaggerating out of his goodwill for you. I hesitate to praise you to your face, but in my view your treatment of this obscure and difficult subject has been crystal-clear, not merely in ample exposition of your views, but also in elegance of expression more marked than is customary in your school.

59 'During my time in Athens, I often attended Zeno's lectures.* In fact our teacher Philo, who used to call Zeno "the Epicurean chorus-leader", himself encouraged me to attend, doubtless so that after hearing the Epicurean doctrines expounded by the leader of their school, I would more readily appreciate how well Philo* refuted their doctrines. The point I wish to make is that Zeno, unlike most of his school and like yourself, spoke with clarity, seriousness, and elegance. Yet in listening to you just now, I experienced the same reaction as I often had when listening to him; I felt irritated that so talented an individual, if you will forgive my saying so, had become associated with such trivial, not to say stupid, doctrines.

60 'Not that I myself will advance anything better at this time, for as I said a moment ago, on almost all topics but especially on natural philosophy I more readily pronounce on what is not true rather than on what is. Should you ask me to identify God or his nature, I shall cite Simonides as my authority: when the tyrant Hiero* posed the same question to him, he asked for a day's grace to consider it privately, and when Hiero put the same question to him next day, he begged two days' grace. After doubling the number of days repeatedly, and being asked by Hiero why he did this, he answered: "The longer I ponder the question, the darker I think is the prospect of a solution." I imagine that Simonides, by all accounts not merely a delightful poet but also more

generally a man of learning and wisdom, was preoccupied by several sharp and subtle thoughts which caused him to hesitate about which was the most valid, so that he despaired of attaining any truth at all.

61 'But has your mentor Epicurus (for I prefer to conduct the argument with him rather than with you) anything at all to say which merits attention even at the level of humdrum commonsense, let alone as philosophy?

'In this investigation of the nature of the gods, the primary issue is whether they exist or not. You say that it is difficult to deny it. I agree, if the question is posed in public, but it is quite easy in this type of conversation conducted between friends. So though I am a *pontifex* myself,* and though I believe that our ritual and our state-observances should be most religiously maintained, I should certainly like to be persuaded of the fundamental issue that gods exist, not merely as an expression of opinion but as a statement of truth; for many troubling considerations occur to me which sometimes lead me to think that they do not exist at all.

62 'But note how generously I intend to deal with you. Beliefs like this one, which you share with other philosophers, I shall not tackle, for virtually all philosophers—and I include myself particularly—like the idea that gods exist. So I do not dispute the fact, but the argument you adduce I do not consider to be sufficiently strong. You advanced, as a sufficiently compelling proof for us to acknowledge the existence of gods, that persons of all communities and nations believe it to be so.* But this argument is not merely unsubstantial in itself, but also untrue. To begin with, what is the source of your knowledge of the beliefs of nations? My own opinion is that many races are so monstrously barbarous that they entertain no suspicion that gods exist.

63 'A second argument. Did not Diagoras, the man they called the Atheist, and after him Theodorus, openly dispense with gods and their nature? As for Protagoras* of Abdera, whom you have just mentioned and who was quite the most important sophist of his day, he prefaced his book with the words "I cannot say whether gods exist or not", and by order of the Athenians he was banished from their city and territory, and had his books

publicly burnt. I personally think that this precedent induced many to be more reluctant to declare similar convictions, for mere expressions of doubt could not guarantee them immunity from punishment.

'Or again, take perpetrators of sacrilege. What judgement shall we make of men who commit impieties or perjure themselves? To quote Lucilius,*

> If Lucius Tubulus at any time,
> Or Lupus, or Carbo, or any of Neptune's sons

64 had believed that gods exist, would they have perjured or polluted themselves so markedly? So this argument is not so conclusive as it seems for confirming the point you wish to make. But because you share it with other philosophers, I shall forgo it for now, since I prefer to confront doctrines peculiar to your school.

65 'I grant you that gods exist; so now inform me of their provenance, location, and the nature of their bodies, minds, and lives. These are the answers I am keen to have. To explain all of them, you exploit the dominion and the free movement of atoms. From them you fashion and create everything on earth, as the saying goes. But in the first place, atoms do not exist; for there is nothing [so small that it cannot be divided; moreover, assuming that atoms exist, they cannot be impelled through the void, assuming that you mean by void that]* which contains no body; so there can be no void, and nothing which is indivisible.

66 'These arguments with which I make free are the cryptic utterances of the natural philosophers. Whether they are true or not I do not know, but they seem more probable than yours.* The reprehensible theories which you mouth emanate from Democritus—perhaps also from his predecessor Leucippus:* that there are tiny bodies, some smooth, some rough, some round, some oblong, some curved and hook-shaped, and that heaven and earth have been formed from these not under the compulsion of any natural law, but by some sort of accidental collision.* You, Velleius, have carried this theory through to our own day; one could dislodge you from your whole life's course sooner than from the authority which you cite, for you decided on becoming an Epicurean before you acquainted yourself with these tenets,

and so you had either to take aboard these outrageous doctrines, or to abandon your claim to the philosophy which you had embraced.

67   'For what would induce you to stop being an Epicurean? "Absolutely nothing", you reply "would make me forsake the rationale of the happy life and the truth." So is this creed of yours the truth? I do not challenge you on your claim to the happy life, for in your eyes even a god does not attain it unless he lives a life of torpid idleness. But where is this truth you claim? I suppose it lies in all those countless worlds of yours, which come into being and fade away at the drop of a hat! Or does it lie in the indivisible particles which without the direction of nature or reason* can fashion such notable structures? But I am forgetting the forbearing attitude which I had begun to show to you a moment ago, and I am challenging too many of your tenets. So I shall let pass your claim that all things are composed of atoms. But what relevance has this when the subject of our investigation is the nature of the gods?

68   'Granted, then, that the gods are composed of atoms, it follows that they are not eternal,* for what is formed from atoms came into being at some time. Now if an atomic compound comes into being, gods did not exist earlier, and if gods have a beginning, they must also die—as you argued a moment ago* yourself in the case of Plato's universe. So where are this much-vaunted blessedness and this eternity of yours, the two criteria which you demand for divinity, to be found? In trying to establish them, you take refuge in a thicket of philosophical jargon, in your statement that a god does not have a body but a quasi-body, and does not have blood but quasi-blood.

69   'This is a frequent practice of your school. When you try to avoid censure for proposing an unlikely theory, you advance a thesis so utterly impossible that you would have been better to concede the matter in dispute than to offer such shameless resistance. For example,* Epicurus realized that if atoms were borne downwards by their own weight, free will would be out of the question, because the movement of the atoms would be fixed and inevitable. So he devised a means of avoiding such determinism (this idea had doubtless not occurred to Democritus); he

70 stated that when the atom was borne directly downward by the
force of gravity, it swerved* ever so slightly. This explanation is
tawdrier than his inability to defend his thesis* would have been.

'He does the same thing in confronting the logicians.* Their
traditional teaching is that in all disjunctive propositions of the
"either true or not" type, one or other of the two standpoints is
true. But Epicurus was afraid that if he granted the validity of
the statement "Epicurus will be alive tomorrow, or he will not",
one or other conclusion would be necessary; so he denied that
the entire category of "either true or not" was necessary; what
can possibly be more asinine than that? Arcesilaus used to
hammer away at Zeno,* for while he himself labelled all sense-
impressions fallacious, Zeno claimed that some were false, but
not all. But Epicurus feared that if one single sensation appeared
false, none of them would be true, so he stated that all sense-
impressions registered the truth. In none of these doctrines was
he too clever;* while seeking to ward off the lighter punch, he
ran into one heavier.

71 'He does the same thing in discussing the nature of the gods; in
seeking to avoid the charge that they are an accretion of atoms,
with the inevitable consequence of their destruction and disper-
sal, he claims that they do not have bodies, but "quasi-bodies",
and not blood, but "quasi-blood". It seems remarkable that one
augur can look another in the eye without grinning,* but it is
more remarkable still how you Epicureans can restrain your
laughter when in each other's company. "Not bodies, but quasi-
bodies"; I could grasp the meaning of this if they were made of
wax or earthenware, but what a "quasi-body" or "quasi-blood"
is in the case of a god, I cannot imagine. Nor can you, Velleius,
but you are unwilling to admit it.

72 'You Epicureans repeat these doctrines like parrots, as though
they have been dictated to you. Epicurus dreamt them up when
half-asleep, for as we note from his writings, he boasted that he
never had a teacher. Even if he had not proclaimed this, I
myself could readily have believed it of him. He reminds me of
the owner of a badly constructed house who boasts of not
having employed an architect. There is not a whiff of the Academy or the Lyceum* in him, nor even a hint of basic lessons

learnt at school. He could have attended the lectures of Xenocrates,* an impressive enough teacher heaven knows, and some
believe that he did so. But he himself disavowed it, and I prefer
his own testimony to that of others.

'He says that he attended the school of a certain Pamphilus,*
one of Plato's disciples, on the island of Samos, where he lived as
a young man with his father and brothers. (His father Neocles
had gone there* as a settler, but he turned schoolmaster, I
believe, when his little farm provided too precarious a living.)

73 But Epicurus shows extraordinary contempt for this Platonist,*
so fearful is he of appearing ever to have been taught anything.
But he is caught red-handed in the case of Nausiphanes,* a follower of Democritus; he does not deny that he heard him lecture,
but he harries him with all manner of abuse. Yet if we assume
that he had not attended these teachings of Democritus, what
others could he have attended? What is there in the natural
philosophy of Epicurus which does not stem from Democritus?
It is true that he changed a few things, as for example the
swerve of the atoms which I mentioned a moment ago, but the
main lines are the same: atoms and void, images, infinity of
space, countless worlds, their emergence and extinction—in
fact, almost the entire range of natural philosophy.

74 'But tell me: what *do* you understand by "quasi-body" and
'quasi-blood'? Not merely do I admit that your knowledge in
these matters is superior to mine, but I am readily reconciled to
the fact. But once this view has been enunciated, why should Velleius be able to understand it, while Cotta cannot? I understand
the nature of body and of blood, but what "quasi-body" and
"quasi-blood" are I utterly fail to understand. It is not that you
are hiding things from me, as Pythagoras used to do from outsiders;* nor do you purposely make things obscure as Heraclitus
did.* Let us be frank with each other; you do not understand

75 the doctrine either! I am aware that your contention is that
gods have a certain appearance, embodying nothing compact
or firm, nothing securely fashioned or outlined, but what is
clear, light, and transparent. So we shall liken it to the *Venus of
Cos.** Hers is not a body, but the representation of a body; that
blush which pervades and colours her snow-white complexion is

not blood, but a sort of representation of blood. Likewise Epicurus' god has no reality, but merely a semblance of reality.

76   'Assume for a moment that I accept this quite incomprehensible notion. Explain to me, please, the outline and shape of these shadowy gods of yours. You have a number of arguments to advance here, in the attempt of your school to demonstrate that gods have human shape. First, you claim that we have an inbuilt, preconceived notion in our minds, so that when we think of "god", the human form is what presents itself to us. Second, since the gods' nature excels all things, its shape must likewise be the most beautiful, and no shape is more beautiful than the human. Third, you adduce the argument that in no other shape can a mind have a home.

77   'So first you must analyse the nature of each of these claims. It seems to me that you Epicureans arrogate as your rightful possession an assumption which is wholly improbable.

'To begin with, was anyone ever so blind in his survey of realities as not to see that these human shapes have been ascribed to the gods for one of two possible reasons? Either some strategy of philosophers* sought to divert more easily the minds of the unsophisticated from debased living towards observance of the gods; or superstition ensured that statues were furnished for men to worship in the belief that they were addressing the gods themselves. Poets, painters, sculptors have nurtured these attitudes, because it was not easy to preserve the impression that gods were active and creative if they were represented by non-human shapes.

'There was also a belief of yours perhaps reinforcing this, that to a human person nothing seems more beautiful than another human being. But you as a natural philosopher must see how nature plays the role of a seductive brothel-madam, a procuress recommending her wares. You surely cannot imagine that there is a single beast on land or sea which does not take delight above all in one of its own species? If this were not the case, why should a bull not seek to couple with a mare, or a horse with a cow? Do you perhaps suppose that an eagle or lion or dolphin* prefers any other shape to its own? So it is hardly surprising that nature has similarly prevailed on humans to believe that nothing is more beautiful than a human being. [It is likely that this is why the gods have been thought to resemble men.]*

78 'Do you not acknowledge that if beasts had reason they would one and all have ranked their own species highest? Even as it is, to speak frankly, in spite of my self-regard I do not presume to claim to be more handsome than the bull which bore off Europa!* The point at issue in our discussion here is not of course our native intelligence or powers of expression, but our appearance and shape; yet if we had the choice of fashioning and forming a combination of shapes, you would refuse to resemble the famous merman Triton,* who is depicted as propelled by sea-creatures which are attached to his human frame. I am treading on difficult territory here; such is nature's power that no one wants to resemble anything but another human being, just as every ant wishes to resemble another ant.

79 'Yet what sort of human shape would we like? There are very few handsome people. During my time in Athens, it was hard to find a single handsome lad in every platoon of national servicemen.* I know why you're grinning,* but my observation is true. A further point: those of us who take our cue from the philosophers of old, and enjoy the company of young men, often find even their physical defects attractive. For Alcaeus,* the mole upon a young lad's wrist appeals; though a mole is a physical blemish, the poet considered it a beauty-spot. Quintus Catulus,* the father of the Catulus who is my fellow-pontiff and friend, was an intimate of your fellow-townsman Roscius;* indeed, he addressed these lines to him:

> To greet the rising Dawn I chanced to stand,
> When Roscius suddenly rose at my left hand.
> Ye gods, without offence I must declare:
> No god beside that mortal seemed so fair!

In Catulus' eyes Roscius was more handsome than a god, though he had (and still has) the most terrible squint. Yet it hardly mattered, for Catulus found that very feature amusing and charming.

80 'But let me get back to the gods. Do we picture any of them, I don't say as cross-eyed as that, but with a slight squint? Or any

of them with a wart? Or any that are snub-nosed, or flap-eared, or beetle-browed, or with large heads, like some humans? Or are all these defects straightened out among the gods? Let's grant you that they are—but surely the gods' features are not all identical? The point is that if they vary in appearance, one must be more handsome than another, and from this it follows that some among them are not outstandingly beautiful. If on the other hand they all look alike, the Academy must be flourishing in heaven,* for if one god is indistinguishable from another, recognition and perception are out of the question.

81   'Then again, Velleius, will you maintain that risible stance of yours, if we find that it is wholly untrue that when we think of a god, the sole appearance that comes to mind is that of a human being? It perhaps works out as you say in the case of Romans like ourselves, for from childhood onward we identify Jupiter, Juno, Minerva, Neptune, Vulcan, Apollo, and the other deities with the features which painters and sculptors have decided to plant on them; not only do they give them standard features, but the equipment they carry, the clothes that they wear, and their time of life do not vary. But Egyptians, Syrians, and virtually all the uncivilized world do not envisage gods in this way; you can observe that they maintain more passionate beliefs in the divinity of certain animals than we manifest in our most hal-
82 lowed shrines and statues of the gods. We see, do we not, many shrines plundered,* with statues of the gods being removed from their most venerable niches; but we do not get reports even by hearsay of a crocodile or ibis or cat* suffering violence at the hands of an Egyptian. You must surely concede that the sacred ox Apis* seems as much a god to the Egyptians as your celebrated Sospita seems to you, the goddess whom even in deep sleep you never see without her goatskin, spear, small shield, and turned-up slippers; yet the Juno* at Argos, and again the Juno at Rome are quite different. So Juno has one appearance for the Argives, but another for the Lanuvians; and indeed Jupiter appears to us in one guise on the Capitol, but in another to the Africans as Jupiter Ammon.*

83   'So are you, the natural philosopher who with gimlet eye hunts down the secrets of nature, not ashamed to look for evidence of

the truth in minds steeped in familiar convention? If we accept
your arguments, it will be right to claim that Jupiter always
sports a beard, while Apollo is always clean-shaven; that Minerva's eyes are grey-green, but Neptune's are dark blue. And
another thing: we praise the representation of Vulcan, the work
of the sculptor Alcamenes* which is found at Athens. The god is
standing fully clothed, and carries a not unseemly limp; so we
shall assume that the god is lame, since this is the tradition
which we have inherited concerning Vulcan.

84   'And tell me this: are we also to assume that the gods bear the
names which we allot to them? Yet they have as many names as
there are human languages. Wherever you go, your name
remains Velleius, but unlike you, Vulcan does not bear the same
name* in Italy, France, and Spain. Then again, even our pontifical registers* do not contain numerous names, whereas the
number of gods is beyond counting. So are there anonymous
gods? You are forced to make such an admission, for since they
are look-alikes, what point is there in a plurality of names? How
splendid it would be, Velleius, if you were to admit ignorance of
what you do not know, rather than puking and feeling disgust
with yourself for uttering such balderdash! You cannot genuinely
believe that a god is in my likeness or yours; of course not.

'So, reverting to the point you made, am I to call the sun a god,
or the moon, or the sky? If so, they too are blessed—but what
85 pleasures do they enjoy?—and wise. These are your Epicurean
arguments. So if, as I have shown, gods do not have a human
appearance, and if, as you firmly believe, they are unlike anything in the heavens, why do you hesitate to deny that they
exist? You lose your nerve, and it is wise of you to do so, though
your fear on this account is not of the people but of the gods themselves. I know Epicureans who worship every little statue; but I
note that some people think* that Epicurus gave merely nominal
assent to the gods' existence, while dispensing with them in reality, to avoid incurring the Athenians' displeasure. So in those
carefully chosen, pithy maxims of his, which your school calls
*The Principal Doctrines,** I gather that the first one runs: "What is
blessed and immortal experiences no trouble itself, and causes
no trouble to anyone." Some believe that the maxim was deliber-

ately formulated in this way, but in fact it was the result of Epicurus' inability to express himself clearly. He was no calculating scoundrel, and their imputation is unjust.

86   'It is not clear whether he is saying that there *is* something blessed and immortal, or that *if any such thing exists*, it possesses such attributes. But his critics do not notice that whereas his statement here is ambiguous, in several other places both he and Metrodorus* expressed themselves as clearly as you did just now. Epicurus does indeed believe that gods exist. In fact I have never met anyone with more fear of the things which he said we should not fear, namely death and the gods. He is loud in his claim that the whole of mankind is inwardly scared of things which in reality do not worry normal people overmuch.* Thousands on thousands commit robbery with violence in spite of the death penalty, and others plunder every shrine they can lay hands on; those footpads, I suppose, are alarmed by fear of death, and these plunderers by religious panic!

87   'I shall now address Epicurus himself; since you do not dare bring yourself to deny the gods' existence, what prevents you from assigning a place among the gods to the sun, or the universe, or some eternal Mind? He counters: "But I have never seen a rational, purposeful mind in any form but the human." But surely you have seen nothing to match the sun either, or the moon, or the five planets. The sun accomplishes its course* year by year, confining its progress within the two extreme limits of the one orbit. The moon, which is fired by the sun's rays, encompasses the same route as the sun within a month. The five planets maintain the same circular course, some being closer to and others more distant from the earth, but from the same starting-point they cover the same distance in varying lengths of time. Epicurus, you can have seen nothing similar to this.*

88   'Let us assume, then, the non-existence of the courses of the sun, moon, and planets,* since nothing can exist except what we have touched or seen. But you have not had sight of God himself, have you, so why believe in his existence? On this basis we must dispense with everything brought to our notice by history or science; it leads to the conclusion that folks in the hinterland do not believe in the existence of the sea. What downright

narrow-mindedness this is! It is like imagining that you were born on Seriphus* and had never left the island, where you were used to seeing small creatures like hares and foxes—and refusing to believe in lions and panthers when they were described to you. As for the elephant, if anyone told you about it, you would believe that you were the butt of a joke!

97   'To press this argument* still further, can any statement be more childish than the claim that the types of beasts found in the Indian Ocean or in India* do not exist? Yet even the most diligent of researchers cannot gather information about all the many animals which dwell on land and sea, in marshes and rivers. So are we to claim that they do not exist because we have never set eyes on them?

89   'As for you, Velleius, you have expressed the substance of your argument not after the normal practice of your school, but using the technique of the logicians,* of which your tribe is wholly ignorant. You assumed that the gods are happy; we grant that. You argue that none can be happy without virtue; this too we concede, and gladly. Virtue, you claim, cannot exist without reason; to this too we are forced to assent. But as for your next step, that reason exists only in the human form, who do you imagine will grant you that? If this were indeed the case, why should it have been necessary to reach it by successive stages? You could have assumed it on your own terms, but how is it relevant to the chain of argument? I understand your progress step by step from the gods' happiness to virtue, and from virtue to reason, but how do you advance from reason to the human form? That is a headlong plunge, not a logical step.

90   'Frankly I do not understand why Epicurus prefers to say that gods are like men, rather than that men are like gods. You will ask what the difference is, saying that if the first are like the second, the second are like the first. I realize that, but my point is that the outline of the human shape did not pass from men to the gods, for the gods have always existed,* and were never born, as they were to be eternal. But men are born, so the human form existed before the human race did, and the immortal gods were endowed with that form. Accordingly we must

state not that the gods have human shape, but that our human form is divine.

'But I leave this to you Epicureans to cope with as you will. What I seek to know, since your school claims that nothing in the natural world has come to pass by design, is the extraordin
91 ary chance, the remarkable accident which resulted in so fortunate a fusion of atoms that men were suddenly born in the image of gods. Are we to believe that divine seeds tumbled down from heaven to earth, and that this was how men sprang into existence resembling their sires? I should be delighted with such an explanation from you, for to acknowledge kinship with the gods would not go against the grain. But the account you offer is not like that, for you say that our similarity to the gods is the result of chance. Do we need to seek proofs to reject such absurdity? I only wish that I could divine the truth as easily as I can refute such falsehood.

'It was with pleasure and surprise at a Roman's possessing such wide knowledge* that I heard you recounting in detail the opinions of philosophers from Thales of Miletus onwards, con
92 cerning the nature of the gods. But did you regard all of them as maniacs because they claimed that a god can exist without hands and feet?

'When your school reflects on the usefulness and convenience of limbs for human beings, does not even this convince you that the gods have no need of such human limbs? Why should they need feet when they do not walk, or hands if they need grasp nothing, or an allocation of all our bodily parts? None of these is without point or purpose, none is superfluous; we conclude that no human skill can emulate the expert touch of nature. So will God have a tongue yet not speak, and teeth and palate and throat, yet to no purpose? As for the parts which nature has attached to our bodies for procreation, will God possess them but have no use for them? And likewise the internal as well as the external organs, heart, lungs, liver and the rest—what beauty do they possess if you discount their usefulness? I ask this because you Epicureans argue that God possesses them for their beauty.

93 'These were the dreams of yours which lent assurance not only to Epicurus, Metrodorus, and Hermarchus* when they

challenged Pythagoras, Plato, and Empedocles, but also to Leontium,* that mere courtesan, who had the effrontery to write a riposte to Theophrastus—mind you, she wrote elegantly in good Attic, but still, this was the licence which prevailed in the Garden of Epicurus. And yet you Epicureans are often thin-skinned. Zeno even had recourse to law, and I need not mention the case of Albucius. As for Phaedrus,* most urbane and cultivated of men, the old fellow would grow hot with rage if I ever said anything to needle him. Yet Epicurus buffeted Aristotle* with fearful insults, heaped despicable abuse on Socrates' pupil Phaedo, wrote whole volumes to cut down to size Timocrates, brother of his associate Metrodorus, merely for expressing some philosophical disagreement, showed lack of generosity to Democritus, the very man whose doctrines he had adopted, and doled out harsh treatment to his own teacher Nausiphanes, from whom he claimed to have learnt nothing. As for Zeno, not only did he revile his contemporaries Apollodorus, Sillis,* and the rest, but he labelled Socrates, the very father of philosophy, an Attic trifler, using the Latin word *scurra*, and invariably he referred to Chrysippus as Chrysippa.* When you yourself a moment ago were calling the roll of philosophers like a censor reciting the list of senators, you repeatedly stigmatized men of distinction as simpletons, fools, and madmen. Yet if not one of them discerned the truth about the nature of the gods, we must fear that there is no such thing at all.

'As for this Epicurean account of yours, it is utter eyewash, hardly worthy of the old women who spin yarns by candlelight. You simply do not realize how much you let yourselves in for if you extract from us the admission that men and gods are identical in shape. You will have to allot to a god all the physical cares and concerns* that we ascribe to a man—walking and running, reclining and bending, sitting down and grasping things, and to crown all, even chatting and declaiming. As for your thesis that deities are both male and female, you realize the significance of that! I for my part never cease to wonder how your famous founder came to hold those beliefs.

'But your interminable cry is that we must cleave fast to the doctrine of the divine blessedness and immortality. But what prevents a god being happy even if he is not endowed with two legs? Why cannot this blessedness, however you like to term it— whether we are to use the word *beatitas* or alternatively *beatitudo*,* both quite hard on the ears, but we have to soften words by use—be applied to the sun up yonder, or to this world of ours, or to some eternal Mind possessed of no bodily shape or limbs?

96 Your only response is: "I never saw a happy sun or a happy world." So have you ever set eyes on a world other than this? You will say you have not. Why, then, had you the temerity to maintain the existence not merely of thousand upon thousand, but of worlds beyond counting? You reply: "Reason has taught us this." So in your search for the nature that is truly outstanding, blessed, and eternal, which alone possesses the attributes of divinity, will reason not also instruct you that just as divine nature surpasses us in immortality, so too it surpasses us in mental excellence—and not only in mental but also in physical excellence? So why are we peers of the gods physically, when we fall behind them in all other respects? One would have thought that human beings attained closer likeness to the gods in virtue than in appearance.*

97 'In any case, the physical likeness in which you take the greatest pleasure has no bearing on the argument. Does not a dog resemble a wolf? (And as Ennius remarks,* "An ugly brute the ape may be, / But how he resembles you and me!") Yet the two have different habits. No beast surpasses the elephant in sagacity,

98 but what animal is more monstrous in appearance? I instance animals, but is it not true that human beings of closely similar appearance differ widely in behaviour, and that those with similar manners differ in appearance?

'Indeed, Velleius, once we embark on this type of argument, observe where it leads. Your assumption was that reason can exist only in the human form; but someone else will take it for granted that it exists only in an earthly creature, in one who has been born, has grown to maturity, has been schooled, is made up of a soul and a transient, feeble body—in short, that it exists only in human persons doomed to die. If you set your face against all these limiting factors, why should shape alone preoccupy you? You acknowledged that reason and intelligence exist in man only if those determinants which I have proposed are present; yet you state that even if they are stripped away, you can recognise a god as long as the physical features remain. This conclusion of yours emerges not from reflection, but from a lottery.

99   'But perhaps you have not noted even this: not merely in a man, but also in a tree, anything superfluous or without a function is an impediment. It is a dreadful nuisance to have an extra finger, and why? Because the five which we have do not require a sixth for appearance or for use. But the god you posit has no mere finger surplus to requirements, but a head, neck, spine, sides, belly, back, hams, hands, feet, calves, and thighs. If these are provided to make him immortal, what relevance have limbs or even facial features for sustaining life? More important are the brains, heart, lungs, and liver, for these are the vitals; facial appearance is unimportant for maintaining life.

100   'Another thing: you directed withering criticism* at those who took account of the magnificent and pre-eminent works of creation, who contemplated the universe itself and its parts—the sky, lands, and seas, and their adornments the sun, moon, and constellations—and who recognized the developments, changes, and transformations of the seasons, and accordingly conjectured that there was some outstanding, pre-eminent nature which had created them, and now impelled, governed and guided them. Even if such men are off-target, I can understand their line of thought. But I ask you, what great and outstanding work do *you* adduce,* such as seems to have been created by a divine mind, and which leads you to conjecture that gods exist? You reply: 'I have the notion of God implanted in my mind.' Yes, together with a vision of a bearded Jupiter, and Minerva wearing a helmet. So can you really believe that this is what they are

101   like? How much more sensible is the approach of the ignorant masses to these issues! They credit God not only with human limbs but also with the use of them, for they equip them with bow and arrows, spear and shield, trident and thunderbolt; and if they have no idea of the actions which gods perform, at least they cannot envisage a God who is wholly inactive. We scoff at the Egyptians, but even they have deified only those creatures from whom they could derive some benefit. For example, ibises

dispose of large numbers of snakes, for these birds are tall with stiff legs and long, horny beaks. They keep Egypt clear of the plague by killing and eating the flying serpents borne in from the African desert* by the south-west wind, and as a result the snakes do no harm by their bite when alive, or by their stench when dead. I could go on about the usefulness of Egyptian rats and crocodiles and cats,* but I do not wish to be tedious. I shall merely point the moral that beasts though these are, they have been deified by the barbarians for the benefits they bring, whereas no benefit accrues from your gods—indeed, they do nothing at all.

102 ' "God", says Epicurus, "has no concerns." Like boy-favourites, he clearly likes nothing better than the idle life. But even those boys in their idleness seek enjoyment by playing some physical sport; do we want God to be so idle and sluggish as to make us fear that he cannot he happy if he bestirs himself? That maxim of his not merely deprives the gods of the movements and action appropriate to divinity, but also makes humans lazy, the assumption being that even God cannot be happy if he is doing something.

103 'But let us grant, as you would have it, that God is the image and likeness of man; where is his residence,* his habitat, his native heath? Or again, how does he spend his life? What things make for the happiness which you ascribe to him? For one who is to be blessed must exploit and enjoy his blessings. Even the soulless elements possess their allotted regions: earth occupies the lowest level, water laps over it, the region above it is apportioned to the thicker air, and the topmost area to the aetherial fires. Of creatures, some dwell on earth, some in water, and some that are amphibious dwell in both. Some are thought to be born even in fire,* and are often to be seen fluttering in fiery furnaces.

104 'So my first question is: where does that God of yours dwell? Second, what makes him move from his position, if he ever does? Next, since living creatures have a native tendency to seek what is suited to their nature, what is it that God seeks? For what purpose does he exercise the thrust of his mind and reason? Finally, what form do his blessedness and eternity take?

Touching on any of these issues probes a sensitive spot, for reasoning without a solid premiss cannot attain a proper conclusion.

105   'Your claim was that we envisage God's appearance by thought rather than by the senses, that his form has no substance or continuing measurable identity,* and that our perception of it is such that it is descried in a sequence of similar images. You suggest that there is an unceasing onset of such similar images emerging from a limitless number of atoms, as a result of which, through concentration on these forms, our minds regard the divine nature as blessed and eternal. In the name of the very gods whom we are discussing, what sort of statement, I ask you, is this? If the gods make their impact only on our thoughts, and have no substance or outline, what difference does it make whether we visualize a hippocentaur* or a god? Other philosophers label all such mental constructions as empty experiences, but you call them the onset and entry of images into our minds.

106   When I seem to behold Tiberius Gracchus* haranguing the assembly on the Capitol, and extending the voting-urn to decide the fate of Marcus Octavius, I pronounce this to be an empty figment of the mind, but you argue that the images of both Gracchus and Octavius after their arrival on the Capitol remain present to be transmitted to my mind; and your standpoint is identical in the case of God, for you claim that our minds are struck by repeated images of divinity, so that we come to understand that the gods are blessed and immortal.

107   Even if we grant that there are images to strike our minds (always provided that they have some sort of shape), why should such a manifestation be blessed or eternal?

'But what are these images of yours, or where do they come from? Admittedly such a fanciful notion derives from Democritus,* but he has been criticized by many, and you Epicureans can devise no solution, so that the whole doctrine is halting and precarious. For what can be less probable than that the images of each and every individual should present themselves to me— Homer and Archilochus,* Romulus and Numa, Pythagoras and Plato, and none of them in their original appearance? How, then, did those famous figures reach me? To whom do the images belong? Aristotle informs us that the poet Orpheus never existed, and the Pythagoreans maintain that the Orphic poem now current* was the work of a certain Cercops; yet Orpheus, or as you maintain the image of him, often enters my mind.

108 'Further problems arise: different images of the same person* strike our two minds; we are visited by images of things which certainly never existed or could never exist, like those of Scylla and of the Chimaera, or by images of people, places, and cities which we have never set eyes on; again, images present themselves to me as soon as I desire them, or they come to me unsummoned even when I am asleep. The whole theory, Velleius, is a nonsense, and yet you Epicureans foist the images not only on our eyes but also on our minds. Your prattling is wholly undisciplined and fanciful.

109 ' "There is a constant stream of images flowing past us, so that the many seem to merge into one." I should be ashamed to admit that I do not understand this, if only you apologists for the notion understood it yourselves. How do you establish that the images are continuous, or if they are continuous, that they are never-ending? Epicurus states: "There is a supply of innumerable atoms." You will surely not claim that this establishes that all things are eternal? You have recourse to the theory of equilibrium (we can use this term, if you are agreeable, for the Greek *isonomia*), arguing that since there is transitory nature, there must also be immortal nature. On this argument the existence of mortal men would necessitate the existence of immortal men, and since human beings are born on earth, some would likewise be born on water. "Because there are destructive forces, there must also be forces which preserve." Very well, but they must preserve things that exist, and I am not sure that those gods of yours do exist.

110 'However, leaving this on one side, how does the generality of these images of objects emerge from the atoms? Even if we assume that the atoms exist—in fact, they do not—though they perhaps could strike each other and be stirred by such collisions, they could not shape or fashion things, or endow them with colour and life. So in no way does your school prove the existence of an immortal God.

'Let us now consider blessedness.* It can certainly not exist at all without virtue, but virtue is an active faculty, whereas your

111 God is inactive. He is thus a stranger to virtue, and accordingly he cannot be blessed either. So what sort of life does he lead? "There is a ready supply of good things", you say, "without the hindrance of any evil." What are these good things, then? Pleasures, I suppose, and naturally enough physical ones, for you Epicureans acknowledge no pleasure of the mind unless it has is source and its final effect in the body. I do not imagine that you wish to be like the other Epicureans, who are ashamed of some of the statements of Epicurus, in which he attests that he cannot even envisage any good which is detached from luxurious and lewd pleasures;* he has the gall to enumerate them specifically.

112   'So what foodstuffs and drinks, what musical harmonies or range of blossoms, what pleasures of touch or smell will you assign to the gods so as to steep them in pleasures? The poets for their part furnish nectar and ambrosia and banquets, with Juventas or Ganymede* serving the cups; what plans do you have as an Epicurean? I cannot see from where your God is to procure such things, nor how he is to enjoy them. So humans are better equipped by nature than gods for the life of blessedness, because they enjoy a greater range of pleasures.

113   'Your response is that you regard as more trivial those pleasures which, to use Epicurus' word,* merely titillate the senses. Is there no limit to the games you play? Like me, our teacher Philo* could not brook Epicureans despising effeminate and luxurious pleasures; with his keen memory he used to quote word for word numerous maxims of Epicurus. He would also recount several more shameless utterances of Metrodorus, Epicurus' associate in philosophy; it was this Metrodorus who inveighed against his brother Timocrates for his reluctance to make the belly the criterion of all that relates to the blessed life—and this was no isolated accusation, but one frequently repeated. I see that you acknowledge the point, for the statements are known to you; if you denied it, I could produce the books. I do not at this juncture censure your making pleasure the measure of everything, for that is another question; I am bringing home to you

the fact that your gods are strangers to pleasure, and so by your own counting they cannot be blessed either.

114 ' "But they have no experience of pain." Is *that* sufficient for a life of total blessedness, replete with good things? "God continuously contemplates his own blessedness," they say; "He has nothing else to preoccupy his mind." So ponder and envisage a god whose thoughts throughout all eternity are focused solely on "All is well with me!", and "I am blessed!" Yet I do not see how this blessed God of yours feels no fear of extinction, since he is battered and buffeted without respite by a perpetual onslaught of atoms, and since all the time images emanate from him. So your God is neither blessed nor eternal.

115 ' "Yet Epicurus wrote also about reverence and devotion* for the gods." Yes, but how does he address the issue? You would swear that you were listening to one of our chief priests, to Tiberius Coruncanius or Publius Scaevola,* and not to one who has utterly undermined all religious observance, and has overturned the temples and altars of the immortal gods not by violence, as Xerxes did,* but by his arguments. What reason can you offer that men should worship the gods, when the gods not merely show no regard for men, but take absolutely no responsibility or action of any kind?

116 ' "But their nature is in some sense so outstanding and preeminent that of its very self it must entice the philosopher to worship it." Yet how can there be anything outstanding in the nature which takes joy in its own pleasure, and whose existence—past, present, and future—is one of total inactivity? Moreover, what devotion is the due of one from whom we have received nothing, or what can possibly be owed to one who has not deserved well of us? Piety means giving the gods their due; but what religious law can we follow, when humans and gods have no common bond? Religious observance is expertise in divine worship, but I fail to understand why the gods should be worshipped if we neither obtain nor anticipate any blessing from them.

117 'As for admiring the gods' nature, why should we revere it when we see in them no outstanding quality? You Epicureans often boast that you free men from superstition,* but that is easily achieved once you have deprived the gods of all their

power—unless perhaps you think that Diagoras or Theodorus, who flatly denied the gods' existence, could have been superstitious, though my own view is that even Protagoras,* who could not decide whether the gods existed or not, was not troubled that way. The maxims of all these thinkers banish not only the superstition which induces groundless fear of the gods, but also the religious observance embraced by devoted worship of them.

118   'Then again, some have said that belief in the immortal gods was a total invention by sages in the interests of the state, so that those who could not be impelled by reason should be constrained by religious awe to a sense of duty; surely they too have utterly undermined all religion? Or take Prodicus of Ceos,* who stated that all things which brought benefit to our human lives are numbered among the gods; what remnant of religious observance did he leave?

119   'Again, there are those who record that valiant, renowned, or powerful individuals joined the company of gods at death, and that these are the persons whom we usually worship, implore, and revere; surely these thinkers too are divorced from all religious sense? Euhemerus was the chief to espouse this theory, but our Ennius most conspicuously translated him* and followed in his footsteps. Now Euhemerus* proves that gods died and were buried; does he appear, then, to have strengthened religious belief, or to have utterly and totally demolished it? I refrain from mentioning the sacred and venerable shrine of Eleusis,

> where the most far-flung nations of the earth
> become initiates;

I take no account of Samothrace, and the rites on Lemnos*

> which men attend by night, and celebrate
> in secret, in the depths of woodland glades.

For if we explain and rationalize these rituals, we gain more knowledge of natural philosophy than of gods.

120   'In my opinion even that outstandingly great man Democritus,* from whose springs Epicurus watered his little plots, seems to dither about the nature of the gods, for at one moment he proposes that images endowed with divinity are at large in the uni-

verse, and at another he states that elements of Mind, also existing in the universe, are gods; at another, that there are images
endowed with life that regularly help or harm us; at another,
that there are certain images of such massive dimensions that
they embrace the entire universe from without. All these doctrines are more appropriate to Democritus' native city* than to
Democritus himself, for who can mentally take aboard such
121 images? Who can look up to them, or account them worthy of
worship or veneration?

'But Epicurus, in refusing to allow the gods to accord help and
favour to men, has wholly uprooted religion from human
hearts; for though he states that the divine nature is best and
most outstanding of all, he further says that God manifests no
favour, and thus he removes what is chiefly characteristic of the
best and most outstanding nature. For what better or more outstanding quality is there than the kindness which confers benefits? When your school envisages a God lacking this quality, the
message you preach is that no one, divine or human, is dear to
God, that no one is held in love and affection by him. The conclusion is that not only is the human race of no concern to the gods,
but the gods themselves are of no concern to each other.

'How much better is the attitude of the Stoics,* whom you censure! They maintain that the friendship of the wise extends even
to the wise men with whom they are not acquainted; for nothing
is more lovable than virtue, and the person who has acquired it
122 will be held in our affection no matter where he lives. But what
harm you Epicureans do by regarding kindness and goodwill as
weaknesses! Leaving aside the gods' impact and nature, do you
suggest even that humans would not have shown beneficence
and affability if it had not been for their weakness? Does no natural affection exist between persons who are good? The very
word *amor* (love), from which the word *amicitia* (friendship)
derives, carries an affectionate sound. But if we exploit that
friendship for our own advantage, and not in the interests of the
person we love, it will cease to be friendship,* and become a
kind of trafficking in the benefits it offers. We show regard for
meadows and fields and herds of cattle, because profits are
derived from them, but affection and friendship between

human beings are spontaneous; how much more, then, is the friendship shown by the gods, for they lack nothing, and they both show mutual affection and have the interests of mankind at heart. If this were not so, what point would there be in our revering and imploring the gods, or in priests presiding over sacrifices, and augurs over the auspices, or in petitioning and making vows to the immortal gods?

123   'You object that Epicurus too wrote a book on reverence. The man makes sport with us, though he is not so much a wit as one undisciplined with the pen. How can there be reverence if the gods take no thought for human affairs? How can a nature be invested with life, yet remain wholly insensitive?

'So undoubtedly closer to the truth is the claim made in the fifth book of his *Nature of the Gods* by Posidonius,* whose friendship we all share: that Epicurus does not believe in any gods, and that the statements which he made affirming the immortal gods were made to avert popular odium. He could not have been such an idiot as to fashion God on the lines of a poor human, even if merely in broad outline and not in substantial appearance, yet endowed with all the human limbs but without the slightest use of them, an emaciated, transparent being conferring no gifts or kindness on anyone, and in short discharging no duties and performing no actions.

'First, such a nature cannot exist. In his awareness of this, Epicurus in actuality discards the gods, while paying lip-service to them. Second, should such a god actually exist, prompted by no favour or affection for mankind, I bid him farewell. There is no point in my urging him "Be gracious", for he can be gracious to no one, since all favour and affection, as you Epicureans state, is a mark of weakness.'

Book Two

1 When Cotta finished this discourse, Velleius remarked: 'How unwary I was in attempting to join issue with an Academic, and a rhetorician* at that! I should not have feared to confront a tongue-tied Academic, nor again a rhetorician, however fluent he was, if he was unversed in your philosophy; for I am not disconcerted by a flow of empty words, nor again by acute observations if expressed in arid language. But you, Cotta, have demonstrated twin strengths; all you lacked was a circle of listeners* and a jury! But I shall respond to these arguments of yours on another occasion; let us now give the floor to Lucilius, if he is agreeable.'

2 Then Balbus said: 'For myself, I should have preferred to listen to Cotta further, this time presenting the true gods with the same eloquence with which he has dispatched the false. A man like Cotta, both philosopher and priest,* should have a conception of the immortal gods which is not the erroneous and vacillating vision of the Academics, but the steady and firm conviction which we Stoics hold. Enough, and more than enough, has been said to refute Epicurus; I am keen to hear your own opinion, Cotta.'

'You surely have not forgotten my opening remarks,'* Cotta rejoined, 'that I can express what I do not hold more easily than what I do, and especially when discussing topics of this kind? 3 But even if I had some clear-cut thesis to present, I should much rather listen to you in turn, since I myself have spoken at such length.'

Then Balbus said: 'Well then, I shall humour you, and make my case as briefly as I can, for now that the mistaken views of Epicurus have been refuted, I can dispense with a sizeable part of my discourse. In general, our school divides this whole question of the immortal gods into four parts,* teaching first, that gods exist; second, their nature; third, that they order the universe; and finally, that they have the interests of the human race at heart. In this present discussion, let us take up the two earlier points. The third and fourth are larger issues, and I think that we should postpone them for another occasion.'

'I wholly disagree', said Cotta, 'for we have time on our hands, and this subject which we are discussing should take precedence even over our daily duties.'

4   Then Lucilius said: 'The first point seems scarcely to need affirming. What can be so obvious and clear, as we gaze up at the sky and observe the heavenly bodies, as that there is some divine power of surpassing intelligence by which they are ordered? If this were not the case, how could Ennius* have won general assent with the words

> Behold this dazzling vault on high, which all
> Invoke as Jupiter!

and not merely as Jupiter, but also as the lord of creation, governing all things by his nod, and (to exploit Ennius's words again) as "father of gods and men", an attentive and supremely powerful God? I completely fail to understand how anyone who doubts this can avoid also doubting whether the sun exists or

5   not—for in what way is the sun's existence more obvious than God's? If this realization was not firmly implanted in our minds, such steadfast belief would not have endured nor been strengthened in the course of time, nor could it have become securely lodged in succeeding generations* and ages of mankind. We see, do we not, that other beliefs when false and unfounded melt away with the years. Who now credits that the hippocentaur or the Chimaera* ever existed? Is there a single old woman to be found who is so unhinged as to be sorely afraid of those monsters in the nether world* in which people once believed? Time obliterates falsehoods of common belief, and strengthens the judgements which nature inculcates.

6   'The result is that in our own society, as in that of all others, ritual worship of the gods and religious observances are continually enhanced in quantity and quality. This does not happen at random nor by chance, but for two reasons. First, the gods often

make their effective presence felt. For example, during the war with the Latins at Lake Regillus,* when the dictator Aulus Postumius was engaging in battle with Octavius Mamilius of Tusculum, Castor and Pollux appeared fighting on horseback in our battle-line. A more recent recollection: these same sons of Tyndareus brought tidings of victory over Perseus.* Publius Vatinius, the grandfather of our young contemporary,* was on his way to Rome from his magistracy at Reate* when two young men mounted on white horses told him that king Perseus had been captured that day. When he reported this to the senate, he was initially thrown into prison for making reckless claims about state business, but then a letter arrived from Aemilius Paulus confirming that very day of victory, and the senate conferred on Vatinius a gift of land and exemption from military service. A further example: when the Locrians won a very considerable battle over the Crotonians at the river Sagra,* it is reported that on that very day the outcome of the fighting was heard at the games at Olympia. Voices of Fauns have often been overheard, and apparitions of gods have often been seen; these have compelled each and everyone who is not dull-witted or sacrilegious to admit that gods were at hand.

7   'Second, there are prophecies and premonitions of future events. These constitute nothing less than a declaration that the future is being revealed, indicated, portended and predicted to men; hence the words "revelation", "indication", "portent", and "prediction". Even if we regard the stories of Mopsus,* Teiresias, Amphiaraus, Calchas, and Helenus as falsehoods of romantic fantasy (and if the facts had been totally opposed, they would not have been incorporated as seers into those legends), will we refuse to accept the divine power as established even when we are enlightened by examples from home? Will we not be struck by the rash behaviour of Publius Claudius in the First Punic War? His mockery of the gods was meant as a mere joke; when the chickens were let out of their pens, but refused to feed, he ordered them to be thrown into the water to make them drink since they were unwilling to eat. But that pleasantry was the cause of many tears to Claudius himself, and of great calamity to the Roman people, for the fleet suffered overwhelming

defeat. And did not Claudius' fellow-consul Lucius Junius*
during that same war lose his fleet in a storm because he had not
observed the auspices? The outcome was that Claudius was con-
8   demned by the people, and Junius took his own life. Coelius
records that Gaius Flaminius* perished at Trasimene through
neglect of religious observances, and did great harm to the state.
The ruin of these men can help us understand that the interests
of our state were enhanced when the top commands were held
by men who obeyed the dictates of religion.

   'If we seek to compare our Roman ways with those of foreign-
ers, we shall find that in other respects we merely match them or
even fall below them, but that in religion, that is, in worship of
9   the gods, we are much superior. Or are we to sneer at that
famed augural staff of Attus Navius,* with which he traced out
the boundaries of sections of his vineyard in order to locate his
pig? I could believe that the sneer would be justified, were it not
that king Tullus Hostilius made him take the auspices before he
waged large-scale wars. But nowadays the indifference of the
nobility has led to the science of augury being abandoned; we
adhere to the mere forms of the auspices, and despise the truth
that they teach. The result is that the most important activities
of the state, including the wars that ensure its safety, are conducted without taking the auspices. We no longer take them
when crossing rivers, or witnessing flashing spear-points,* or
when men are summoned* for call-up (and that is why soldiers
no longer make their wills when geared for battle; our commanders begin their military operations only after dispensing with
the auspices).

10   'But in the time of our forebears, the impulse of religion was so
strong that certain commanders* even devoted their own lives
on behalf of the state, cloaking their heads and reciting formal
prayers. I could recount many Sibylline prophecies and many
responses of soothsayers, the fulfilment of which no one should
doubt; but the authentic discipline of our augurs and of Etruscan
soothsayers was demonstrated by the events themselves that
occurred in the consulship of Publius Scipio and Gaius Figulus.*
Tiberius Gracchus in his second consulship was presiding over
their election; just as he was declaring them elected, the senior

poll–clerk suddenly died. Gracchus, however, completed the formalities of the election. But he realized that the election had troubled the religious susceptibilities of the common folk, so he referred the issue to the senate. The senate decreed that the usual officials should be consulted. The soothsayers were brought in, and pronounced that the appointment of the poll–clerk at the elections had been invalid. I had it from my father that Gracchus was furious, and exclaimed: "So I was out of order when as consul, and incidentally as augur, I presided over the voting when the auspices had been taken! And you barbaric Etruscans, I suppose, are the guardians of the law governing the auspices of the Roman people, and are competent to rule on the validity of our elections?" In that spirit he told them to quit the senate chamber there and then. But later he dispatched a letter to the college of augurs from his province. In it he stated that on reading the augural books, he had realized that his choice of the Scipionic gardens for siting his augural tent had been defective; for when he subsequently entered the city precincts to preside over the senate, he had forgotten to take the auspices when crossing the boundary on his return journey, and accordingly the consular elections were invalid. The augurs laid the matter before the senate, and the senate instructed the consuls to resign their office, which they did.

'Do we need seek more conspicuous examples than this? Here was a man of profound wisdom, perhaps the most eminent leader of his time, who preferred to confess his fault, which he could have concealed, rather than allow a religious irregularity to besmirch the body politic; and the consuls preferred to lay down the highest office rather than to retain it for a moment in defiance of religious law.

'Augurs wield great authority, and we must surely grant that the soothsayers' skill is divinely inspired. Any person observing these examples, and countless others of the same kind, would surely be compelled to admit that gods exist. People who employ spokesmen must themselves assuredly exist, and since the gods have spokesmen, we must concede that gods exist. Perhaps it may be objected that all does not turn out as predicted. But we do not argue that there is no art of medicine, simply because all sick persons do not get better! The gods reveal signs of future events, and if individuals go astray in interpreting these, the fault lies not with the nature of the gods but with the inferences made by humans.

'So there is general agreement amongst all persons of every nation. All have an innate conviction that gods exist, for it is, so to say, engraved on their hearts. No one denies that they exist, though there is a range of opinions about their nature.
13 Cleanthes* of our school stated that there are four reasons why conceptions of the gods are imprinted on human minds. The first which he posited was the one which I have just mentioned, arising out of foreknowledge of future events. The second we infer from the abundant blessings derived from our temperate climate, the fertility of our lands, and a host of other advantages.
14 The third is the terror experienced by our minds through lightning, storms, rain-clouds, snows, hailstones, desolation, plague, earthquakes; and also through frequent rumblings, showers of stones and of drops of blood, landslides, sudden chasms, unnatural prodigies both human and bestial, the sighting of shooting-stars and those which the Greeks call "comets" and we term "long-haired stars". Only recently these last presaged great disasters in the war which Octavius raised.* Then too there is the phenomenon of twin suns; my father told me that this occurred in the consulship of Tuditanus and Aquilius, the year in which the light of Publius Africanus,* Rome's second sun, was extinguished. These manifestations caused people to panic, and to suspect the existence of some heavenly and divine power. The
15 fourth reason advanced, and the greatest, is the uniform movement and undeviating rotation of the heavens, the individuality, usefulness, beauty, and order of the sun and moon and stars, the very sight of which is sufficient proof that they are not the outcome of chance. Supposing a person enters a house or athletics-centre or market, and observes the systematic and ordered arrangement of everything there. He could not conclude that this was accidental; he would realize that there was someone in charge exacting obedience. When that person observes the large-scale movements and alternations in the heavens, the ordered patterning of all those massive bodies, which from earl-

iest ages have never in their infinite and boundless existence proved unfaithful, he must all the more come to the view that these mighty movements of nature are controlled by some Mind.

16 'Though Chrysippus* has the sharpest of minds, what he says about this he seems to have learnt from Nature herself, and not to have fathomed it in his own mind. "If there is anything in the universe", he says, "which man's mind and reason, and his human thrust and capacity, cannot achieve, that which creates it is inevitably superior to man. Now the heavenly bodies, and all those objects whose orderly progression is never ending, cannot be created by man. Therefore that by which they are created is superior to man, and what better name can be ascribed to this than God? Indeed, if gods do not exist, there can surely be nothing in creation better than man, for he alone possesses reason, which no other faculty excels. But that a man should exist believing that nothing in the universe is superior to himself would be insanely arrogant. Therefore something superior does exist, so God certainly exists."

17 'Supposing your eyes lit upon a large and beautiful house. Even if you could not descry its owner, no one could force you to believe that it was built by mice and weasels. Well then, if you were to imagine that the highly adorned universe, with its huge variety and beauty of the heavenly bodies, was your home and not that of the immortal gods, would you not seem to be totally out of your mind? Another thing: can we not grasp that all things which are higher are better,* and that the earth is the lowest level of all, shrouded in an impenetrable band of air? For this very reason, the experience which is visited upon certain regions and cities, of having inhabitants who are dimmer-witted because of the denser atmosphere,* has also afflicted the human race, because it is located on earth, the densest region of the universe.

18 'In spite of this mental limitation, our native intelligence must lead us to the view that there is a Mind certainly keener than our own, and also divine. As Socrates asks in the pages of Xenophon,* where did man lay hold of the intelligence which he possesses? If someone seeks to know the source of the moisture and the heat* circulating in our bodies, and the earthy solidity of

our flesh, and lastly the breath that animates us, the answer of course is clear: one of these we have obtained from the earth, another from water, the third from fire, and the fourth, which we call our breath, from the lower air. But where did we light upon and obtain the faculty which transcends all these? I refer to the reason, or if you wish to express it more fully, the mental processes of deliberation, reflection, and forethought. Are we to say that the universe possesses all the rest, but not the one which is of the greatest value? Yet beyond all doubt no existing thing is better, more outstanding, or more beautiful than the universe; indeed, not only is there nothing better, but there is nothing conceivably better. Now if there is nothing better than reason and wisdom, these qualities must exist in that which we concede is best of all.

19   'Consider again the harmony, unanimity, and unbroken affinity in nature; this will surely compel one and all to express agreement with my case? How could the earth at one time blossom, but then in turn become rigidly barren? How could the approach and departure of the sun at the summer and winter solstices be signalled by a spontaneous transformation in so much of nature? How could the sea-tides and the confined waters in the straits be affected by the rising and setting of the moon? Or the diverse courses of the stars be maintained in the single rotation of the entire heavens? What is certain is that these processes could not take place through harmonious activity in all parts of the universe, unless they were each embraced by a single divine, all-pervading, spiritual force.*

20   'When these arguments are propounded in a richer and more flowing style, as I intend to present them, they more easily escape the captious criticism of the Academics; but when they are expressed more briefly and sparingly as Zeno used to do,* they are more exposed to rebuttal. A river in spate suffers little or no pollution, whereas an enclosed pool gets easily sullied; and likewise the critic's censure is diluted by a stream of eloquence, whereas the narrow confines of circumscribed argument cannot readily defend themselves. These expansive arguments of ours

21   were condensed by Zeno like this:* "That which employs reason is better than that which does not. Now nothing is super-

ior to the universe; therefore the universe employs reason." By a similar argument it can be established that the universe is wise, and blessed, and eternal, for all embodiments of these attributes are superior to those without them, and nothing is superior to the universe. This will lead to the conclusion that the universe is God.

'Zeno also produced this argument: "Nothing which is devoid
22 of sensation can contain anything which possesses sensation. Now some parts of the universe possess sensation; therefore the universe is not devoid of sensation." He goes further, pressing the argument more closely: "Nothing which lacks a vital spirit and reason can bring forth from itself a being endowed with both life and reason. Now the universe does bring forth creatures endowed with life and reason. Therefore the universe is endowed with life and reason." He also pressed home his argument with his favourite technique of the simile, like this: "If flutes playing tunefully were sprouting on an olive-tree, you would surely have no doubt that the olive-tree had some knowledge of flute-playing; again, if plane-trees bore lutes playing in tune, you would likewise, I suppose, judge that plane-trees were masters of the art of music. Why then is the universe not accounted ani-mate and wise, when it brings forth from itself creatures which are animate and wise?"

'Earlier I stated* that this, the first of my four topics, needed
23 no elaboration, because it was crystal-clear to everyone that gods exist; but as I have begun to ignore that initial declaration, I should now like to ram home this very point with arguments drawn from physics,* that is, from the world of nature. The simple fact is that all things which are nourished and grow, con-tain within themselves the thermal energy without which they could not be nourished or grow; for everything which is hot and fiery is stirred and driven by its own movement. Now that which is nourished and grows experiences movement which is steady and uniform, and as long as this movement remains within us, we retain sensation and life; but once that heat cools and dies, we ourselves decline and are snuffed out.

'Cleanthes* deploys further arguments to demonstrate the
24 degree of thermal heat in every body. He states that no food is so

solid as not to be digestible within a day and a night, and some heat still remains even in the residue which nature expels. Then again, our veins and arteries never cease to throb with the sensation of fiery movement; and as has often been observed, when the heart has been plucked out of a living creature, it pulsates with such rapid movement as to resemble a flickering flame. Therefore every living thing, be it animal or vegetable, lives because of the heat enclosed within it. This forces us to the conclusion that the elemental heat possesses within it a life-sustaining force which extends throughout the whole universe.

25 'We shall visualize this more readily if we explain more precisely this entire element of fire which pervades all matter. All parts of the universe, then (but I shall specify only the largest), are supported and sustained by heat. This can be observed first of all in the element of earth; so we see fire ignited by striking or rubbing stones together, or again, earth when freshly dug steams with heat. Then too water drawn from well-springs is hot, especially in winter-time, because a great concentration of heat is contained in subterranean caves, and since the earth gets denser in winter, it compresses more closely the heat stored within it.

26 'It would need a lengthy discourse with a host of arguments to succeed in demonstrating that all the seeds which the earth harbours in her womb, and the plants which she herself spontaneously generates and take root in her, owe their origin and their growth to the due proportion of heat within her. As for water, the very fact of its fluidity demonstrates that heat mingles with it as well; it would not freeze over in cold weather, nor harden into cold or frost, unless it also melted, thawed, and liquefied through the intermingling of heat. So the moisture both solidifies when cold winds from the north or the other quarters impinge upon it, and in turn it softens when warmed, and it melts with the heat. The seas too, when stirred with winds, become warm, and we can readily conclude from this that heat is stored within those massive waters. We are not to imagine that the warmth enters from outside; rather it is stirred up by violent movement from the innermost depths of the sea. A similar thing happens to our own bodies; through movement and exer-

tion they become warm.

'As for the lower air, which is by nature the coldest of the elements, it is certainly not devoid of heat—indeed, there is a great deal of it intermingling within, for the air itself comes into being by exhalation from the waters. In fact we are to regard the air as a kind of vaporized water; the vapour emerges through the action of the heat resident in the waters. We can observe a similar development when water comes to the boil through resting on fire below it.

'The fourth and remaining element in the universe is by nature wholly composed of fire, which bestows its health-giving, animating heat on all the other elements. The conclusion we infer from this is that since all parts of the universe are sustained by heat, it is this same element or its equivalent which likewise keeps the universe itself in being throughout the long ages; and all the more so because we are to realize that this hot, fiery substance percolates the whole of nature in such a way that it becomes both the forceful begetter and the cause of bringing into existence, the means by which all living creatures, and the plants rooted in the earth, are to be brought to birth and nurtured.

'So there is an element which holds together and protects the entire universe, an element moreover not devoid of sensation and reason; for every organism in nature, provided that it does not stand alone and is not a single substance, but is complex and composite, must have within it some ruling principle. In man this is the mind, and in beasts something similar to the mind, which awakens their inclination for things. In the case of trees and of plants which spring from the earth, the ruling principle is thought to reside in their roots.* I use the term "ruling principle" (*principatus*) for what the Greeks call *hegemonikon*;* there is nothing in each and every class of object which can or should overshadow it. From this it must follow that the element containing the ruling principle in the whole of nature is the best of all things, and is supremely worthy of power and dominion over the whole universe.

'Now we observe that some parts of the universe possess sensation and reason; I say "parts of the universe", for there is nothing in its entirety which is not a part of the whole. It must accordingly follow that those faculties exist in the part wherein the ruling principle of the universe resides, and indeed that they are keener and greater there. The universe itself must accordingly be wise, and the element which embraces and secures the whole of reality must be supremely endowed with perfect reason. So the universe must be God, and its entire energy must lie in that element which is divine.

'Moreover, the fiery heat of the universe is much purer, more radiant, and more supple, and accordingly better adapted to stimulate our senses, than is that heat which we ourselves experience and which is the agent by which objects known to us are kept in being and nurtured. So since humans and beasts are con-
31 trolled by this heat of ours, and are thereby enabled to experience movement and feeling, it would be nonsense to claim that the universe lacks sensation, for the heat which controls it is undiminished, free-ranging, pure, and in addition supremely keen and mobile. What reinforces this contention is that this heat within the universe is not engendered by any foreign force from outside, but is spontaneously moved by its own efforts; for what force can exist more powerful than the universe, or is capable of lending impetus and movement to the heat by which the universe is preserved in being?

'Here we must lend an ear to Plato, the god so to say among
32 philosophers.* His view is that motion is of two kinds, the first self-propelled and the second directed from without; and that which is achieved spontaneously of its own accord is more divine than that awakened by the thrust of another. Spontaneous motion he attributes only to souls; in his view, it is from them that all motion takes its rise. So since all motion has its origin in the heat within the universe, and since such heat is achieved spontaneously and not by an external thrust, that fiery heat must be a living soul. In other words, the universe is alive.

'A further consideration will enable us to realize that the universe possesses understanding: the universe is certainly better than any individual element. Just as there is no part of our own bodies which is not of lesser account than our full selves, so the entire universe must be of greater importance than any part of the whole. If this is accepted, the universe must be wise; for if it were not, we would have to say that a human being, though a part of the universe, is of greater worth than the entire universe because he has a share of reason.

33   'A further argument: if we seek to move forward from the first undeveloped levels of being to the furthest and most perfect, we inevitably arrive at the nature of the gods. At the lowest level we observe that nature sustains plants sprung from the earth, and she bestows on them nothing more than her protective nurture and growth. On beasts she has conferred feeling and move-

34 ment, and a kind of inclination which prompts them to seek what is good for them, and to avoid what is baneful. On humans she bestowed something more noble than this, with the additional gift of reason, to enable them to control their mental inclinations, giving them free rein at one time and holding them in check at another. But the fourth and highest level is of beings who by nature are begotten good and wise; from the outset there is implanted in them the reason which is steady and true. We must visualize this as beyond the reach of the human race, and assign it to God, that is, to the universe, in which that total perfection of reason must reside.

35   'Furthermore, it is undeniable that in each and every compartment of life there is some ultimate perfection. Take as examples the vine and cattle: unless it meets some obstructive force, nature follows its own route to reach its final perfection. Or again, the arts of painting, architecture, and the other crafts seek their goal of consummate workmanship. Similarly, and indeed to a much greater degree, the entire realm of nature is the scene of such achievement and perfection. Though the individual facets of nature can encounter many external obstacles to impede their perfection, nothing can hinder the progress of nature as a whole, since she constrains and contains all those facets within herself. And this is why the fourth level which is highest of all must exist, so that no external force can approach it. This is the level on which the nature of the universe rests, and

36 since it both presides over all things and cannot be hindered by any of them, the universe must be both intelligent and indeed also wise.

  'What greater mark of ignorance can there be than to refuse to grant the title of "best" to the nature which embraces all things? Or if conceding that it is best, to deny first of all that it is alive, second, that it is endowed with reason and purpose, and finally that it is wise? For how else can it possibly be best? If it is comparable to plants or even to the brute beasts, one cannot regard it as best rather than worst. Even if it had a share of reason, but had not been wise from the outset, the status of the universe would clearly be worse than that of human beings; for a man can become wise, whereas the universe assuredly will never attain wisdom if it has lacked it throughout the eternity of the past. So it would be inferior to man; but since this is absurd, the universe must be accounted as having been wise and divine from the beginning.

37   'The universe alone has no deficiencies. It is compacted closely together, and is perfect and complete in all its aspects and parts. Chrysippus* puts it neatly when he says that just as the cover is made for a shield, and the sheath for a sword, so all else with the exception of the universe has been created for other things. So cereals and fruits of the earth grow for the benefit of living creatures, and animals exist to meet men's needs—the horse as mount, the ox for ploughing, the dog for hunting and guard-duty. Man has emerged for the contemplation and imitation of the universe; though he is in no way perfect, in a sense he is a fragment of perfection. By contrast the universe is perfect in every

38   aspect, for it incorporates all things, and nothing exists which does not lie within it. How then can it be devoid of what is best? And since nothing is better than intelligence and reason, the universe cannot lack these.

'Chrysippus appends analogies to make this point well. He states that all things improve in creatures which have attained the perfection of full growth. So they are better in a horse than a foal, in a dog than a pup, and in a man than a boy. Hence that which is best in the universe as a whole must reside in what is perfect and complete. Now nothing is more perfect than the uni-

39   verse, and nothing is better than excellence,* so excellence rightly belongs to the universe. Man's nature is not perfect, yet man achieves excellence; how much more readily, then, does the universe achieve it! So the universe possesses excellence, and

is therefore wise, and in consequence divine.

'Once we have recognized that the universe possesses this divinity, we must assign that same divinity to the stars,* for they are sprung from the most fluid and pure sector which is the aether, with no admixture of any other element. They are entirely translucent heat, so that with perfect truth we can say that they too are living beings with sensation and understanding. That the heavenly bodies are composed wholly of fire Cleanthes 40 believes is confirmed by the evidence of two of our senses, those of touch and sight. For the sun's heat and brightness are more brilliant than those of any fire, since it shines so far and wide over the boundless universe, and its impact is so powerful that it not merely warms but also often burns; neither of these effects could it achieve if it were not made of fire. "Therefore," says Cleanthes, "since the sun is made of fire and is nurtured by moisture from the Ocean* (for no fire could continue to burn without some form of nourishment), it must be like the fire which we exploit for our own use and sustenance, or like that which is contained in the bodies of living creatures. But whereas the fire 41 which we need for daily living destroys and consumes everything, and causes chaos and scatters everything in its hostile path, the heat in our bodies is life-enhancing and health-giving; it preserves, nurtures, increases, and sustains all things, and endows them with feeling." He therefore concludes that there is no doubt which of these fires the sun resembles, since it too ensures that all things blossom and ripen, each according to its kind. So since the sun's fire is similar to the fires which inhere in the bodies of living creatures, the sun too must be alive, and likewise the other celestial bodies, for they are sprung from that heat of the heavens which we call the aether or the sky.

'Since, then, some forms of life come into existence on earth, 42 others in water, and others still in the lower air, Aristotle regards it as nonsensical* to think that no living being is born in the region best adapted for begetting living things. Now the region of the aether is occupied by the stars, and since it is extremely rarefied, and constantly shifting and active, any living being begotten in it must have the keenest of senses and the swiftest of movements. So since the stars have their origin in the aether, the logical inference is that they possess feeling and understanding, which is why the stars must be numbered among the gods.

'We observe, do we not, that those who dwell in lands where the atmosphere is clear and rarefied have minds that are sharper and more intelligent than those whose climate is thick and cloying. Then too the general belief persists that the relative sharp-
43 ness of our minds depends on what we eat. On these grounds it is probable that the stars have surpassing intelligence, for on the one hand the sector of the universe in which they dwell is the aether, and on the other, the vapours from seas and lands which sustain them are rarefied by the huge distance which they travel. What especially denotes that the stars are conscious and intelligent is their consistent regularity and the absence of random or fortuitous variation, for no such rational, ordered movement can be conducted without planning. Now this systematic regularity of the stars through all eternity is an indication of no mere natural process,* for it is wholly rational, nor is it the operation of chance, which loves change and abhors consistency. So it follows that their movement is self-induced, brought about by their own consciousness and divinity.

'We must praise Aristotle* also for his doctrine that the move-
44 ment of all objects is to be ascribed to nature, or force, or will. In stating that the sun, moon, and all the heavenly bodies are moved, he observes that things moved by nature are borne either downward by their weight or upward by their lightness, but that neither of these applies to the stars, because their progress is circular. Again, it can hardly be suggested that the stars are moved by the impact of some greater force opposed to their own nature, for what greater force can there be? So the only possibility remaining is that their movement is voluntary.

'The person who observes these facts would display not merely ignorance but also impiety if he said that the gods do not exist; and there is very little difference between denying that they exist and depriving them of any stewardship or activity,* for in my eyes a person who is not active seems not to exist at all. To sum up, the existence of the gods is so crystal–clear that I regard anyone who denies it as being virtually out of his mind.

'My remaining task* is to consider what the gods are like. Now

45   it is supremely difficult to detach our inward vision from the usual testimony of our bodily eyes; this difficulty makes the naïve public—and philosophers similarly naïve*—unable to visualize the immortal gods without forming them in human shape. This shallow-mindedness has already been censured by Cotta, and needs no further words from me. But in our minds we hold the sure conviction first that God is a living being, and second that nothing surpasses him in the whole of nature; and in my view nothing so aptly accords with these preconceived convictions as the conclusion that the universe first and foremost* is alive and divine, for nothing more outstanding can exist.

    'Epicurus can crack jokes at this if he likes; mind you, the
46 amusing sally is not his forte, for he has not even a pinch of Attic salt. He can say that he cannot envisage what a whirling, tubby god is like, but he will never budge me from this conviction; indeed, he himself approves it, for he accepts the existence of gods on the grounds that there must be some outstanding nature than which there is no better. Now clearly nothing is better than the universe; and there can be no doubt that a living being with consciousness and reason and intelligence is better than anything devoid of these. It therefore follows that the uni-
47 verse is alive, and endowed with consciousness, intelligence, and reason; and the logical conclusion from this is that the universe is God.

    'This, however, will be more immediately obvious in a moment, upon consideration of the actual things which the universe creates.* Meanwhile, Velleius, please do not parade the utter ignorance of learning of your school. You say that you regard the cone and cylinder and pyramid as shapes more beautiful than the sphere. In this you betray the same curious judgement in aesthetics which you show in all else. Let us suppose, however, that these shapes *are* more beautiful in appearance. This is not a view that I share; for what can be more beautiful than the shape which alone embraces and gathers in all other shapes, which can exhibit no rough surface, no jagged projection, no angular indentations or bends, no protuberances or yawning gaps? There are two shapes which excel all others: in solid bodies, the globe (*globus* is the word I use to render the Greek

sphaera), and in planes the circle or orb, the Greek word for which
is *kuklos*. These two shapes alone are closely similar in all their
parts, with the circumference equidistant from the centre at all
points. Nothing can be better ordered than that. Still, if you Epi-
48 cureans do not realize this because you have never traced dia-
grams in the dust of the schools, could you natural
philosophers* not have grasped even this, that the uniform
movement and regular positions of the stars could not have
been preserved in any other shape? So nothing could be more
ignorant than the usual assertion of your school; for you claim
that it is not certain that this universe of ours is round, since it
has possibly another shape, and you maintain that there are
countless other worlds of varying shapes. If only Epicurus had
49 learnt that twice two makes four, he could certainly not have
argued this, but his criterion of what is best was his own palate,
and he failed to raise his eyes to Ennius' "palate of the sky".*

'Now there are two types of heavenly bodies.* The first type
travels from east to west over the same unchanging regions,
never at any time making the slightest alteration to their course.
The second type covers the same expanse and the same route in
two revolutions* without a break between them. The two types
reveal to us both the rotatory movement of the universe, achiev-
able only because it is spherical in shape, and the circling revolutions of the stars.

'Take the sun first, which has pride of place among the heavenly bodies. In its course it first fills the lands with abundant
light, and then shrouds them successively in shade, for night
results when the earth's shadow blocks the sunlight. Its journeys
in darkness have the same regularity as those in daylight. The
sun also regulates the limits of cold and heat by drawing slightly
nearer and retiring slightly further. The round of the year is completed by some 365¼ daily circuits* by the sun; and by adjusting
its course* now northward, now southward, the sun creates
summer and winter, and the two seasons which follow the tail-
ends of winter and of summer. The transformation of the four
seasons ensures the birth and the rationale of all things which
are begotten on land and sea.

'Next, the moon in her monthly circuit traverses the course

50 over which the sun takes a year. When she draws nearest to the
sun, her light becomes dimmest, and her orb is fullest when she
is most distant. Not merely do her appearance and shape
change, as she waxes and then by gradual diminution returns to
her original form, but she alters her position in the sky. Her position in north or south creates in her course the equivalent of the
winter and summer solstices;* she is the source of the many
effluences* which result in the nurture and growth of living creatures, and which cause the plants which sprout from the earth to
swell and ripen.

'Most remarkable, too, are the movements of the five planets,
51 mistakenly labelled "those which stray";* mistakenly, because
nothing can be said to "go astray" which through all eternity
maintains in a steady, predetermined pattern its various movements forward, backward, and in other directions. What is all
the more remarkable in these bodies under discussion is that at
one moment they disappear, and at another reappear; now they
draw close, and now retire; at one time they draw ahead, and at
another lag behind; they alternatively accelerate and decelerate;
on occasion, they cease to move at all, and remain still for some
time. Mathematicians have exploited the varying movements of
the planets to calculate the length of the Great Year,* which is
accomplished once the sun, moon, and five planets have completed all their revolutionary courses, and have returned to the
same relative positions.

'The actual length of the Great Year is a difficult question, but
52 it is undoubtedly a fixed and delineated period. The planet bearing the name of Saturn, which the Greeks call *Phaenon* ("shin-
ing") is furthest from the earth. It takes about thirty years for it
to complete its journey, in the course of which it does many
remarkable things. It goes ahead, and then falls back; it disap-
pears during the hours of evening and shows itself again in the
matutinal hours; and yet in age after age throughout eternity it
never varies, but behaves identically at the identical times.
Below Saturn and closer to the earth the planet Jupiter speeds
on its way; men call it *Phaethon* ("blazing"). Jupiter completes
the same circuit through the twelve signs of the zodiac every
twelve years, and in its course it indulges in the same variations

as Saturn does. The nearest circuit below this is covered by *Pyr-*
53   *oeis* ("fiery"), which is called the star of Mars; this planet completes in, I think, some six days short of twenty-four months the
same round as the other two. Below Mars lies the star of Mercury, called *Stilbon* ("gleaming") by the Greeks, which takes
about a year to circle through the zodiac; it never distances itself
from the sun more than one sign's length, sometimes leading
ahead and sometimes falling behind. Lowest of the five planets
and nearest to the earth is the star of Venus, in Greek called *Phos-*
phoros ("light-bringing"), and in Latin when it precedes the
sun, Lucifer, but Hesperus ("at evening") when it follows
behind. Venus completes its course in a year; it traverses the
breadth as well as the length of the zodiac as also do the planets
above it, and it never departs more than two signs' distance*
from the sun, sometimes lying ahead, and sometimes behind.

'This is why I cannot envisage such regular behaviour in the
54   stars, and such remarkable coincidence of timing in their varied
paths throughout eternity, as existing without intelligence,
reason, and planning; and since we observe these qualities in heavenly bodies, it is impossible for us not to number them among
the gods.

'It is the same with the so-called fixed stars: they too evince the
same intelligence and foresight. Every day they revolve with
due and dependable regularity. It is not that they merely revolve
with the aether, or that they cling close to the firmament, as is
assumed by many who are ignorant of the laws of physics; for
the composition of the aether is not such that it grips the stars
and twists them round by its force, since it is rarefied and diapha-
nous and endowed with uniform heat. Thus it seems unsuited to
be a receptacle for the stars. Accordingly the fixed stars have
55   their own spheres,* separated from and free of attachment to
the aether. Their perennial and unceasing journey, traversed
with a wondrous regularity beyond belief, makes manifest the
divine force and intelligence which resides within them. Hence
anyone who fails to realise that they possess the power of gods
seems incapable of any kind of observation.

'So the heavens contain no chance or random element, no
56   erratic or pointless movement; on the contrary, all is due order

and integrity, reason, and regularity. All that lacks these qualities, and misleads with falsehood and abounds in error, belongs
to the vicinity of earth below the moon,* the lowest of the heavenly bodies, and to earth itself. Therefore any person who imagines that the heavens are mindless, when their remarkable order
and regularity beyond belief ensure the total preservation and
well-being of everything in the universe, must himself be
regarded as out of his mind.

57 'This inclines me to the view that there is little chance of my
going astray if I take my lead in this discussion from the leading
investigator of the truth. Zeno,* then, defines nature like this:
he says that it is "the creative fire advancing on its path towards
generation". His thesis is that it is the particular role of any art
to create and to generate, and that nature performs much more
creatively all that our handiwork achieves in the works of art we
perform. Nature, as I have said, is the creative art which teaches
all other arts. On this reasoning, every aspect of nature is creative, because it has what we may call a prescribed path to
follow; whereas the nature of the universe itself, which constrains
58 and contains everything within its embrace, it said by Zeno to
be not only creative, but in fact the creator,* taking thought
and making provision for all that is useful and apposite. And
just as the several departments of nature are sprung from their
own seeds, and thrive within the limits prescribed by them, so
the nature of the universe as a whole has its own chosen movements, those impulses and desires which the Greeks call *hormai*,*
and it directs its actions in accordance with these, just as we ourselves do when we are stirred by our spirits and feelings. Such,
then, is the mind of the universe, and for this reason it can be
justly termed "Prudence" or "Providence" (for its name in
Greek is *Pronoia*);* hence its chief provision and preoccupation
is to ensure first, that the universe is most suitably ordered for survival; secondly, that it is deficient in no respect; and above all,
that its beauty is outstanding in its universal adornment.

59 'I have dealt with the universe as a whole, and also with the
heavenly bodies, so that now virtually visible before our eyes
stands a host of gods who are neither in retirement nor straining
with irksome and troublesome toil at the tasks they perform.

For they are not constrained by veins and sinews and bones, and they do not feed on the kinds of foodstuff and drink as cause a concentration of acidic or curdled humours. Their bodily make-up is not such as to make them afraid of tumbling down or of receiving blows, or to be apprehensive of illnesses brought on by physical exhaustion (it was fear of such frailties which led Epicurus to concoct his shadowy, inactive gods).* These true gods

60 are endowed with most beautiful shapes; their abode is in the most unsullied sector of the heavens; and as they speed along, they control their courses in such a way that they appear to have conspired to preserve and to protect all things.

'With some justification, however, both the wisest men of Greece and our own ancestors have set up and lent names to many other divine natures because of the great benefits which they have conferred. They did this because they believed that anything which bestows some great service on the human race did not originate without divine beneficence. So they then applied the name of the deity itself to what that deity had brought forth. This is why we call corn Ceres, and wine Liber, as in that tag of Terence:*

> Ceres and Liber, if not there,
> The heat of Venus do impair.

'A further instance is when some concept embodies a greater
61 significance; its title then acknowledges that significance as divine.* Examples are Faith and Mind, both of which we observe have ben recently enshrined on the Capitol by Marcus Aemilius Scaurus, Faith having earlier been lent divine status by Aulus Atilius Caiatinus. Before your eyes stands a temple of Virtue and Honour, which was restored by Marcus Marcellus, and which was dedicated many years earlier by Quintus Maximus during the war with Liguria. Need I mention the temples of Wealth, Safety, Concord, Freedom, Victory? In each case the impact of these concepts was so great that it could be controlled only by a god, and thus the concepts themselves gained the titles of gods. Desire, Pleasure, and Sexual Joy have similarly been deified; these are vicious and unnatural forces, even if Velleius thinks otherwise, for these very vices rage too fiercely, and

banish our natural instincts. So these gods which spawned these
62 several blessings have owed their divine status to the great benefits which they bestowed, and the power residing in each deity is
indicated by the names which I cited a moment ago.

'Our human experience and the common practice have
ensured that men who conferred outstanding benefits* were
translated to heaven through their fame and our gratitude.
Examples are Hercules,* Castor and Pollux, Aesculapius, and
Liber as well (by Liber I mean the son of Semele, not the Liber
whom our ancestors solemnly and piously deified with Ceres
and Libera, the nature of whose worship can be gathered from
the mysteries. Because we call our children *liberi*, the offspring of
Ceres were named Liber and Libera; the sense of 'offspring' has
been retained in the case of Libera, but not in that of Liber).
Romulus is a further example; people identify him with Quirinus. These men were duly regarded as gods because their souls
survived to enjoy eternal life, for they were both outstandingly
good and immortal.

'Another line of thought which derives from the world of
63 nature has given rise to numerous gods. These have been clothed
in human form and have provided fables for poets, cramming
our lives with every kind of superstition. This category was discussed by Zeno, and Cleanthes and Chrysippus* have elabo-
rated upon it at greater length. To offer an example: there was
an ancient belief* pervading Greece that Caelus was mutilated
by his son Saturn, who was himself clapped in irons by his son
Jupiter. Behind these sacrilegious fables lies a scientific explana-
64 tion which is quite sophisticated. The point they make is that
the ethereal or fiery element which lies at the summit of heaven
and brings forth all things unassisted does not possess that
bodily part which has to fuse with another body for the purpose
of procreation. By Saturn they seek to represent that power
which maintains the cyclic course of times and seasons. This is
the sense that the Greek name of that god bears, for he is called
Kronos, which is the same as Chronos or Time. Saturn for his
part got his name because he was "sated" with years; the story
that he regularly devoured his own children is explained by the
fact that time devours the courses of the seasons, and gorges

itself "insatiably" on the years that are past. Saturn was
enchained by Jupiter to ensure that his circuits did not get out of
control, and to constrain him with the bonds of the stars. What
of Jupiter, a name deriving from "helpful father" (*iuvans pater*),
and whom in the oblique cases we refer to as Jove, from the verb
to help (*iuvare*)? The poets call him "Father of gods and men",*
and our ancestors described him as "Best and Greatest", putting
"best" before "greatest" because "best" implies "most benefi-
65 cent"—service to all men being greater, or at any rate more
greatly appreciated, than possession of great wealth. Ennius, as
I mentioned earlier,* cites him in these words:

> Behold this dazzling vault on high, which all
> Invoke as Jupiter!

This is more explicit than the same poet's description elsewhere:

> By this sky's light, whatever it may be,
> I'll curse that man with all my strength . . .

Our augurs too cite him in their formula, "If Jove sends lightning
and thunder", by which they mean "If the sky sends lightning
and thunder"; and Euripides among many striking passages has
this terse description:

> You see outspread on high the boundless aether,
> Folding our earth within its soft embrace;
> This you must deem the highest god, our Jupiter.

66

'Now the Stoics argue that the lower air, which lies between
sea and heaven, is deified under the name of Juno, sister and
spouse of Jupiter, because it bears a resemblance to the aether,
and is joined closely to it. They have made it female and assigned
it to Juno because nothing is softer than it. Juno, I believe, gets
her name from the verb to help (*iuvare*).*

'Other than these joined elements there remained water and
earth; thus the fables established a division* into three kingdoms.
So the first of these, the entire kingdom of the sea, was assigned
to Neptune (we like to call him Jupiter's brother); just as Portunus* is lengthened from *portus* (harbour), so Neptune is derived
from *nare* (to swim), with a slight change to the initial letters.

The entire range and element of earth has been consecrated to father Dis; his name means rich (*dives*) like that of his Greek equivalent Pluto, because all things dissolve into the earth and spring up from it. With Dis they link Proserpina, who has a Greek name, for she is identical with Persephone in Greek; they regard her as the seed of the harvest, and the story they invent is that she was kept out of sight and sought by her mother Ceres,

67 who in turn gets her name from bearing (*gerendis*) the crops; her name is actually Geres, but the initial letter has suffered accidental change, just as happened in the case of the Greeks, who in similar fashion have named her Demeter, standing for *Ge Meter* ("mother earth"). Mavors is so called because he causes great turmoil (*magna vertere*), and Minerva because she either humbles (*minuere*) or threatens (*minari*).

'In all matters, beginnings and ends are the vital features. This is why they cite Janus first in sacrifices, for his name is derived from the verb *ire*, to go; hence the word *iani* for archways, and *ianuae* for the gates of secular buildings. As for Vesta, her name is adopted from the Greeks, being identical with their Hestia. Her province is altars and hearths, and this is why the goddess is invoked at the end of all prayers and sacrifices, because she guards the things deep within. Not far removed from her role is

68 that of the household gods (*Penates*), who either get their name from *penus*, connoting everything which humans eat, or from the fact that they reside deep within (*penitus*); this last is why the poets label them *penetrales* ("the innermost"). Apollo's name is Greek; he is commonly identified with the sun; and people regard Diana and the moon as one and the same. The sun gets its name (*sol*) either because its great size is unique (*solus*) among the heavenly bodies, or because when it rises all the stars are hidden and it alone (*solus*) is visible; the moon (*luna*) is so called from the verb to shine (*lucere*). Lucina is identified with it, which is why in our country they invoke Juno Lucina in childbirth, just as the Greeks call on Diana the Light-bearer. Diana also has the name *Omnivaga* ("wandering everywhere"), not because of her hunting but because she is numbered as one of the seven planets; her name Diana derives from the fact that she turns

69 darkness into daylight (*dies*). She is invoked at childbirth because

children are born occasionally after seven, or usually after nine, lunar revolutions, which are called months (*menses*) because they complete measured (*mensa*) distances.

'Timaeus,* in recording that on the night of Alexander's birth the temple of Diana at Ephesus was burnt down, commented with his usual felicity that this was hardly surprising, since Diana was away from home, having opted to attend the confinement of Olympias. Our folk have coined the name Venus for the goddess who comes (*venire*)* on all occasions; she does not derive her name from *venustas* ("attractiveness"), but the converse is the case.

'So do you now realize how the admirable and useful discoveries about the natural world have resulted in the creation of false and fictitious deities? This process has given rise to false beliefs, confused misapprehensions, and superstitions which are virtually old wives' tales. We are informed what the gods look like, how old they are, what clothes they wear and what arms they bear, as well as about their family backgrounds, marriages, and kinships; all these details about them are reduced to the level of human frailties. They are even presented as being emotionally disturbed, for we are told of their lusts, anxieties, and outbursts of anger; those tales have it that they also participate in wars and battles, not merely as in the Homeric accounts where they separate and take sides on behalf of opposing armies, but also waging their private wars, for example with the Titans, and with the Giants.* These idiotic narratives induce idiotic beliefs; they are utterly unprofitable and frivolous.

'But though we reject these stories with contempt, we shall be able to identify and grasp the nature of the divinity pervading each and every natural habitat, as Ceres on earth, as Neptune on the seas, and as other deities in other areas; and we shall acknowledge the significance of the names which custom has imposed on them. These are the deities which we are to revere and worship; our worship of the gods is best and most chaste, most holy and totally devout, when we revere them with pure, sincere and untainted hearts and tongues.

'It was not merely the philosophers, but also our ancestors who distinguished superstition from religion.* Those who spent all

72 their days praying and sacrificing in the hope of having their children survive them (*superstites*) were called superstitious* (*superstitiosi*), a word which subsequently took on a wider sense. But those who scrupulously rehearsed and so to say studied afresh all the ritual involved in divine worship were called religious* (*religiosi*), a word which derives from the verb to review (*relegere*)—just as elegant people are so called because they make choices (*elegantes ex eligendo*), diligent people because they are attentive (*ex diligendo diligentes*), and intelligent people because of their understanding (*ex intellegendo intellegentes*). All these words contain the same force of "choosing" which is present in the adjective "religious". So the word "superstitious" came to note something deficient, and "religious" something praiseworthy. But I think that I have now said enough to demonstrate both the existence of the gods and their nature.

'My next task* is to show that the world is ordered by the gods'
73 providence. This is indeed a large issue, and one which members of your school, Cotta, strongly contest, so that undoubtedly we have to conduct the argument with you Academics. As for your school, Velleius, you are unaware of the meaning of the various terms; for you read and hug only your own writings, and all others you condemn unheard. For example, yesterday* you stated that Stoics present Pronoia or Providence as an old hag who tells fortunes, a misapprehension attributable to your belief that they visualize Providence as a goddess in her own right who guides and governs the entire universe. But in fact "Provi-
74 dence" is shorthand. A person might remark that the Athenian state was governed by "the Council", without adding "of the Areopagus";* in the same way, when we state that the universe is ordered by Providence, you must mentally supply "of the gods". You are therefore to regard the fully developed formulation as "the universe is ordered by the providence of the gods". So I do beg you all kindly to refrain from wasting that wit of yours in jeering at us—after all, it is in short supply in your tribe! Take my advice, for heaven's sake, and don't even try to be funny. It is demeaning, and you haven't the knack; you aren't up to it. This criticism doesn't apply to you personally, for you have the polished manners of your family, and the elegance

on which we Romans pride ourselves; I am referring to the rest of your school, and in particular to your founding father, that uncultivated and illiterate fellow who fires off at everyone, and has not a shred of pungency or moral weight or charm.

75 'I am claiming, then, that the universe and all its parts were initially ordered and are perennially controlled by the providence of the gods. Those of our school usually divide this thesis into three parts. Of these the first is an extension of the argument which demonstrates that gods exist; if this is granted, the admission must follow that the universe is ordered by their discernment. The second teaches that everything in creation is controlled by sentient nature,* which disposes everything most beautifully; once this is established, it follows that nature was sprung from elements that are alive. The third is the argument inspired by wonder at the things of heaven and earth.

76 'To start with, then, we must either deny that gods exist, which in a sense is what Democritus does by introducing "phantoms", and Epicurus with his "appearances",* or if we grant their existence, we must admit that they are active, and that what they achieve is outstanding. Now nothing is more outstanding than the ordering of the universe, so it must be ordered by the gods' discernment. If this is not the case, something must certainly exist which is better and endowed with greater power than God, whatever it is, whether inanimate nature or necessity impelled by some mighty force towards the creation of the most beautiful works which we behold. If that is true, the gods' 77 nature is not supremely powerful or outstanding, since it is subject to that necessity or nature by which sky, seas and lands are governed. Nothing, however, is more outstanding than God, and hence the universe must be governed by him. So God is obedient or subject to no nature; therefore he himself governs all nature.

'The truth is that if we allow that the gods have intelligence, we also grant that they make provision even for the greatest things. So are they unaware of what those greatest things are, and how they are to be handled and maintained, or do they not possess the capacity to support and wield such great responsibilities? Such ignorance on the one hand is surely foreign to the gods' nature; and on the other, it would be quite contrary to the gods' majesty if weakness made it difficult for them to perform their duties. It follows from this that the universe is ordered by the providence of the gods, which is the point I wish to make.

78 'Now since gods exist (given that they do, as is certainly the case), they must inevitably be alive; and not only alive, but also endowed with reason, and united with each other in what we may call civic harmony and fellowship, ruling the universe as a single unit, as if it were some shared state and city. From this it

79 follows that they possess the same rational faculty as is possessed by the human race, that gods and men alike subscribe to the same truth and the same notion of law which recommends what is right and rejects what is wrong. What we gather from this is that both wisdom and intelligence have passed from the gods to human beings; this accounts for the fact that our ancestors established the custom of deifying and publicly enshrining as deities Mind, Faith, Virtue, and Concord;* and since we venerate august and sacred statues of these, how can we decently deny them a place in the Pantheon? Now if intelligence and faith, virtue and concord exist in the human race, from where could these have emanated down to earth except from the gods above? Again, since we possess good counsel, reason, and wisdom, the gods must have these qualities in greater measure, and not merely possess them, but also employ them in the activities which are greatest and best. Now nothing is greater or

80 better than the universe; so the universe must be ordered by the discernment and providence of the gods.

'In short, now that we have sufficiently demonstrated that those beings whose notable power and distinguished appearance we behold, namely, the sun, moon, planets, and fixed stars, and the heavens and the universe itself, and the aggregate of all that is contained in the entire universe for the great service and welfare of the human race, are gods, it follows that all things are governed by divine intelligence and wisdom. So the first part of my threefold thesis has now been adequately covered.

'My next step is to demonstrate that all things are subject to

81 nature, and are most beautifully administered by her. But I must first briefly outline what nature itself is, so that what I seek

to explain can be more readily understood. Some philosophers hold that nature is a kind of non-rational force which induces necessary movements in material bodies. Others again* say that nature has a share in reason and order, and advances, so to say, on a fixed path; she clearly indicates what she does to produce each effect which she seeks, and what she aims to attain. No technique, no handiwork, no craftsman can match her skill by imitating her; take the thrust of a seed,* for example. Though tiny, it is so potent that if it enters some receptive substance which houses it, and if it obtains the food necessary for its nurture and growth, it fashions and creates the product proper to its kind. In some cases such a product is merely nourished through its roots, but others can experience movement, sensation, appetite, and the ability to reproduce organisms like themselves.

82　　'Other philosophers use the term nature to describe all existing things. Epicurus, for example, apportions it between atoms and void, and their interpenetration. But when we Stoics say that the universe both coheres and is ordered by the work of nature, we do not regard it as being like a clod of earth, or a pebble, or something of that kind which lacks organic unity, but rather to be like a tree or a living creature which does not present a haphazard appearance, but bears clear evidence of order and similarity to human design.

83　　'Now if plants which are rooted in the earth thrive and flourish by nature's skill, surely earth herself is sustained by the same power, for when she is impregnated with seeds, she brings forth from her bosom an abundant harvest; she embraces and nurtures the roots of plants, and makes them grow, and is herself nourished in turn by natural forces above and without. The exhalations from the earth nurture both the lower and the upper air, and all that lies in them above. And if the earth is sustained and flourishes through the agency of nature, the same process is at work throughout the rest of the universe; plants are rooted in the earth, and living creatures are sustained by inhaling the air, which itself shares with us our faculties* of sight, hearing, and utterance, for air is indispensable to all these. Indeed, the air even moves when we do; for wherever our movements take us, it appears to give place and to yield to us.

84   'All that is borne* to the mid-point of the universe, which is its lowest region, or from that mid-point to the region above, or that moves in rotation round the centre, comprises the one linked nature of the universe. Now the elements are of four kinds, and as these change from one to another, the nature of the universe continues to cohere; for water is formed from earth, air from water, and the aether from the lower air; and in turn there is the reverse process, as the lower air is formed from the aether, water from the air, and earth, the lowest element, from water. Thus the fusion of the parts of the universe is maintained by these elements, of which all things are composed, as they journey up and down and to and fro.

85   'This process, as we now see it displayed, must be either eternal or at any rate exceedingly long-lasting, enduring for a lengthy, almost immeasurable period of time. Whichever of the two is the case, it follows that nature orders the universe. Compare the navigation of a fleet of ships, or the deployment of an army, or (to revert to the comparison with what nature herself performs) the growth of a vine or a tree, or the fashioning and physical harmony of a living animal; does any of these reflect the degree of inventive talent of nature shown by the universe itself? We are therefore driven to admit either that nothing at all is governed by a conscious nature, or that the universe is so governed. Indeed, since the universe contains within it all other aspects of
86   nature and their seeds, how can it fail to be controlled by nature? Take an example: if someone were to say that teeth and hair were the product of nature, but that the man who owned them was not, that would be a failure to understand that things which are productive possess natures more perfect than the things which they produce.

'Now the universe is, so to speak, the sower, planter, begetter, tutor, and nurturer of all things ordered by nature; it gives nourishment and support to all things, for these are in a sense its limbs and parts. But if the parts of the universe are governed by nature, then the universe itself must likewise be governed by it. The way in which it is governed contains no feature which can attract censure, for what could best be achieved from the pre-

existing elements has already been achieved. So let anyone who
87 can, seek to demonstrate that the universe could have been
ordered better; no one will ever be able to do so. Whoever tries
to make any improvement in the universe will either make it
worse or will attempt the impossible.

'But if all the parts of the universe have been so appointed
that they could neither be better adapted for use nor be made
more beautiful in appearance, we must investigate whether this
is accidental, or whether the condition of the world is such that
it certainly could not cohere unless it were controlled by the
intelligence of divine providence. If, then, nature's attainments
transcend those achieved by human design, and if human skill
achieves nothing without the application of reason, we must
grant that nature too is not devoid of reason. It can surely not
be right to acknowledge as a work of art a statue or a painted
picture, or to be convinced from distant observation of a ship's
course that its progress is controlled by reason and human skill,
or upon examination of the design of a sundial or a water-clock
to appreciate that calculation of the time of day is made by
skill and not by chance, yet none the less to consider that the
universe is devoid of purpose and reason, though it embraces
those very skills, and the craftsmen who wield them, and all
else beside.

'Our friend Posidonius* has recently fashioned an orrery; each
88 time it revolves, it makes the sun, moon, and planets reproduce
the movements which they make over a day and a night in the
heavens. Suppose someone carried this to Scythia or to Britain.*
Surely no one in those barbaric regions would doubt that the
orrery had been constructed by a rational process? Yet our opponents here profess uncertainty whether the universe, from which
all things take their rise, has come into existence by chance or
some necessity, or by divine reason and intelligence. They
believe that Archimedes was more successful in his working
model of the heavenly revolutions than was nature who achieved
them, even though nature's role is considerably more ingenious
than are such representations.

'The shepherd in Accius'* play offers a parallel. Never having
89 seen a ship before, when from a distant mountain-top he beheld

that novel vessel of the Argonauts which was a gift from heaven, he expressed his astonishment and his fright like this:

> See how that massive pile glides on!
> It roars along, unleashing from the deep
> Resounding rumblings with a blaring blast.
> It rolls the waves before it, and its thrust
> Whips up great whirlpools; then it dips and drops,
> Spattering and blowing back a shower of spray.
> You would think a fractured raincloud rolled along,
> Or that some rock was caught and borne aloft
> By winds or storms, or whirling water spouts
> Were forming, smitten by the warring waves.
> Perchance the sea wreaks havoc on the land,
> Or Triton, active with his three-pronged spear,
> Upturns the deep-set caverns from their roots
> Down in the billowing waters of the sea,
> And from the depths throws up a massive crag
> Towards the sky.

At first he is uncertain what this unknown creature that he sees can be. Then, when he observes young men aboard, and hears the sailors singing, he adds:

> Like swift and nimble dolphins do they snort

and so on and so forth:

> Unto to my listening ears sounds forth a tune
> Like that played by Silvanus.*

'This shepherd at first sight imagines that he sees something 90 without life or feeling, but later, when the signs are clearer, he begins to suspect the nature of what had puzzled him. Philosophers ought to have reacted in the same way. If the first sight of the universe happened to throw them into confusion, once they observed its measured, steady movements, and noted that all its parts were governed by established order and unchangeable regularity, they ought to have realized that in this divine dwelling in the heavens was one who was not merely a resident but also a ruler, controller, and so to say the architect of this great structural project. But as things stand, they seem to harbour not even a suspicion of the immense marvels of sky and earth.

'To begin with, the earth, set at the mid-point of the universe,
91 is surrounded on all sides by that living element which we
breathe. The name it bears is *aer* (air), a Greek term but one
which our compatriots have adopted in everyday use, for it commonly passes for Latin. In turn, the air is encompassed by the
boundless aether, which is composed of fires lying at the furthest
height; we Romans can borrow this word "aether" as well, and
express it as Latin just as we do *aer*, though Pacuvius* translates
it:

> Greeks call it aether, but we speak of heaven above.

The joke is that a Greek speaks this line! You will retort: But he is
speaking in Latin. True, but we are to imagine him saying it in
Greek, for he says elsewhere:

> My words declare that I'm a native Greek.

'But let us return to the main theme. We were speaking of the
92 aether. From it come into existence countless fiery stars, chief of
them the sun, which brightens all things with its most brilliant
light, and is many times greater and more impressive than the
entire earth; and in addition there are the other heavenly bodies
boundless in extent. Yet these huge and numerous fires not only
do no harm to lands and things on earth, but are actually beneficial. The proviso is, however, that if they were moved from their
locations, and if they ceased to be controlled and moderated,
the earth would inevitably burst into flames from such great
heat.

'I cannot but express astonishment at this, that anyone could
93 convince himself that certain solid, indivisible bodies are borne
along by their thrust and weight, and that from the chance collision of these bodies is created a universe supremely embellished
and beautiful. In my view, anyone who imagines that this could
have happened, must logically believe that if countless numbers
of the twenty-one letters of the alphabet,* fashioned in gold or
in some other substance, were thrown into the same receptacle
and then shaken out upon the ground, they could form the
Annals of Ennius made immediately readable before our eyes.

Yet I doubt if as much as a single line could be so assembled by chance. Now our Epicurean friends maintain that the universe has been formed from atoms endowed with no colour or quality (the Greek term for quality is *poiotes*) or feeling*—or rather, that countless worlds at every moment of time come into being or perish. But if a collision of atoms can form the universe, why not a colonnade, a temple, a house, a city—all of them less laborious tasks—or many things even easier to create?

94

'In fact these people talk such nonsense about the universe that it seems to me that they have never gazed upwards at the remarkable embellishment of the heavens lying before their very eyes. As Aristotle sagely comments:*

Imagine that there were people who had always dwelt below the earth in decent and well-lit accommodation embellished with statues and pictures, and endowed with all the possessions which those reputed to be wealthy have in abundance. These people had never set foot on the earth, but through rumour and hearsay they had heard of the existence of some divine power wielded by gods. A moment came when the jaws of the earth parted, and they were able to emerge from their hidden abodes, and to set foot in this world of ours. They were confronted by the sudden sight of earth, seas, and sky; they beheld towering clouds, and felt the force of winds; they gazed on the sun, and became aware of its power and beauty, and its ability to create daylight by shedding its beams over the whole sky. Then, when night overshadowed the earth, they saw the entire sky dotted and adorned with stars, and the phases of the moon's light as it waxed and waned; they beheld the risings and settings of all those heavenly bodies, and their prescribed, unchangeable courses through all eternity. When they observed all this, they would certainly believe that gods existed, and that these great manifestations were the works of gods.

95

'This is as far as Aristotle takes it; but let us further envisage a darkness as dense as that which, when the volcano erupted at Aetna,* is said to have blotted out the neighbouring districts. For two days no one could recognize his neighbour, and when on the third day the sun broke through, people felt that they had come to life again. Now supposing after an eternity of darkness we suddenly and similarly beheld the light of day, how would the heavens appear to us? But as things stand, because we

96

routinely see them every day and they are a familiar sight, our minds grow inured to them, so we do not experience wonder, or seek to explain what lies always before our eyes. It is as if novelty rather than the majesty of creation is what must rouse us to investigate the causes of the universe. Who would regard a human
97 being as worthy of the name, if upon observing the fixed movements of heaven, the prescribed dispositions of the stars, and the conjunction and interrelation of all of creation he denied the existence of rationality in all these, and claimed that chance was responsible for works created with a degree of wisdom such as our own wisdom fails totally to comprehend? When we observe that some object—an orrery, say, or a clock,* or lots of other such things—is moved by some mechanism, we have no doubt that reason lies behind such devices; so when we note the thrust and remarkable speed with which the heavens revolve, completing with absolute regularity their yearly changes, and preserving the whole of creation in perfect safety, do we hesitate to acknowledge that this is achieved not merely by reason, but by reason which is preeminent and divine?

'At this point we can abandon the refinements of argument,
98 and concentrate our gaze, so to say, on the beauty of the things which we declare have been established by divine providence.

'Let us first envisage the earth in its entirety, situated at the world's centre as a solid, spherical, compacted ball through the gravitation of its parts. It is clothed in flowers, grass, trees, and harvest-produce, all in their astonishing abundance and inexhaustible variety. Consider also cool streams that never dry up, limpid river-waters, their banks clad in the fairest green; the hollowed recesses of caves, the jagged rocks, the lofty overhanging mountains, the boundless plains. Again, think of the hidden veins of gold and silver, and the limitless quantities of marble.

'Reflect on the species of tame and wild animals in all their
99 variety, the gliding courses and songs of birds, the pastures for cattle, the forests which offer a livelihood for wild beasts. Need I mention the human race, whose imposed task, so to say, is to cultivate the earth? They do not permit it to degenerate into wild haunts for savage beasts, nor to be ravaged by thorny thickets. By their labour, the fields, islands, and coastlines are brightly

dotted with houses and with cities. If we could only gaze on these with our eyes as we mentally picture them, none of us as we contemplate the wide world could doubt the existence of a divine intelligence.

100 'How beautiful again is the sea, and how splendid in its entirety, with its crowd and variety of islands, its picturesque coastlines and beaches! It is the home of so many different species of marine life, partly dwelling under water, partly floating and swimming on the surface, and partly encrusted on the rocks with its shells. The sea itself, in its longing to embrace the land, sports on its shoreline, so that the two elements seem to merge into one.

101 'Next the air, lying closest to the sea, alternates between daylight and darkness. At one point it rises aloft, thin and rarefied; at another, it thickens into clouds, and as it gathers moisture it enriches the earth with rain; at another, it forms the winds as it flows this way and that. The air too institutes the yearly variations between cold and heat. It also supports the birds in their flight, and nurtures and sustains living creatures when they inhale it.

'Finally, there is the element most remote from us, set at the greatest height above our dwellings. This is the vault of heaven, which girds and confines the whole of creation. Its other name is the aether; it forms the remotest border and limit of the universe. In it the fiery shapes of the heavenly bodies mark out their ordered courses in most wondrous ways, among them the sun,*

102 which in size surpasses the earth many times over. It encircles the earth, and as it rises and sets makes day and night. First it draws near and then it retires, as each year it makes the twin journeys to and from its furthest point. In the course of this, it causes the face of the earth to contract in a sort of melancholy, and in turn makes her joyful, so that she seems to rejoice with the sky.

'As for the moon, which the mathematicians calculate is more

103 than half the size of the earth,* it roams over the same courses as the sun, at one time converging with the sun's course, and at another diverging from it. The light which it has received from the sun it directs upon the earth, and manifests changes in its own light. Moreover, at one time it lies below the sun and facing

it, so that it hides from us the sun's rays and light; at another, when facing the sun it passes into the shadow of the earth, so that its light suddenly fades, because the earth interposes itself and blocks its access to the sun.

'Those stars which we call planets likewise travel round the earth on the same course. They rise and set similarly, now accelerating* and now slowing down, sometimes even coming to a halt. There is no more strange or beautiful sight than this. In 104 addition there is a vast number of fixed stars,* their groupings so clearly defined that they have acquired their titles because they resemble familiar objects.'

At this moment Balbus looked over at me, and said: 'I shall now cite some lines of Aratus.* Your translation of them, which you made when you were still a stripling,* gives me so much pleasure because they are in Latin that I can recall many of them from memory. So here goes,* as illustration of what we continually observe with no change or variation:

> The other stars of heaven glide swiftly on;
> By day and night they circle with the sky.

'A person desirous of contemplating the regularity of nature 105 can never have his fill of the contemplation of those heavenly bodies:

> The furthest point of the axis at either end
> Is called the pole.

Around that pole the two constellations of the Bears* course and never set:

> The Greeks call one of them the Cynosure;
> The other bears the name of Helice.

The stars in the second of these are visible all night long, and they are very bright:

> The name we give to them's "the Seven Oxen".

'The smaller constellation, the Cynosure, has the same number 106 of stars similarly arranged, and it patrols the same pole of heaven:

> In this Phoenicians on the deep confide their trust.

> Though brighter gleam the other's stars arrayed,
> So widely visible, as darkness falls,
> Yet this, though smaller, aids the mariner;
> It circles on an inner, shorter round.

What makes the sight of these constellations more wonderful is that

> Between the two, like river in full spate,
> The frowning Dragon,* flexing sinuous coils,
> Glides over and beneath them . . .

107 'Its whole appearance is striking, but especially eye-catching is the shape of the head and the glowing eyes:

> No single shining star adorns its head,
> For dual brightness studs its countenance.
> From its fierce eyes twin flashing lights blaze forth;
> A single gleaming star ignites its chin.
> Its head is slanted, bent from tender neck;
> You'd swear it gazes on the Great Bear's tail.

108 'Whereas the rest of the Dragon's body is visible to us all night long,

> Its head of a sudden partially screens itself,
> Where rising and setting equally claim their place.*

But encroaching on that head,

> The wearied phantom of the Grieving Man*
> Circles around.

That phantom the Greeks

> Have termed Engonasin; it journeys on its knees.
> Here shines the surpassing radiance of the Crown.*

This lies behind the Serpent. Close to its head is the Serpent-holder:*

> The Greeks endowed him with that glorious name.
109 > He grasps the snake with pressure of both hands,
> Yet is himself bound by its twisted coils,
> For the Serpent circles round below his breast.
> Yet straining hard, he presses with his foot,

Trampling upon the Scorpion's eyes and breast.

'Behind the Seven Stars* follows

> Arctophylax,* called Ploughman by the mob,
> He urges on the Bear yoked to the pole.

'The next lines describe the Ploughman's neighbour:

110

> A star with gleaming rays, a famous name,
> Arcturus,* who seems planted 'neath his breast.

Speeding along beneath his feet,

> Bright Virgo* clasps her famous ear of corn.

'Note how the constellations are so marked out that their spacious organization indicates the divine genius:

> Close to the Bear's head you can see the Twins;
> The Crab's beneath its belly; at its feet
> Great Leo* brandishes his trembling flame.

'The Charioteer

> Will glide round, shrouded by the Twins' left flank.
> Him Helice with aspect fierce confronts.
> At his left shoulder Capra* brightly shines.

What follows next is:

> Yes, Capra's sign is gleaming bright, and vast;
> The Kids* by contrast cast a paltry light.

Beneath the Charioteer's feet

> The hornèd Bull* strains with his massive frame.

Its head is spangled with myriad stars:

111

> The Greeks gave these the name of Hyades,

because they bring rain (*huein* in Greek means "to rain"), whereas our countrymen ignorantly call them "The Sucking-pigs", being under the impression that the term Hyades* derives from the word for pigs and not from the word for rain-showers.

'Behind the Lesser Bear follows Cepheus, his hands open and

extended:

> For close behind the Lesser Bear he wheels.

Preceding him is

> Cassiepia, whose stars are scarce discerned;
> And close beside her, body twinkling bright,
> Andromeda* sadly shuns her mother's gaze.
> The Horse, her neighbour, shakes its glistening mane,
> Brushing his flank against her head. These two
> A single star with common light unites,
> Seeking to bind them indissolubly.
> Close to them clings the Ram* with twisted horns.

Next to the Ram

> Appear the Fish;* one glides some way ahead
> More subject to the chilling North Wind's breeze.

'Perseus is depicted at Andromeda's feet:

112

> The North Wind blasts him from its topmost pole.
> Close by his left knee you will next descry
> The Pleiades,* shedding unsubstantial light,
> Next to them, sloping outward, is the Lyre.

And beyond the Lyre,*

> The winged Bird,* beneath the sky's broad vault.

Closest to the head of the Horse is Aquarius'* right hand, followed by his entire figuration. Next

> Comes Capricorn, half-bestial; he breathes
> The Arctic cold from out his mighty breast
> Within his zone, clothed in enduring light
> By Titan* on his zig-zag wintry course.

'Visible here is

113

> The Scorpion, appearing in the height,
> Drawing the bent Bow* with its powerful tail

Adjacent to it,

> The Bird, reclining on its wings, glides round,

Hard by, the Eagle,* body blazing, wheels.

Next comes the Dolphin,* and then

Orion,* straining with his body bent.

After him,

114   The Dog-star,* glowing hot with stellar light.

The Hare* follows behind,

Which never wearies, never halts its course.
At the Dog's tail creeping Argo* glides along,
Protected by the Ram and scaly Fish,
With its bright body hugging River's banks.*

You will observe the River, flowing on its long and creeping course,

And see the extended Chains which bind the Fish,
Positioned at their tails. Next, near the sting
Of gleaming Scorpion, you'll see close by
The Altar,* soothèd by the South Wind's breath.

'Next to these is the Centaur,* who

Eager to join the Horse's parts to the Claws,
With hand outstretched controlling the mighty beast,
Unsmiling heads towards the gleaming Altar.
Here Hydra* looms up from the lower realms.

Her body extends wide;

Within her folds, the Wine-bowl* brightly gleams;
The feathered Crow* strains hard to peck her tail.
Close to the Twins appears the Dog's forerunner—
The Greeks give it the name of Procyon.*

Can any person imagine that this overall pattern of constella-
115   tions, this massive embellishment of the heavens, can have been
the outcome of atoms careering at random in various chance
directions? Or that any other natural process devoid of intelligence or reason could have achieved a creation which not
merely required the use of reason, but whose working cannot be
understood without its utmost application?

'The constellations are admirable in themselves, but nothing is

more impressive than the existence of a universe so steady and
compact that one can imagine nothing better calculated to
endure, for all its parts from every quarter strive uniformly to
grasp the centre. Now bodies which are interlinked endure long-
est when drawn together by some bond which encompasses
them; this binding is achieved by the nature which pervades the
entire universe, ordering all things with intelligence and reason,
and drawing and turning the outermost elements towards the
centre.

116 'If, then, the universe is spherical, and if all its parts are
balanced throughout and joined with each other of their own
volition, it necessarily follows that the same is true of the earth;
all its parts incline to the centre, the lowest point of the sphere,
and no obstruction can possibly cause this great impulse of gravity and weight to break up. By the same process the sea, though
higher than the land, seeks the mid-point of the earth, and gathers all round it in balanced order; it never spills over* or over-
flows.

117 'The air which is contiguous with the sea is borne upwards,
since it is light, but it spreads outwards in all directions. So it
both remains closely harnessed to the sea, and naturally rises
towards the heavens. There it blends with the thin heat of the
sky above, and thus provides living creatures with the breath
which ensures their life and health. The air is circumscribed by
the highest region of heaven which we call the aetherial element.
This both preserves its own rarefied heat, which does not coalesce
or mingle with any other substance, and it adjoins the upper
limits of the air.

118 'It is through the aether that the stars wheel on their way.
Their own pressure draws them together, enabling them to
maintain their positions, and their shape and figuration dictate
their movements, for they are spherical, and as I think I said earlier,* the spherical shape is the least susceptible to damage. The
stars are made of fire, and they are accordingly fed by moisture
from the earth and sea and the other waters; the sun extracts it
from the fields when they grow warm, and from the waters.
When the stars and the aether generally have been nourished
and refreshed by the moisture, they disgorge it, and then they

take it up again from the same sources. Virtually none of the moisture is lost, or at any rate only a minute fraction is consumed by the fiery stars and the flaming aether. Our Stoic spokesmen (they used to concede that Panaetius registered doubts* about this) believe that the ultimate outcome will be that the entire universe will go up in flames;* for once the moisture has evaporated, the earth cannot obtain nourishment, and the air cannot circulate, since it cannot rise when all the water has dried up, with the result that nothing is left but fire. Then the universe will be restored from this living and divine element of fire; it will come into being embellished as before.

119   'I do not wish to appear long-winded to you in this account of the stars, particularly those which are said to wander;* the harmony from their totally dissimilar movements is so cohesive that though Saturn in the highest position remains cold, and Mars at midway below is afire, yet Jupiter which lies between them is bright and moderately warm; and the two planets below Mars obey the injunction of the sun.* The sun itself fills the entire universe with its light; and the moon, which draws its light from the sun, is the agent of pregnancies and births and periods of ripening. If a person is not struck by this association, or if you like, agreement, in creation to achieve the unimpaired progress of the universe, I am quite certain that he has never reflected on these matters.

120   'Now let us turn from the things of heaven to those of earth: is there a single one among them in which the design of an intelligent nature is not obvious? Take for a start the stems of plants which spring from the earth. They both lend stability to the produce which they sustain, and they extract from the earth the sap for the plants which are held in position by their roots. Moreover, they are shielded by bark or cork to give them better protection against cold and heat. Then again, vines cling to their supports with their tendrils which serve as hands, and in this way they raise themselves upwards as though they are living creatures; and further, people claim that if they are planted close to cabbage-stems,* they avoid them as baneful and harmful, refusing to have any contact with them.

'Next, living creatures; what a huge variety they manifest, and

121 how powerful is the impulse in them to remain true to their kind! Some of them have coverings of hide; others are clothed in wool, and others still in coarse bristles. We observe that some are clad in feathers, and others in scales; again, some are equipped with horns, while others have wings to enable them to escape. As for food for animals, nature has provided an abundance of what is suitable for each species. I could easily detail how living creatures are fashioned to obtain and to digest their food. How clever and sophisticated is the allocation of their parts, and how remarkable the make-up of their limbs! Every organ enclosed within their bodies is so shaped and positioned that not one is surplus to requirements, or unnecessary for the maintenance of life.

'Nature has additionally granted the beasts both sensation and appetite, the second to induce them to forage for their natural
122 food, and the first to discriminate between what is harmful and what is health-giving. Some animals seek their food on foot, some creeping on their bellies, some on the wing, and some by swimming. Some seize their food by opening their mouths and using their teeth, others grab and grip it with their claws, and others still use their hooked beaks. Some suck down their food, and others mangle it; some bolt it down, while others chew it. Some species are so stunted that they readily collect food from the ground with their beaks, while others, which are taller, like geese, swans, cranes, and camels, have the advantage of long
123 necks. Elephants are equipped even with hands,* because the huge size of their bodies makes it difficult for them to get to grips with their food. Those beasts which seek their sustenance by feasting on other species have been endowed by nature with either strength or speed of movement.

'Some creatures are even endowed with technological expertise or inventiveness; so some spiders weave a kind of net so as to finish off any insect caught in it, while others keep watch* [to catch their victim] off their guard, and they seize and devour whatever comes their way. What the Greeks call the *pina*, a mollusc exposed between two large shells, forges an alliance with the tiny pea-crab to obtain its food: when tiny fish have swum between the open shells, the pea-crab nips the mollusc which then snaps the shells shut. Thus these little creatures, so different

from each other, seek their food in common. The interesting
question is whether the alliance is the outcome of an agreement
124   between them, or whether it is a process of nature which begins
at birth.

'Another remarkable phenomenon is to be seen in aquatic
creatures born on land, for example, crocodiles, river-tortoises,
and certain snakes, which are hatched away from water, but
head for it as soon as they can make their way there. Another
curious feature is observable in our custom of setting ducks' eggs
to hatch out under hens.* When the chicks emerge, the hens
which have hatched and nurtured them give them initial
sustenance. But then, as soon as the ducklings are able to set
eyes on the water which they regard as their natural habitat,
they abandon the hens, and make off from them when the hens
pursue them. So strong is the charge of self-preservation
implanted by nature in living creatures.

'In my reading* I have further discovered how the bird called
the spoonbill obtains its food. It trails those birds which dive
into the sea; when they emerge with their prize of a fish, the
spoonbill forces down their heads by pecking them until they
drop their catch, which it then grabs. According to the written
account, this same bird* often stuffs itself with shellfish, and
when its stomach's heat has enabled it to digest them, it regurgi-
tates them, and selects from them the morsels which are good to
eat.

'The tradition about sea-frogs* is that they bury themselves in
the sand, and then make their way to the water's edge. Then the
125   fish approach them, thinking that they are food, whereupon the
frogs kill and devour them.

'The kite and the crow* conduct a species of natural warfare
with each other; whenever one comes across the eggs of the
other, it destroys them.

'A further curiosity noted by Aristotle, from whom most of
these examples are taken, must occasion universal surprise.
When cranes travel across the seas in search of warmer climes,
they fly in triangular formation.* The apex of the triangle
brushes aside the air which confronts them, and the birds mount
gradually upwards, using their wings on either side as oars. The

base of the triangle in the cranes' formation is aided by tail-winds, and the birds in the rear rest their necks and heads on the backs of those flying in front. The leading bird cannot do this, since he has nowhere to lay his head, so he flies back to the rear to take a break, and one of the birds which is rested takes his place. This interchange continues throughout the journey.

'I could cite many examples of this type, but you understand the kind of thing I mean. Even better known are the ways in
126 which animals protect themselves, keeping a wary eye while feeding, and lying doggo in their lairs. Then there is the remarkable fact that dogs cure their sickness by vomiting, and Egyptian ibises by purging their bowels;* our doctors, clever as they are, discovered this technique only recently, just a few generations ago. It is claimed that panthers in foreign countries, when taken in by poisoned meat, devise some remedy to rescue them from death; that wild goats in Crete, when pierced by poisoned arrows, search out a plant called dittany, which when swallowed causes the arrows to be expelled from their bodies; and that shortly before giving birth, does* purge themselves with a little
127 plant called hartwort. Another feature which we observe is how different species defend themselves with particular weapons against violence and terror; bulls use their horns, boars their tusks, lions their tread.* Others protect themselves by flight or by concealment. The cuttlefish ejects a black fluid, the stingray* induces paralysis, and many animals shake off pursuers by emitting an insufferably foul smell.

'Divine providence has taken great pains to ensure that the universe is enduringly embellished. The various types of animals, trees, and all plants rooted in the earth never die out, for all of them contain within themselves the seed whose thrust ensures that each one multiplies. This seed lies enclosed deep within the fruits which sprout from each tree, and the same seeds both feed the human race in abundance, and replenish the lands with renewed growth of plants of the same kind.

'Need I mention the ambitious design which we see in animals to ensure the preservation of their kind? To begin with, they are
128 male and female, which is nature's way of ensuring their survival; second, their bodily parts are supremely equipped for both

procreation and conception. Both male and female exhibit notable urges to copulate. Once the seed is in place, it appropriates
almost all the nourishment, and while enclosed there it gives
shape to the embryo. In the case of creatures nurtured by milk,
once the offspring emerges smoothly from the womb, virtually
all the food absorbed by the mother turns into milk; and the
new-born creature requires no teacher, for under nature's guidance it makes for the teats, and gets its fill from their abundance.
We are enabled to understand that none of this happens by
chance, and that all is achieved by the provision and genius of
nature, from the fact that those animals which produce a multiplicity of offspring, like pigs and dogs, are endowed with numerous teats, whereas those which give birth to few have fewer teats.

'Need I mention the great love which animals show in rearing
and protecting the young which they have borne, until the time
when they can tend for themselves? True, we are told that fish
abandon their eggs once they have laid them, but then those
eggs readily float on the water, and hatch out.

'Tortoises and crocodiles* are said to lay their eggs on land, to
bury them, and then to make off, leaving their young to hatch
out and to rear themselves without assistance. As for hens and
the other birds, they seek out a peaceful place to lay their eggs,
and there they build nesting-boxes or nests for themselves, and
line them with the softest material they can find, to ensure that
the eggs are most easily kept safe and sound. Once the chicks
are hatched out, the mothers protect them by keeping them
warm under their wings, to ensure that the cold does not harm
them, and in hot weather they shield them from the sun. Once
the fledglings can flap their tiny wings, their mothers attend
them as they fly, but thereafter they are freed from other duties.
Human ingenuity and industry also contribute towards the preservation and welfare of some animals and produce of the earth;
for there are many domestic animals and plants which would
not survive if humans did not tend them.

'Numerous aids, which differ according to the region, are
available to men to ensure plentiful cultivation. Egypt is irri-
gated by the Nile; throughout the summer it completely covers
the earth, and then the waters recede, leaving the fields soft and

mud-covered for the sowing season. The river Euphrates makes
Mesopotamia fertile; every year it renews the fields. The
Indus,* greatest of all rivers, not merely fertilizes and softens
the lands, but also sows the seed in them, for it is said to carry
down with its current a great quantity of seeds which resemble
corn. I could cite many other favourable features in diverse
places, and many other fertile lands which produce a variety of
131 crops.

'How friendly nature is in bestowing such an abundance and
range of succulent food to eat, and not merely at the one season
of the year! The result is that we have the continuous pleasure of
an abundance of varied produce. How timely and health-giving
are the Etesian winds,* which nature has provided not merely
for the human race but also for the animal world, as well as for
all the plant life which springs from the earth! Their breezes
moderate the extreme heat, and for sea-journeys they guarantee
a swift and steady course. I recount these many benefits, but
there are equally many which I must leave unmentioned, for I
132 cannot catalogue those which rivers bring, the constant ebb and
flow of sea-tides, the mountains clothed with woodland, the
salt-beds far removed from the sea-shore, the lands teeming
with health-giving medicines—in short, the countless construc-
tive contributions to the needs for sustenance and life. Then too
there is the interchange between day and night, which preserves
living creatures by assigning a time for activity and a time for
rest.

'Thus all considerations from every viewpoint demonstrate
that everything in the universe is wonderfully ordered by divine
intelligence and design for the welfare and preservation of all.

'Supposing someone asks: who or what is the beneficiary of this
mighty work of creation? Is it the trees and plants, which
133 though without sensation are none the less maintained by
nature? But that would be absurd. Or is it the brute beasts? But
it seems no more likely that the gods laboured so hard on behalf
of dumb creatures without understanding. So for whom is one
to say that the universe has been created? It is surely for those
living creatures who enjoy the use of reason, namely gods and
men, than whom nothing better exists in the world, for reason is

the faculty that excels all others. This is what makes it credible that the universe and all within it have been created for the benefit of the gods and the human race.*

'This thesis, that the immortal gods have made provision for mankind, will be more readily grasped if we examine the make-up of man in the round, and the entire shape and perfection of humankind. The lives of living creatures are sustained by three things, food, drink, and breath. To take in all these the mouth is

134　supremely suitable. The proximity of the nostrils allows access of breath, and the teeth implanted in the mouth are given charge over food, which is fragmented and softened by them. The front teeth are sharp, and they break up the food by biting; the back teeth, which are called molars, complete the mastication, a process seen to be aided also by the tongue. The food taken by the mouth slips first into the gullet,* which adjoins the

135　tongue, for it is attached to its roots. On each side the gullet is bounded by the tonsils, and it extends as far back as the inner-most part of the palate. Through the activity and movements of the tongue, it receives the food which is passed and, so to say, thrust down into it, and which it dispatches further down. The parts of it which lie below the food being swallowed expand, while the parts above it contract.

'The windpipe, called "rough"* by the physicians, has an orifice adjoining the roots of the tongue, just above the junction of

136　tongue and gullet; it extends as far as the lungs, and receives the inhalation of breath, which it also exhales and passes out from the lungs. It has a sort of cover over it, which is designed to ensure that the breath is not blocked by any food which chances to fall in it. Lying below the gullet is the stomach, which is the receptacle for food and drink, whereas the lungs and the heart outside it breathe in the air. The stomach is the seat of many remarkable functions, principally the work of muscular fibres; it is complex and twisted in structure, and it both constrains and contains the dry and the moist food which it receives, so that it can be assimilated and digested. At one time it contracts, and at another is relaxed. It compresses and intermingles all that it can take in; and in consequence, by reason of its abundant heat,* by its fragmentation of the food, and by the additional effect of breathing, it digests and absorbs it all, and distributes it through-out the rest of the body.

'The lungs are porous and soft like sponges, and they are accordingly well suited to take in air. At one time they contract as they inhale, and at another they expand as they exhale, so that there is a regular intake of that nourishing air by which living creatures are chiefly sustained.

'A nourishing juice detaches itself from the rest of the food in the stomach, and flows from the intestines into the liver. It
137   passes along certain channels and passages directly from the middle intestine* to the so-called "gates" of the liver; these ducts belong to and are attached to the liver. There are other channels leading out of the liver, and the food which passes out of it travels along them. The bile separates itself from the food, together with the liquids which pour from the kidneys. The remainder turns into blood, and flows to those same "gates" of the liver to which all its passages connect. When it has slipped through these "gates", the food at this point pours into the vein which is called "hollow";* by now it is totally absorbed and digested, and flows along this hollow vein to the heart. From the heart it is distributed over the whole body by means of numerous veins which extend to every part of our human frame.

'It would not be difficult to explain how the superfluous food is expelled from the bowels as they contract and loosen, but I must
138   pass over this to avoid unsavoury discussion. Instead, let me expound the astonishing craftsmanship of nature. The air which we draw into our lungs by breathing is warmed initially by our breath, but then also by contact with the lungs. Some of it is returned when we breathe out, but some is absorbed by that part of the heart which is called the cardiac ventricle. Joined to this is another like it, into which the blood from the liver flows through the hollow vein which we have mentioned. In this way and from these organs the blood is distributed* through the veins to the whole of our bodies, and so too is the breath through the arteries. These veins and arteries are numerous and close-packed, winding through the whole body; they bear witness to the astonishing complexity of this highly skilled and divine work-manship.

'What am I to say of the bones, which provide the body's frame? They are equipped with remarkable joints which are
139 both suited to lend the body stability, and are ideal as boundaries for the limbs; they facilitate the movement and the entire activity of the body. Consider, too, the sinews which hold our limbs together, and their complex structure which pervades the whole body. Like the veins and arteries, they issue from the heart, and they spread to every part of the body.*

'I could cite many further instances of this assiduous and sophisticated provision of nature, to make clear the extent of
140 these outstanding gifts of the gods to mankind. To begin with, she has raised men from the earth and made them stand tall and erect, so that by gazing on the sky they could acquire knowledge of the gods. Human beings are sprung from the earth not as natives and dwellers there, but to survey the heavenly realm above, an insight granted to no other species of living creatures. Our senses have been created and located in the citadel, so to say, of our heads, for necessary purposes; they identify and give notice of external objects. The eyes are our watchmen, and so they occupy the highest vantage-point, from where they have the clearest vision for the performance of their duties. The ears too are rightly set aloft in our bodies, for they are to catch the
141 sounds which naturally travel upwards. Again, the nostrils are both aptly set high because every smell is borne upwards, and with good reason they are aligned with the mouth, because they have an important role in discriminating food and drink. As for the palate, since it must sample the types of food which we eat, it has its home in that part of the face in which nature has opened a passage for items of food and drink. The faculty of touch is evenly spread throughout the whole body, to enable us to be aware of all blows and of the excessive impact of cold and heat. Finally, just as architects in constructing residences remove from the eyes and noses of their owners the drainage which would inevitably be rather squalid, so nature has removed the physical equivalent in our bodies well away from the organs of sense.

'I ask you: what craftsman other than nature, whose cleverness nothing can surpass, could have demonstrated such great

142 ingenuity in the creation of the senses? To begin with, she enclosed the eyes with a covering of most delicate membranes, which she first made transparent so that we could see through them, and secondly made strong enough to keep the eyes in place. The eyes themselves she made slippery and mobile, so that they could avoid contact with anything harmful, and could readily switch their gaze in any desired direction. The actual organ of sight, which is called the pupil,* is so small that it easily avoids things which may damage it; and the eyelids, which afford a covering for the eyes, are extremely soft to the touch to avoid damage to the pupil. They are also most conveniently designed both to close the eyes, so that nothing can buffet them, and to open them. Nature has made provision for this movement to be repeatedly performed with the greatest speed. The eyelids moreover are protected with what we may call a rampart of eyelashes. These exclude any intrusion into the eyes when open; and when they are closed in sleep, during the period

143 in which vision is not required, the eyes can be tucked in and allowed to rest. Then too the eyes are set back to advantage, being protected all round by protruding features. To start with, the parts above them screened by the eyebrows ward off the sweat which flows down from the head and forehead. Then the cheeks lying below project slightly, and offer protection; and finally the nose appears to be set between the eyes like a defensive wall.

'The organ of hearing remains always open, for we need this sense even when asleep; we are roused even from slumber when

144 we hear a sound. The passage within the ear is winding, to prevent anything from entering, which would occur if access were direct and straight. A further precaution guards against the attempted entry of minute insects, for they are trapped in the wax secreted in the ear, as though in bird-lime. Outside this passage project the ears properly called, whose purpose is to cover and to protect the faculty of hearing, and to prevent the impact of sounds from slipping away and going astray before they strike the organ of sense. Their apertures are hard and horny,* and also sinuous; such qualities amplify the sounds that strike them. This explains why the sound of lyres is amplified by the tortoise-

shell or horn;* and again, why winding and enclosed compart-
ments make for greater reverberations.

    'The nostrils, which remain permanently open for their neces-
sary functions, likewise have narrower apertures so that no
145 harmful substance can penetrate them; and mucus is always present in them, which serves to dispose of dust and many other substances. The palate is particularly well protected, for it is
enclosed in the mouth for its proper use, and to preserve it from
damage.

    'All these human organs of sense are much superior to those of
brute beasts.* In the first place, our eyes attain a more refined
perception of many objects in the fields of art for which the eye
is the judge—paintings, sculptures, and engravings, and also
bodily movements and gestures. Moreover, our eyes assess
beauty and order and the propriety, so to say, of colours and
shapes. They also pass judgement in matters of greater import,
for they distinguish virtues from vices, the angry person from
the well-disposed, the brave from the coward, the bold man
from the craven.

    'Our ears too possess the admirably skilful capacity to distin-
guish differences of tone, pitch, and timbre in both vocal and
146 instrumental music. These numerous categories of sound—the
tuneful or the flat, the smooth or the rough, the deep or the
shrill, the wavering or the uniform—only human ears can distinguish. Then again, our nostrils, our palate, and to some extent
the faculty of touch have great powers of discrimination. Numerous skills have been developed—indeed, more than I could have
wished—to entice and to indulge these senses, for it is clear to all
how far we have advanced in our blending of perfumes, season-
ing of foodstuffs, and embellishment of our bodies.

    'To turn now to our fundamental possessions of mind, intelli-
gence, reason, prudence, and wisdom, any person who does not
147 realize that these have been brought to perfection by divine
supervision seems to me to lack those very qualities. I only wish,
Cotta, that your eloquence was granted to me* in my exposition
of this topic, so that I could emphasize as you would what keen
perception we possess, what power of combining and understanding premisses and consequences. I mean the ability to state

what conclusions are reached from what premises, and to draw such conclusions by reasoning, and to define individual concepts and limit their application. From this we come to realize the force and nature of knowledge; even God possesses no more sublime a faculty than this.

'But how great also are the faculties which you Academics seek to invalidate and dismiss! I mean our ability to discern and understand external reality* by the use of our senses and judgement. By conjoining and comparing these experiences, we devise the further techniques essential for practical living and

148   for recreation. How splendid too and divine is the power of utterance, which your school is wont to label "the controlling faculty". In the first place, it provides the means of learning things which we do not know, and of teaching others the things which we do know; and second, we employ it to cajole and to persuade, to console the afflicted and to dispel the fears of the apprehensive. We deploy it to rein in the impetuous, to snuff out immoderate desires and flashes of anger. It is this which has united us in the fellowship of justice and laws and citizenship, and has weaned us* from the barbaric life of savagery.

'By careful observation alone can we lend credence to nature's extensive mechanism which provides the faculty of speech. To

149   begin with, an artery runs from the lungs to the recesses of the mouth. The sounds initially formed in the seat of the intelligence* are intercepted by this artery, and issue through it. Second, the tongue, which is situated in the mouth and confined by the teeth, lends shape and control to those inarticulate sounds. By its impact on the teeth and on other parts of the mouth, it makes the sounds sharp and compact. Hence the men of our school often compare the tongue to the plectrum,* the teeth to the strings, and the nostrils to the horn which gives resonance to the strings when a tune is played.

'Consider too how well suited for the exercise of numerous skills* are our hands, which nature has bestowed on us. Because

150   our joints are so flexible, it is easy to close and open our fingers, for manipulation of them is effortless. This ready movement of the fingers gives the hand scope to paint, to mould, to carve, and to make music on strings and flutes. Such use of them is for

recreation, but other applications provide necessities; I refer to cultivation of the fields, construction of dwellings, weaving or sewing garments which clothe us, and all creative work in bronze and iron. It is clear, then, that all that the brain has devised and the senses have envisaged we have attained by the hands of craftsmen, and we are thus enabled to be housed and clothed, to live in security, and to build our cities, walls, and temples.

'Moreover, the labours of men performed by their hands have procured for us great variety and abundance of food. The fields
151   bear much produce which is gathered by hand for immediate consumption or for storage to be eaten later. Then too we catch or rear by hand the creatures of land and water and air for our tables. Further, we tame four-footed animals to transport us, and their speed and strength bestow strength and speed on us. There are certain beasts on which we impose burdens, or the yoke, and we exploit for our benefit the remarkably sharp senses of elephants,* and the keen wits of dogs.

'We also ease out from subterranean caverns the iron necessary for cultivation of the fields, and we search out deeply hidden veins of copper, silver, and gold, both for practical purposes and for embellishment. We put trees to use,* exploiting every kind of timber both cultivated and wild; we burn it to keep ourselves warm and to cook our food, and we use it also for building, so that we can ward off the cold and heat in the shelter of our dwellings.

'The timber is also highly useful for building ships, and the voyages they undertake supply from every quarter all the
152   resources which we require for living. Because of our knowledge of seamanship, we humans alone cope with the most violent forces which nature unleashes, namely those of sea and winds, and we enjoy and exploit the fruits of the sea. Total dominion over the produce of the earth lies in our hands. We put plains and mountains to good use; rivers and lakes belong to us; we sow cereals and plant trees; we irrigate our lands to fertilize them. We fortify river-banks, and straighten or divert the courses of rivers. In short, by the work of our hands we strive to create a sort of second nature within the world of nature.

'Then again, has not our human reason advanced to the skies?
Alone of living creatures we know the risings, settings, and
153 courses of the stars. The human race has laid down the limits of
the day, the month, the year; they have come to recognize
eclipses of the sun and moon, and have foretold the extent and
the date of each occurrence of them for all the days to come.
Such observation of the heavens allows the mind to attain knowledge of the gods, and this gives rise to religious devotion, with
which justice and the other virtues are closely linked.* These virtues are the basis of the blessed life which is equivalent and analogous to that enjoyed by the gods; it yields to them only in their
immortality,* which has no relevance to the good life.

'I think that I have sufficiently demonstrated by my explanation of these matters how greatly man's nature transcends that
of all other living creatures. This forces us to realize that the
shape and arrangement of our bodily parts, and the considerable
powers of our intellect and mind, could not have been the outcome of chance.

'It remains finally for me to show in my peroration that all
things in this universe of ours have been created and prepared
154 for us humans to enjoy. So first, the universe itself was made for
the benefit of gods and men. All that is in it has been provided
and devised for us to enjoy; for the universe is, so to say, the
shared dwelling of gods and men, or a city which houses both,*
for they alone enjoy the use of reason, and live according to justice and law. So just as we must believe that Athens and Sparta
were founded for the Athenians and Spartans, and that everything in those cities is rightly claimed to belong to those peoples,
so all that exists in the entire universe must be regarded as the
possession of gods and men.

'Again, the revolutions of sun, moon, and other heavenly
bodies admittedly form part of the organic structure of the uni-
155 verse, but they also offer a spectacle to the human race. This is
supremely the sight of which we never tire; it is more beautiful
and reflects greater reason and intelligence than all others, for
by measuring their courses, we become aware of the due arrival
of the seasons, and of variations and changes in them. Since only
humans have this awareness, we must infer that this is a dispensa-

tion made for their sake.

'The earth again teems with grain and with a huge array of vegetables, which it pours out in the greatest profusion; I ask 156 you, is it for the beasts or for humans that she is seen to produce them? Need I mention vines and olives, seeing that their most fertile and abundant fruits are of no interest whatever to beasts? A further point: animals have no knowledge of sowing, cultivating, harvesting, and gathering in the produce in due season, nor of preserving and storing it; man alone takes thought for and enjoys the use of all these.

'Just as we should acknowledge that stringed instruments and flutes have been made for the benefit of those who can play 157 them, so we must likewise admit that the produce I have mentioned has been provided only for those who exploit it. Animals may steal and plunder some of it, but this will not lead us to concede that it has been grown for their benefit. Men do not store their corn for mice and ants to devour it, but for their wives and children and domestics. This is why animals use stealth in feeding on it, whereas owners eat it openly and freely.

'Hence we must admit that this universal abundance has been provided for us humans—unless perhaps the plenty and variety 158 of fruits, with their delicious taste, fragrance, and appearance, raise doubts that nature has conferred them on mankind alone! So far from their having been provided for the brute beasts, we observe that those very animals have been created for man's benefit. What purpose have sheep, other than to clothe us with their fleeces when processed and woven? They could certainly not have been reared or kept alive by their own efforts, nor could they have produced anything themselves without human cultivation and care. As for dogs which mount faithful guard, fawn affectionately on their masters, show such detestation of strangers, exhibit an astonishing ability to pick up a scent, and show such enthusiasm for the hunt, what does all this denote except that they are bred for the benefit of the human race?

'Need I mention oxen? The figuration of their backs shows that they are not fashioned to carry burdens; instead, their 159 necks are formed for the yoke, and their broad and lusty shoulders for drawing the plough. This is why men of the golden age,* according to the poets, never used violence against them, for by splitting the clods they subdued the fields:

> Then, on a sudden,* the race of iron emerged.
> They first presumed to forge death-dealing swords;
> The steers their hands had disciplined and yoked
> Became their food . . .

People believed that the oxen rendered them such useful service that to eat their flesh was thought to be criminal.

'It would be a long story to recount the services rendered by mules and asses, but they were undoubtedly created for the use of men. As for the pig, what role has it other than to become our food? Chrysippus* in fact remarks that life was bestowed on it to serve as salt, to prevent its going bad. It was because it was so suitable for human consumption that nature made it more prolific than other domestic animals. I need not mention the horde of mouth-watering fish and birds, which afford us such pleasure that there are times when our Stoic Providence seems to have become an Epicurean! Note too that the only way these creatures can be caught is by human intelligence and guile. However, our belief is that certain birds, in the language of our augurs "birds of flight" and "birds of utterance",* have been created to presage the future.

'As for the monstrous wild beasts, we hunt them down both for food and for exercise in the chase, for this offers a training analogous to war. Some of these animals we also exploit when they are tamed and disciplined, for example elephants. Further, from their carcasses we obtain many cures for illnesses and wounds,* as we do also from certain roots and herbs whose usefulness we have come to appreciate through protracted use and experiment. Survey, if you will, with your mind's eye the whole land-mass and all the seas: on the first you will see fertile plains extending endlessly, thickly wooded mountains, and flocks at pasture, and on the second, ships ploughing the waters at astonishing speed.

'The innumerable things afforded us do not lie merely above ground; they also lurk in the earth's darkest recesses. These too have been created for men's use, and they are uncovered by men alone.

'I now turn to a claim which you will both perhaps seize upon for censure—you, Cotta, because Carneades* used to enjoy baiting the Stoics with it, and you, Velleius, because Epicurus scoffs at prophecy of the future more than at anything else—but which above all else seems to me to prove that the gods in their wisdom take thought for human affairs. I refer to divination, which assuredly demonstrates such forethought; it is manifest in many places at many times in both the public and the private domain. The *haruspices* have many insights; the augurs* foresee many future events; numerous prophetic indications are

163 revealed by oracles, prophecies, dreams, and portents. Acknowledgement of these has brought the fulfilment of many human aspirations and benefits, and the repulse of many dangers. Hence this power or skill or natural faculty certainly leads to knowledge of future events, and it has been bestowed by the immortal gods on men alone. Each of these arguments individually may perhaps fail to persuade you, but their interconnection and combination must in sum surely do so.

'The welfare and provision of the immortal gods regularly extends not merely to mankind as a whole, but also to each one

164 of us, for we can whittle down the human race by stages, first to smaller groups and finally to individuals. If for the reasons we have mentioned we pronounce that the gods do consult the interests of all human persons throughout the world, whatever the shore or region distant from this nexus of lands where we dwell, then they also see to the welfare of our fellow-dwellers in these lands extending from east to west. Now if the gods seek the interests of all who dwell in the great island, so to say, which we call

165 the earth, they likewise look to the welfare of those who occupy individual areas of that island, namely Europe, Asia, and Africa. They therefore show regard for both cities in these continents such as Rome, Athens, and Sparta, and for the individuals as distinct from the communities of these cities; for example, for Curius, Fabricius and Coruncanius* in the war with Pyrrhus, for Caiatinus, Duillius, Metellus, and Lutatius* in the First Punic War, and for Maximus, Marcellus, and Africanus* in the Second; and following after these, for Paulus, Gracchus, and Cato,* or again the men whom our fathers recall, Scipio and

Laelius,* as well as for many other outstanding sons of our state and of Greece. We must surely believe that none of them became such heroes without divine aid.

166 'This was what induced the poets, notably Homer, to allot to their leading heroes Ulysses and Diomedes, Agamemnon and Achilles,* certain gods to accompany them in their crises and dangers. Then too the frequent epiphanies of the gods themselves, such as I have already related, attest their concern for both cities and individuals. We come to realize this also through the revelations of future events made known to us both in sleep and when we are awake; we are given many warnings by portents, sacrificial entrails, and by the many other indications which lengthy experience has designated as establishing the art of divination.

167 'Our conclusion is that no great man ever existed without a measure of divine inspiration. We are not to reject this thesis just because a storm has damaged someone's cornfields or vineyards, or because misfortune has deprived a person of one of life's benefits, inducing us to consider the recipient of such misfortune as the victim of divine hatred or neglect. The gods attend to important issues, and disregard minor things. The great men always experience success in all their affairs—that is, if the men of our school and that prince of philosophy Socrates have adequately pronounced on the bounty and abundance which virtue brings to us.

168 'Such, more or less, are the thoughts occurring to me which I thought I should put into words concerning the nature of the gods. If, Cotta, you were to heed my advice, you would argue the same case. You would reflect upon your position as leading citizen and as priest;* and since adherents of your school can argue for and against, you should adopt my position and prefer to devote to it that fluency in discourse deriving from your rhetorical exercises which the Academy has enriched. To argue against the existence of gods, whether from sincerity or the sake of argument, is a debased and impious practice.'

Book Three

1   At these words of Balbus, Cotta smiled and said: 'Your advice to me, Balbus, on the position I should defend has come too late, for in the course of your disputation I have been pondering my possible response, seeking not so much to refute you as to ask about points which I failed to understand. Each of us must make his own assessment, so I find it difficult to embrace the view which you would prefer.'

2   Velleius interposed: 'Cotta, you cannot imagine how much I look forward to hearing you. Your criticism of Epicurus was music to our friend Balbus' ears, so I in turn shall eagerly listen to your attack on the Stoics. I hope that you come well prepared for this, as you usually do.'

3   To this Cotta replied: 'I certainly need to be, Velleius, for my debate with Lucilius is on a different plane from that which I conducted with you.'

   'How so?' asked Velleius.

   'Because in my view your teacher Epicurus does not grapple seriously with the problem of the immortal gods. His sole concern is not to presume to deny their existence, in case he incurs some odium or indictment. Indeed, when he maintains that the gods are wholly inactive and inattentive, and that though endowed with human limbs they make no use of them, he seems to trivialize the argument, regarding it as sufficient to say that there exists some blessed and eternal nature.

4   'But I am sure that you appreciated the wide range of Balbus' observations, which even if untrue are supportive of and consistent with each other. This is why it is my intention, as I have said, not so much to refute his discourse as to seek guidance on the points I did not understand. So I leave it to you, Balbus, whether you prefer to answer my queries individually on the questions I did not clearly follow, or to hear out my whole discourse.'

At this Balbus replied: 'Well now, if you would really like an explanation of any individual point, I am happy to supply it. But if you want to question me not so much to elicit information as to refute me, I shall do whatever you prefer, either responding to the individual queries as you raise them, or to your entire argument when you have rounded it off.'

5   'Fine,' said Cotta, 'so let us proceed as the discussion leads us. But before I broach the topic, let me say a word about my own position. I take considerably to heart your authority, Balbus, and the comments at the close of your discourse, in which you urged me to remember that I am not just Cotta, but also a priest. The point you were making, I imagine, was that I should defend the beliefs about the immortal gods which we have inherited from our ancestors, together with our sacrifices, ceremonies, and religious observances. I shall indeed defend them,* and I have always done so; no words from any person, whether learned or unlearned, will ever budge me from the views which I inherited from our ancestors concerning the worship of the immortal gods. In any discussion of religion, my guiding lights are Tiberius Coruncanius, Publius Scipio, and Publius Scaevola,* all of whom were chief priests, and not Zeno or Cleanthes or Chrysippus, and my inspiration is Gaius Laelius,* augur and a philosopher to boot; I would rather lend an ear to him, in that celebrated discourse of his on religion, than to any Stoic authority.

'The religion of the Roman people in general has two separate aspects, its ritual and the auspices, to which a third element is added when, as a result of portents and prodigies, the interpreters of the Sibyl or the diviners* offer prophetic advice. I have never regarded any of these constituents of our religion with contempt; I have come to the firm view that Romulus by his auspices, and Numa by establishing our ritual,* laid the foundations of our 6 Roman state. Certainly Rome could never have achieved such greatness without the supreme benevolence of the immortal gods. So much, Balbus, for the sentiments of Cotta the priest; now acquaint me with your own views. Since you are a philosopher, I must exact from you a rationale for religion, whereas I am to lend assent to our forebears even when no rationale is offered.'

At this Balbus asked: 'So what explanation, Cotta, are you seeking from me?'

'Your discourse', replied Cotta, 'was divided into four parts. You first sought to demonstrate that gods exist, and you next discussed their nature. Third, you argued that gods govern the universe, and finally that they take thought for the concerns of us humans. That was your division, if I remember rightly.'

'True enough,' said Balbus, 'but I still wait to hear what you want of me.'

7   'Then Cotta said: 'Let us advance each in turn and investigate it. Your first thesis, that gods exist, is generally agreed by all except out-and-out unbelievers, and no cautery can dislodge it from my mind. Yet you provide me with no justification for this belief which I hold on the authority of our forebears.'

'But if you already believe it', responded Balbus, 'why should you want to be instructed by me?'

Cotta rejoined: 'I am approaching this discussion as if I have never heard a word about the immortal gods, or given a thought to them. Just regard me as a rough and raw pupil, and answer my questions.'

8   'Tell me then what they are,' said Balbus.

'My first question is this. After saying that this part of your discourse needed no elaboration, because it was obvious and universally agreed that gods exist, why did you labour the point at such length?'

'For the same reason', said Balbus, 'that you, Cotta, when speaking in court,* saddled the judge with every possible argument, as long as the case allowed you to do so; I have often watched you at this. Philosophers in general indulge in this practice, and I too have done it as best I could. Your question is the equivalent of asking me why I fix you with both eyes, and don't close one, since I can achieve the same result with only one.'

9   'The aptness of that comparison', remarked Cotta, 'I leave to your judgement. In fact, when I'm at the bar I don't usually seek to prove what is self-evident and generally agreed, for a clear issue is trivialized by argument; and even if I indulged in such practices at the bar, I should not do the same in a sophisticated discussion here. There would be no point in your shutting

one eye, since the two offer you the same vision, and since the world's nature, which you hold to be wise, has seen fit for us to have the two avenues of light from the mind to the eyes. But because you were not sure that your thesis was as clear-cut as you would like, you sought to adduce many proofs to demonstrate the existence of gods. For me it would have been enough merely to state that this was the teaching bequeathed by our fore10 bears. But you despise authoritative utterances, and engage with the weapon of reason; so permit my reason to battle with yours.

'By deploying all these arguments for the existence of gods, you succeed in casting doubt on what in my view is crystal–clear; for I have committed to memory not merely the sum total of your arguments, but also the order in which you presented them. Your first was that when we raise our eyes to heaven, we at once realize that there is a divine power controlling the realm above. This was the occasion for the quotation which you cited:*

> Behold the dazzling vault on high, which all
> Invoke as Jupiter!

11 But does anyone among us apply the name Jupiter to the heavens, rather than to the god of the Capitol? Is it self-evident and universally agreed that the heavenly bodies are divine, when Velleius and many more besides refuse to grant you that they are even alive? You regarded it as a weighty argument that the belief in the immortal gods both is universal and becomes more widespread every day. So are you happy to entrust such profound issues to the judgement of idiots,* especially as you claim that such individuals are off their heads?

'You object* that we witness the presence of gods before our eyes, as Postumius did at Lake Regillus, and Vatinius on the Via Salaria;* there is also the vague tale about the battle fought by the Locrians at the river Sagra. So do you actually believe that those whom you yourself styled sons of Tyndareus, that is, human sons of a human father who Homer, living shortly after them, says are buried at Sparta,* were confronted by Vatinius as they rode along on white nags without attendants, and that they preferred to announce the victory of the Roman people to

Vatinius, a countryman, rather than to Marcus Cato, the senatorial leader* of the day? And do you therefore credit that what
12 today looks like a hoof-mark on the rock overlooking Lake Regillus was made by Castor's horse? You must surely prefer to believe
what is susceptible to proof,* that the souls of outstanding men
like the sons of Tyndareus are divine and eternal, rather than
that, having been cremated once and for all, they could have
ridden horses and fought in the battle-line. Alternatively, if you
claim that this could have happened, you must explain how,
without having recourse to old wives' tales.'

13   Lucilius rejoined: 'So you regard them as fairy-stories, do you?
But surely you observe in the forum the shrine dedicated to
Castor and Pollux* by Aulus Postumius? Surely you know, too,
of the decree which the senate passed honouring Vatinius?* As
for the Sagra, why, there is even a proverb* widely current
among Greeks, so that when they want to maintain the truth of
a statement, they say it is "more certain than what happened at
the Sagra". You must surely be impressed by witnesses like
these?'

    To this Cotta replied: 'Balbus, you are carrying the fight to me
with rumours as your weapons; I am asking you for rational
proofs . . .'

*[On predictions and premonitions of the future]**

14   '. . . next comes the question of the future, for no one can escape
what is to come. Often it is not even advantageous to know the
future; it is a wretched plight to suffer to no avail without even
the ultimate consolation of the hope* which we all share. This is
particularly the case, since you Stoics further maintain that all
that happens is fated to come to pass, for fate is that which has
been true from all eternity. What point is there, then, in knowing
that something is to happen, or how does that help us to take pre-
cautions against it, since it is definitely going to happen?

    'A further point: how did this divination of yours originate?
Who first demonstrated the fissure* in the liver? Who remarked
on the raven's call? Or who first cast lots? I myself do lend credence to these signs, and I cannot bring myself to scoff at the
augural staff* of Attus Navius which you mentioned, but what I

must ascertain is the interpretation put on these matters by philosophers, especially as in so many instances these diviners of
15 yours mislead us. It is true, as you remarked, that physicians too
are often wrong.* But how can medicine, whose rationale I
understand, be compared with divination, the basic principles
of which I fail to grasp?

'Furthermore, you claim that the gods were appeased by the
self-immolation of the Decii.* How could gods have been so
unjust that reconciliation with the Roman people could be
attained only if such splendid men perished? In fact, however,
the Decii were employing the technique of generalship which
the Greeks call a stratagem; they were commanders who sacrificed their lives in the interest of their country. Their thinking
was that the army would rally behind a general who spurred his
horse and launched himself against the enemy, and that indeed
proved to be the outcome.

'As for the utterances of a Faun,* I myself have never heard
one, but I am willing to believe you if you say that you have,
even though I have no idea what a Faun is. So your explanation
up to this point, Balbus, does not convince me that gods exist. In
fact I believe that they do, but Stoics do not prove it.

16 'As you mentioned, Cleanthes believes* that notions of gods
are formed in our minds in four ways. The first of these is the
one which I have sufficiently discussed already; it takes its rise
from premonition of future events. The second is that unleashed
by the violent impact of storms and by other physical convulsions. The third springs from the convenience and abundance of
material goods available to us, and the fourth from the ordered
progress of the stars and the regularity of the heavens. I have
already discussed premonition. So far as disturbances in the sky,
on earth, and at sea are concerned, I have to admit that when
such things occur, many people fear them, and think that they
17 are the work of the immortal gods. But the question before us is
not whether some people think that gods exist, but whether they
do exist or not.

'As for the other reasons adduced by Cleanthes, the one being
the abundance of benefits which we obtain, and the other the
due order of the seasons and the regular motions of the heavens,

I shall treat them when discussing the gods' providence on which,
18 Balbus, you have discoursed at length. I shall likewise postpone
to that point the argument which you mentioned that Chrysippus presented:* namely, that since there is something in the natural order which man could not create, there must exist
something better than man. I shall also discuss then your comparison of beautiful furniture in a house with beauty in the universe, and your argument about the concord and harmony in
the world as a whole. I shall also put off to the same stage of my
discourse those terse and clever little syllogisms of Zeno;* and at
the same time I shall investigate in their due place all your pronouncements in the field of natural philosophy concerned with
the impetus of fire and the heat from which you claimed all
things were begotten. I shall also hold back for that same occasion all that you said two days ago,* when you wanted to demonstrate that gods exist—namely, how the universe as a whole,
and the sun, moon, and stars individually, enjoy sensation and
19 intelligence. I shall pose the same question to you repeatedly: on
what logical grounds you persuade yourself that gods exist.'

Balbus then remarked: 'In my opinion I have already
addressed these reasons. But your technique of refuting them is
this: when you seem to be on the point of questioning me and I
have braced myself to reply, you suddenly shift the topic, and
give me no chance to answer. In consequence the highly important questions of divination and fate have been passed over without discussion. These issues you dispose of briefly, whereas men
of our school usually treat them at length. However, these are
matters distinct from the question now before us. So please do
not jumble the topics together, so that we can clarify the question
which we are debating.'

20 'Very good,' said Cotta. 'So since you divided the whole topic
into four parts, and we have discussed the first, let us now consider the second. My impression here was that in seeking to
demonstrate the gods' nature, you actually demonstrated that
they do not exist. You stated that it is extremely difficult to
detach the mind from the regular testimony of the eyes,* but
you had no doubt that the universe is good, since there is nothing
in creation better than the universe, and there is nothing more

outstanding than God. That argument might hold good if only we could contemplate a living universe, or rather, visualize this

21 with our minds as we see all else with our eyes. But when you say that nothing is better than the universe, what do you mean by "better"? If you mean "more beautiful", I agree; or if you mean "more adapted to our uses", I again agree. But if you mean that there is nothing wiser than the universe, I profoundly disagree; not because it is difficult to detach the mind from the eyes, but the more I do so, the less I can grasp the conclusion which you seek.

' "There is nothing better in creation than the universe." True, and there is nothing better on earth than this city of ours; but surely you do not thereby assume that our city possesses reason, reflective thought, and intelligence? Or since it clearly does not, you surely cannot believe that an ant is to be rated higher than Rome in all its beauty, merely because our city has no feeling, whereas an ant has not only feeling, but also intelligence, reason, and memory? What we are to consider, Balbus, is not what you yourself wish to take for granted, but what elicits agree-

22 ment with your case. That statement of yours is amplified in that ancient syllogism of Zeno's, so concisely and in your view so cogently expressed. His syllogism goes like this: "That which employs reason is better that that which does not. Now nothing is better than the universe. Therefore the universe employs

23 reason.' Accept this reasoning, and your conclusion will be that the universe seems adept at reading a book; for by following in Zeno's footsteps, you will be able to frame a syllogism like this: "A thing which is literate is better than a thing which is not. Now nothing is better than the universe. Therefore the universe is literate." On this basis the universe will also be eloquent, and a mathematician, and a musician as well; in short, with every branch of learning at its fingertips, the universe will finally be a philosopher!

'Your repeated refrain was that nothing comes into being without God, and that nature has the power to create only things like itself. So am I to grant that the universe is not only alive and wise, but also a harpist and a flute-player, since persons with these skills are its offspring? Hence your founding-father of the Stoics advances no reason why we should regard the universe as rational or even living. So the universe is not God, yet nothing is better than it, for there is nothing more beautiful, nothing more health-giving, nothing more decorative before our eyes, and nothing more regular in its movements.

'Now if the universe as a whole is not divine, neither are the heavenly bodies, which though countless in number you sought to locate in the Pantheon. It was their uniform and eternal movement that captivated you, and I declare justly so, for their regularity is remarkable and beyond belief. And yet, Balbus, we are not to ascribe all that proceeds on a fixed and ordered course to the work of God rather than nature. Can you imagine anything more regular than the repeated ebb and flow of the Euripus* at Chalcis? Or that in the Sicilian strait?* Or in the boiling sea-waters where

24

The greedy wave parts Europe from the Afric shore?*

Or again, can the sea-tides off Spain and Britain, with their regular ebb and flow, not operate without divine agency? I beg you to be circumspect here, for if we claim that every movement, everything maintaining an orderly course at fixed times, is directed by God, we may have to call cases of tertian and quartan fever* heaven-sent, for what can be more regular than their recurring onset? All such happenings require an explanation, but you Stoics in your inability to provide one hasten to seek sanctuary with God.

25

'Chrysippus* too you claimed to be a shrewd spokesman, and he was undoubtedly a quick-witted and practised performer. ("Quick-witted" I use as a term for those quick on the uptake, and 'practised' for those whose minds have hardened with use, like hands* from manual labour.) What he says is: 'If there is anything a man cannot achieve, the one who does achieve it is better than man. Now man cannot create these components of the universe; therefore the one who could create them is superior to man. But who can rise superior to man except God? Therefore God exists."

'This entire argument flounders in the same error as the syllogism of Zeno. Chrysippus fails to define "better" or "superior",

26

nor does he distinguish the difference between nature and reason. He also states that if the gods do not exist, there is nothing in the whole of nature which is better than man. Yet he regards it as supreme arrogance for any man to believe that there is nothing better than man. I grant that it is the height of arrogance for anyone to believe that he is of greater worth than the universe; at the same time, a person who realizes that he possesses sensation and reason, while Orion and the Dog-star* do not, is not only guiltless of arrogance, but also wise.

'Chrysippus also states: "If a beautiful house appeared before our eyes, we would realize that it had been built by the owners, and not by mice; so we must likewise realize that the universe is the home of the gods." I should certainly agree, if I thought that the universe had been built, rather than, as I shall show,* fashioned by nature.

27 'But you will object that Socrates in the pages of Xenophon* asks: "If the universe has no soul, from where did we lay our hands on ours? I counter by asking: from where did we learn to speak, and to count, and to make music? But perhaps we think that the sun chatted with the moon on drawing near to it, and that the universe creates harmonious music, as Pythagoras believes!* Such things, Balbus, are the work of nature; not nature "treading the craftsman's path" as Zeno has it* (I shall presently examine the purport of this statement), but nature stirring and awakening all things by movements and changes within itself. So I liked that part of your discourse in which you spoke of the concord and harmony of nature, which you described as "association and interconnection by relationship";* but I disapproved of your claim that this could have come to pass only through the cohesion achieved by the unique divine breath.* That coherence and permanence is achieved by the forces not of the gods, but of nature; and within nature lies a sort of fellow-feeling which the Greeks call *sumpatheia*. But the greater the spontaneity of the process, the less must we regard it as the operation of the divine reason.

29 'Tell me, how does your school explain away the objection of Carneades:* "If no body is immortal, no body can be everlasting. But there is no body that is immortal, for none is indivisible,

such that it cannot be separated or prised apart. Again, since every living creature has a nature capable of feeling, there is not one which escapes the necessity of subjection to external stimuli, in other words of suffering and enduring; if every living creature is like this, none can be immortal. In the same way, therefore, if every living creature can be split up and separated, none are indivisible or eternal. Now every living creature is susceptible to sustaining and enduring external force, so every living creature must be mortal, dissoluble, and divisible.'

30   Take an example. If all wax were liable to change, there would be no waxen object incapable of change. Likewise if silver and bronze were by nature liable to change, no silver or bronze object would be immune from change. It similarly follows that if all existing stuff from which all things are formed is liable to change, there can exist no body which is not immune from change. Now the stuff from which all things are formed is changeable, as is clear to you, and so every body is liable to change. If on the other hand some body were immortal, all things would not be liable to change, so it logically follows that every body is mortal. In fact, every body is composed of water, or air, or fire, or earth, or a combination of some or all of these, but none of

31   these elements is immune from destruction, for everything composed of earth is separable, and liquid is so malleable that it can easily be compressed and squashed, while fire and air can be most readily shifted by any pressure, for their nature is especially yielding and easily dispersed. Moreover, each of these elements perishes when transmuted into another, as happens when earth changes into water, when air is formed from water, and aether from air; and similarly when the reverse changes occur. So if the elements, which are the stuff of every living creature, perish, no living creature is everlasting.

32   Even if we disregard these arguments, we cannot encounter any living creature which was never born and which will live for ever; for every living creature has sense-experiences, and so feels heat and cold, and tastes what is sweet and bitter. Such a creature cannot with any of its senses experience pleasurable things without also experiencing the opposite. So if a creature experiences the sensation of pleasure, pain must be experienced as

well, and what is capable of pain must be capable of suffering death. So it must be admitted that every living creature is mortal.

33 'Moreover, any being which does not experience pleasure and pain cannot be a living creature. On the other hand, if every living creature must have such experiences, and for that reason cannot be eternal, it follows that every living creature does experience them, so no living creature is eternal. Again, there can be no living creature which does not have instinctive likes and dislikes; what is sought conforms with nature, and what they avoid does not. Every living creature seeks certain things and eschews others; what is avoided is contrary to nature, and what is contrary to nature has the force of destruction. Every living creature must in consequence perish.

34 'These and other arguments, which can establish that everything that possesses sensation must perish, are countless and compelling. Indeed, the very objects of sensation, such as cold and heat, pleasure and pain, and the rest, destroy us when they are intensified. Now no living creature is devoid of sensation, and accordingly no living creature is eternal, for the nature of every living creature is either simple, being composed of earth, or fire, or breath, or moisture—though one cannot even contemplate what such a creature is like—or is composed of more than one element. Each of the elements has its own zone to which it is attracted by natural force, one to the lowest region, another to the highest, another to the in-between. These elements can remain united for a certain period, but permanent coherence is out of the question, because each element must by nature be attracted to its own region. So no living creature is eternal.

35 'Your fellow-Stoics, Balbus, are in the habit of tracing the source of all things to a fiery force; in this, I believe, they follow Heraclitus, though they do not all interpret him in the same way. But let us not labour the point, since he is reluctant to make his utterances comprehensible.* What you Stoics claim is that the source of all energy in the world is fire, the outcome being that living creatures perish when their heat dissipates, and in all creation heat is the source of life and vigour. I fail to understand how it is that bodies perish with the loss of their heat rather than with the loss of their moisture or their air, especially

36   as a further source of death is excess of heat. So what is claimed for heat is attributable also to other elements. But let us see where the argument leads.

    'What you claim, I believe, is that in nature and the universe at large the only vital force is fire. But why fire rather than breath (*anima*),* which is the life-force of living creatures, and from which the word animal derives? How can you take it for granted that the soul is nothing but fire, when it seems more likely to be a composite substance of fire and breath? But if fire of itself is a living creature, and has no other element fused with it, it cannot itself be devoid of sensation, since its presence in our bodies causes us to have sensation. So we can make the same response* here as earlier: whatever has sensation must experience both pleasure and pain, and the being which is visited by pain is visited also by death. Hence you Stoics cannot demonstrate that even fire is eternal.

37   'Then again, does not your school also argue that all fire needs sustenance,* and that it cannot survive at all without such nurture? You claim that the sun, moon, and other heavenly bodies are in some instances fed by fresh waters, and in others by the salt seas. This is the explanation offered by Cleanthes* for the sun's refusal to advance further on its summer and winter circuits; it does not wish to travel too far from its sustenance. I shall postpone consideration of this whole question for the moment, but let me advance this syllogism: That which can perish cannot be eternal by nature; but fire will perish unless it is fed; therefore fire is not by nature eternal.

38   'Can we conceive of any divine nature which is endowed with no virtue?* If we cannot, shall we then assign to God that prudence which distinguishes things good, things evil, and things neither good nor evil? But if a being does not and cannot partake of evil, what need has he to make a choice between good things and evil things, and what need has he of reason and understanding? We apply these faculties to advance from what is revealed to what is hidden, but nothing can be hidden from God. As for justice, which apportions to each its own, it has no relevance to the gods, for as you Stoics put it, it was born when men banded together in community. Temperance consists in forgoing physi-

cal pleasures; if this virtue has a role in heaven, there must also be scope for physical pleasures there. As for the idea of God manifesting courage, how can we envisage that, seeing that pain or

39 grief or danger does not impinge on God? Yet can we possibly visualize a God who does not use reason, and who is endowed with no virtue?

'To tell the truth, when I contemplate the claims of Stoics, I can no longer despise the ignorance of the naïve herd. Those simple souls include the Syrians, who adore a fish,* and the Egyptians,* who have deified virtually the entire animal kingdom. Why, even in Greece, among the gods they worship are many who were earlier human beings—Alabandus at Alabanda, Tenes at Tenedos, and throughout Greece Leucothea who was formerly Ino, and her son Palaemon.* Then too we have our Hercules, Aesculapius,* the sons of Tyndareus, and Romulus, who together with many others the common folk believe have been admitted into heaven as newly enrolled citizens.

40 'Such, then, are the beliefs of the ignorant; but are yours any better, even though you are philosophers? I need not advert to your truly remarkable tenets; let us merely assume that the universe is God. This, I take it, is the purport of that quotation

> Behold the dazzling vault*on high, which all
> Invoke as Jupiter.

So why do we append other gods, and in such huge numbers? I at any rate regard them as numerous, for you count every star as a god, giving them names either of animals, such as She-goat, Scorpion, Bull and Lion, or of inanimate objects such as Argo,

41 Altar, and Crown.* But granted the existence of these, how can we possibly envisage, let alone accept, the existence of the rest? When we label the harvest as Ceres, and our wine as Liber, we are of course using a familiar turn of speech, but do you imagine that anyone is so mindless as to think that what he eats is a deity? As for those who you say have advanced in status from humans to gods,* I shall be delighted to learn how this could have occurred, and why it no longer does so, if only you explain it. But as things stand, I do not see how, as Accius puts it,* the man beneath whom

The funeral-torch was lit on Oeta's mount

survived that burning to attain

His father's home that stands for ever,

when Homer recounts* how Ulysses encountered him among
the others who had departed this life in the world below.

42   'What I am especially keen to know is which particular Hercules we worship, for we are told by those who scrutinize the
secret and abstruse books* that there are several. The most
ancient was the son of Jupiter—the Jupiter who is likewise "the
most ancient", for in old Greek works we find that there are several Jupiters as well. From this ancient Jupiter, then, and
Lysithoe is sprung the Hercules who, we are told, struggled with
Apollo to seize the tripod.* There is a second Hercules who is
said to be Egyptian, the son of the Nile; they say that he composed the Phrygian writings.* A third Hercules hails from the
Digiti of Mt. Ida, to whom the folk of Cos sacrifice.* There is a
fourth who is the son of Jupiter and Asteria,* the sister of
Latona; he is worshipped especially by the people of Tyre, and
people say that Carthago is his daughter. There is a fifth in
India, who bears the name Belus;* a sixth is the one we know,*
whom Alcmena bore by Jupiter—Jupiter mark three, that is, for
as I shall presently explain,* we are told of several Jupiters as
well.

43   'Now that my discourse has led me on to this topic, I shall
demonstrate that I have gained better instruction on how to worship the immortal gods, guided by pontifical law and ancestral
custom, from those miniature sacrificial bowls, bequeathed to
us by Numa and described by Laelius* in his little speech which
is pure gold, than from the explanations of the Stoics. For if I
adopt your Stoic approach, tell me how I am to reply to one
who poses to me this question: "If the gods exist, are the nymphs
likewise goddesses?" If nymphs are divine, then so are Pans and
Satyrs. But Pans and Satyrs are not deities,* so neither are
nymphs. Yet temples have been vowed and dedicated to
nymphs* by the state, so it follows from this that the rest who
have had temples dedicated to them are not deities either.

'Take the argument a step further. You count Jupiter and Neptune as gods, so Orcus their brother is also a god, and so are the rivers which are said to flow in Hades, namely Acheron, Cocytus, and Pyriphlegethon; then too Charon and Cerberus* are to be
44 regarded as gods. But the notion that these five are gods must be rejected, so it must follow that Orcus is no god either; so what have you Stoics to say about his brothers? These issues were raised by Carneades not to dispose of the gods, for this would be wholly unworthy of a philosopher, but to demonstrate that Stoics do nothing to explain them. So he followed up the argument: "Well, then," he would say, "if these brothers are members of the Pantheon, their father Saturn can surely not be denied a place, for he is popularly worshipped in the lands of the west.* But if Saturn is a god, then we must grant that his father Caelus is one as well, and if this is the case, the parents of Caelus, Aether, and Dies,* must be reckoned as gods, and so must their brothers and sisters. These are named by genealogists of old as Love, Guile, Sickness, Toil, Envy, Fate, Old Age, Death, Darkness, Wretchedness, Lamentation, Partiality, Deceit, Obstinacy, the Fates, the Daughters of Hesperus, and Dreams. They say that all these are the children of Erebus and Night." So we must either put the seal of approval on these monsters, or dispense with the first four we mentioned.

45 'Again, are you willing to nominate Apollo, Vulcan, Mercury, and the rest as gods, but have reservations about Hercules,* Aesculapius, Liber, Castor and Pollux? Yet this second group is accorded equal worship with the first, and in fact some people venerate them much more. So these too must be recognized as gods, though they were born of mortal mothers. And what of Aristaeus, claimed as the inventor of the olive and the son of Apollo, or Theseus,* son of Neptune, or the others who were fathered by gods? Should they not have a place in the Pantheon? And what of those whose mothers were goddesses? I think that they have even a stronger claim, for just as in civil law* the son of a free mother is himself free, so by natural law the son of a goddess must be a god. This is why the islanders of Astypalaea worship Achilles* most devotedly; and if Achilles is a god, so are Orpheus and Rhesus,* since the mother of each was one of the

Muses—unless perhaps a marriage in the deep ranks above one on land! If these individuals are not gods merely because they are not worshipped anywhere, how can those earlier ones be?

46   'The danger is that these divine distinctions may be awarded not to possession of immortality, but to human virtues; indeed, Balbus, you too seemed to be suggesting this. If you regard Latona as a goddess, how can you reject Hecate, who is the daughter of Latona's sister Asteria?* Or is Hecate a goddess too? We have certainly noticed her altars and shrines in Greece. But if Hecate is deified, why not the Eumenides as well? And if they are goddesses—after all, they have a temple at Athens,* and my understanding is that here at Rome the grove of Furina* is named after them—then the Furies are goddesses, with the role of detecting and avenging wicked deeds.

47   'Now if the Furies are goddesses because they intervene in human affairs, then Natio* too must be pronounced a goddess, for when we go on pilgrimage to shrines in the Ardea area, we regularly offer sacrifice to her. She derives her name Natio *a nascentibus*, from those being born, because she protects married women who are in labour. And if Natio is a deity, so are all those abstract figures which you mentioned:* Honour, Faith, Mind, Concord, and following these, Hope, Money, and any concept imaginable. If such an extension is improbable, then so is the point of departure from which these additions take their rise.

'A further point. If these figures which we have accepted and now worship are gods, what objection have you to including Serapis and Isis* in the same category? And if we accept them, why should we reject the deities of the barbarians? So now we shall admit oxen and horses, ibises and hawks, asps, crocodiles and fishes, dogs, wolves and cats, and numerous other creatures into the Pantheon, or if we reject them, we must also reject the basic assumption on which their claim rests.

48   'Again, if Ino* (whom the Greeks call Leucothea, and we name Matuta) is regarded as a goddess because she is the daughter of Cadmus, must we not include also in the retinue of the gods Circe, Pasiphae, and Aeetes,* whose mother was Perseis, the daughter of Oceanus, and whose father was the Sun? After

all, our Roman colonists at Cercei* are devoted worshippers of Circe, as of Matuta. So you accept her as a deity; then what excuse will you make for excluding Medea,* daughter of Aeetes and Idyia, when her two grandfathers were the Sun and Oceanus? Or her brother Absyrtus, who in Pacuvius is called Aegialeus,* though the name Absyrtus is commoner in ancient literature? If Medea and Absyrtus are not deities, I fear for the status of Ino, for the claims of all these persons derive from the same criterion.

49   'Then will Amphiaraus and Trophonius count as gods? Our tax-collectors in Boeotia, when confronted with lands belonging to the immortal gods which were exempted from tax by regulation of the censors, used to rule that those who at one time had been human beings did not qualify as immortals. But if Amphiaraus and Trophonius* are gods, Erechtheus* certainly fills the bill; I witnessed his shrine and his priest at Athens. If we count Erechtheus in, we can surely have no hesitation about Codrus* or the others who fell while fighting for the freedom of their native land. Or if these suggestions are implausible, then the earlier characters analogous to these do not pass muster either.

50   'There are many communities in which the memory of brave men has clearly been hallowed by endowing them with the status of immortal gods. The purpose of this was to promote valour, so that the best citizens would more willingly confront danger on behalf of the state. This is precisely the reason why at Athens Erechtheus and his daughters were numbered among the deities; again at Athens there is the Leonatic shrine, there called the Leocorion.* As for the Alabandans,* they pay more devoted reverence to Alabandus their founder than to any of the well-known deities. It was in that city that Stratonicus* showed the wit so often characteristic of him. When some fellow was being a nuisance, maintaining that Alabandus was a god and that Hercules was not, Stratonicus retorted: "Very well; Alabandus can be cross with me, and Hercules with you!"

51   'When, Balbus, you based your arguments on the heavens and the stars,* you failed to realize the lengths to which they lead you. You stated that the sun and the moon are deities; these the Greeks regard as Apollo and Diana. But if the moon is a goddess,

then Lucifer and the other planets must also attain the Pantheon; and if they are admitted, the fixed stars must enter as well. Then there is the rainbow; what prevents that phenomenon from being enrolled among the gods? It is beautiful, and since that beauty has a remarkable cause, Iris the rainbow* is said to be the daughter of Thaumas ("Wonder"). But if the rainbow is divine in nature, how must you regard the clouds, seeing that the rainbow is created by clouds somehow turning multi-coloured? Moreover one of them is said to have given birth to the Centaurs.* But once you reckon clouds among the gods, you will certainly have to include the weather as well, for it has been deified* in the ritual of the Roman people. It then follows that rain and showers, storms and whirlwinds must be regarded as gods, and indeed our admirals when embarking on sea-journeys regularly sacrifice a victim to the waves.*

52   'Further, if Ceres, as you stated, obtains her name from *gerere*,* bearing fruit, then the earth (*terra*) is a goddess; indeed she is so regarded, since Tellus* is no other. But if the earth is a deity, so is the sea as well, and in fact you have named it Neptune. Rivers and springs* will accordingly also qualify; this was why Maso on his return from Corsica dedicated a shrine to Fons ("Spring"), and we observe in the litany of the augurs the names of the Tiber, Spino, Anemo, Nodinus, and other rivers close to Rome. So our list will trail along without end, or else we shall admit none of these; and since we shall refuse to approve this catalogue of superstition, none of these must be accepted.

53   'It therefore follows, Balbus, that we must also oppose those who, not from fact but from opinion, argue that these gods, all of whom we worship with veneration and devotion, have been advanced from human status into heaven.* To begin with, the theologians so-called enumerate three Jupiters. They say that the first two were born in Arcadia,* that the father of the first was Aether, who sired also Proserpina and Liber, and that the father of the second was Caelus; this Jupiter is said to have begotten Minerva, who is cited as the author and deviser of war.* The third, so the story goes, was Saturn's son from Crete;* his tomb is a showpiece in that island. The Dioscuri* as well lend their names to numerous manifestations among the Greeks. The

first three, who are called "kings"* at Athens, are Tritopatreus, Eubouleus, and Dionysus, sons of the oldest Jupiter (called "King") and of Proserpina. The second Dioscuri* are Castor and Pollux, sons of Jupiter mark three and of Leda. The third are named by several authorities as Alco, Melampus, and Tmolus, sons of Atreus* whose father was Pelops.

54   'As for the Muses,* the first group numbers four, and they are daughters of Jupiter mark two; their names are Thelxinoe, Aode, Arche and Melete. The second set are nine in number, and are the daughters of Jupiter mark three and of Mnemosyne. The third gathering, the offspring of Pierus and Antiope, are usually named by the poets as Pierides and Pieriae; they are identical in number and in names with the previous set.

'You state that the sun (*Sol*) got his name* because he is unique (*solus*), but in fact the theologians uncover a plethora of suns. The first was the son of Jupiter and grandson of Aether. The second was the son of Hyperion. The third was the son of Vulcan, whose father was the Nile; according to the Egyptians, it is to this sun that the city of Heliopolis is dedicated. The fourth is the one said to have been born to Acantho at Rhodes in the era of the heroes, and to have been the sire of Ialysus, Camirus, and Lindus, the founding fathers of the Rhodians. The fifth is the one who they claim fathered Aeëtes and Circe at Colchis.

55   'Then again there are several Vulcans.* The first was the son of Caelus, and the father by Minerva of Apollo, who ancient historians say was the protector of Athens. The second was the son of the Nile, and was called Opas by the Egyptians, who claim him as the guardian of Egypt. The third is the son of Jupiter mark three and of Juno; according to tradition, he was in charge of the smithy at Lemnos. The fourth was the son of Maemalius, and lord of the so-called Volcanian islands off Sicily.

56   'Mercury* the first had Caelus for his father, and Dies for his mother; he is depicted rather lewdly with penis erect in excitement at the sight of Proserpina. The second is the son of Valens and Phoronis, identified with Trophonius as a subterranean deity. The third is the son of Jupiter mark three and of Maia; the story goes that he fathered Pan by Penelope. The fourth is

the son of the Nile; the Egyptians regard it as sacrilegious to utter his name. The fifth, venerated by the folk of Pheneus, is said to have slain Argus; they claim that this murder caused him to flee to Egypt, where he bestowed laws and letters on the Egyptians. The Egyptians call him Theuth, the name which they give also to the first month of the year.

57   'As for the sundry figures called Aesculapius,* the first is the son of Apollo and is worshipped by the Arcadians; he is said to have invented the probe, and to have been the first to use splints for healing. The second is the brother of Mercury mark two. The story goes that he was struck by lightning, and that he is buried at Cynosura. The third, the son of Arsippus and Arsinoe, was reputedly a pioneer in the application of purgatives and the extraction of teeth. His tomb and grove are open to inspection in Arcadia, not far from the river Lusius.

'Of the various Apollos,* the oldest is the one who I said a moment ago was the son of Vulcan, and the guardian of Athens. The second, the son of Corybas, was a native of Crete; record has it that he contested possession of the island with Jupiter himself. The third was the son of Jupiter mark three and of Latona; they say that he was an arrival at Delphi from the people of the far north. A fourth is found in Arcadia; the people there call him Nomio, because they claim that they derive their laws from him.

58   'Again, there are several Dianas.* The first is the daughter of Jupiter and Proserpina, and she is said to be the mother of the winged Cupid. The second is more familiar to us, having been born, we are told, from Jupiter mark three and Latona. Tradition has it that the father of the third was Upis, and that her mother was Glauce; the Greeks often call her Upis after her father.

'We have a host of gods called Dionysus.* The first is the son of Jupiter and Proserpina, the second the son of the Nile and allegedly the assassin of Nysa; the third, the son of Cabirus, was said to have been king of Asia, and to have had the Sabazian festival inaugurated in his honour. The fourth was the son of Jupiter and Luna; the Orphic rites are believed to be an offering to him. The fifth, the son of Nysus and Thyone, is thought to have established the triennial festival.

59   'The first Venus* was the daughter of Caelus and Dies; her shrine at Elis I have myself seen. The second was sprung from the sea-foam; we are told that she and Mercury were parents of Cupid mark two. The third, the daughter of Jupiter and Dione, was married to Vulcan, but her son Anteros is said to have been fathered by Mars. The fourth was the offspring of Syria and Cyprus; her name is Astarte, and she is said to have married Adonis.

'As for Minervas,* the first is the one who we said was the mother of Apollo. The second, the daughter of the Nile, is worshipped by Egyptians at Sais. The third we mentioned earlier as the daughter of Jupiter. The fourth is the offspring of Jupiter and Coryphe, daughter of Oceanus; the Arcadians call her Koria, and claim that she introduced the four-horse chariot. The fifth is the daughter of Pallas, and is said to have killed her father when he tried to rob her of her virginity. Artists attach winged anklets to her.

60   'The earliest Cupid* is said to be the son of Mercury and Diana mark one, the second to be the son of Mercury and Venus, and the third, who is identified with Anteros, to be the offspring of Mars and Venus mark three.

'These and other fables of the same kind have been gathered from long-standing Greek traditions. You realize that we must rebut them, so that our Roman rituals may not fall into disrepute. Yet the men of your school do not merely refrain from rejecting them; they positively approve of them by rationalizing the message derived from each. But let us now return to the point from which this digression led us.*

61   'Surely, then, you cannot imagine that we need more sophisticated arguments to refute these tenets? Mind, Faith,* Hope, Virtue, Honour, Victory, Safety, Harmony, and other concepts of the same kind we must envisage as in essence abstractions, not as gods; for they are either qualities that reside within us, such as mind, hope, faith, virtue, and harmony, or they are aims to which we aspire, like honour, safety, victory. I appreciate that these are beneficial qualities, and I note that statues are dedicated in their honour; but why divine powers should reside in them I shall understand only when my researches reveal it.

Fortune has the strongest of claims to inclusion in this category of
deities, yet no one will claim to distinguish it from what is fickle
and random, and these are qualities quite unworthy of a deity.

62   'Another issue: why do you Stoics take such pleasure in rationalizing fables, and in pursuing the etymologies* of names?
You defend the castration of Caelus by his son, and the shackling
of Saturn also by his son, and stories of this kind, so enthusiastic-
ally that those who originated them are regarded not merely as
sound in mind, but even as philosophers! As for your delving
into the meaning of names, your strained interpretations are
quite pathetic. "Saturn is so called because he is sated with
years; Mars, because he overturns might (*magna vertit*); Minerva,
because she diminishes (*minuit*), or alternatively, threatens (*mina-
tur*); Venus, because she visits (*venit*) all things; Ceres, because
she bears fruit (*gerere*)." What a hazardous procedure this is!
Many names will pose problems for you: what can you make of
Veiovis, or of Vulcan?* Mind you, bearing in mind that you
think that Neptune gets his name from *nando*, swimming, there
will be no name for which you cannot offer a derivation based
on a single letter! You seem to me to be more at sea in this pursuit
than is Neptune himself.

63   'First of all Zeno, followed by Cleanthes and then by Chrysippus,* landed themselves in great and wholly unnecessary difficulties in seeking to make sense of lying fables, and in seeking to
explain the reasons for the names of individual things. By so
doing, you Stoics are surely admitting that the facts are at odds
with popular beliefs, for figures dignified with the title of gods
turn out to be properties in nature, and not personal deities at
all. This misconception has gone so far that even destructive
things have been assigned gods' names, and have in addition
been invested with religious ritual. For example, on the Palatine
we find a shrine to Fever, and close to the temple of the Lares
there is one to Bereavement; and on the Esquiline there is an
altar dedicated to Ill-fortune.*

64   'We must therefore banish from philosophy all such misapprehensions, so that in discussion of the immortal gods we may
utter words worthy of them. I know my own views about them,
but I cannot bring myself to agree with yours. You say that Nep-

tune is a soul with intelligence that permeates the sea, and you offer a similar account of Ceres.* It is not just that I fail to grasp the notion of an intelligence pervading the sea or the earth; I do not have even an inkling of it. So I must look for other explanations to enable me to learn of both the fact of the gods' existence, and their nature, for your conception of them . . .'

65 'Let us investigate our next topics: first, whether the universe is governed by divine providence, and second, whether the gods concern themselves with the welfare of humans. These are the two aspects remaining for me to discuss from your earlier division of the subject. These I think I must treat with greater precision, if you people do not mind.'

'As for myself', said Velleius, 'I very much approve. Not only do I strongly support your discussion up to now, but I am expecting even greater things.'

Balbus then remarked: 'I don't wish to interrupt you, Cotta. We must seek another occasion, at which I will certainly extract a confession from you. However . . .'

*

[Cotta]: 'Such arguments should not be publicly aired in case discussion of this sort subverts the practice of the state religion.'

*

[Cotta]: 'We cannot be induced to believe that the immortal and pre-eminent nature of divinity is divided into male and female.'

*

[*Cotta's discussion of the first of the two remaining themes is lost. Its structure is as follows:*

    Is the universe governed by divine providence?
1. *The abundance of blessings which we obtain.*
2. *The due order of the seasons, and the regularity of the heavens.*
3. *Arguments proposed by Chrysippus: comparison of a beautiful house with the beauty of the universe; concord and harmony of the entire universe.*
4. *The syllogisms of Zeno.*

5. *The thrust of fire, and the heat from which all things are begotten.*
6. *Do the universe as a whole, and the sun, moon, and stars, have sensation and intelligence?*
7. *The stars' need of nurture.*
8. *Nature's structured progress.*
9. *The universe not built but shaped by nature.*]

'First of all, then,* it is unlikely that the material stuff from
which all things arose was created by divine providence; more
likely it has and had its own dynamic and nature. So just as a
craftsman when embarking on a building project does not himself create his materials, but exploits those available (and likewise the person who models in wax), so that divine providence
of yours must have had materials to hand, not created by itself
but available to be taken over. Now if God did not make that
material itself, he did not create earth, water, air, and fire.

*

'. . . and that snakes are begotten* from the marrows of human
bodies. It was said of the Spartan Cleomenes . . .'

*

[*Whether the gods concern themselves with human welfare*]
'. . . why, if God has made all things* for the benefit of mankind, many objects are found which are inimical, hostile and
baneful to us, both on sea and on land. The Stoics, through their
failure to observe the truth, have countered this objection in a
most unenlightened way. They state that in plants and in the
ranks of animals there are many properties which as yet lie
hidden, and will come to light in the process of time, just as our
need and experience have made many discoveries unknown to
earlier generations. But what benefit, I ask, can be observed in
mice or cockroaches or snakes, all of them troublesome and
destructive to the human race? Or perhaps some cure lies unde-
tected in them? If this is the case, I pray that it may be discovered
as an antidote to ills, though men grumble that these creatures
bring nothing but harm. People say that the ashes of the viper
when burnt are a remedy for snake-bite; but how much better it

would be if the viper did not exist at all, rather than that a cure should be sought from the viper itself.'

*

'Either God wishes to remove evils and cannot, or he can do so and is unwilling, or he has neither the will nor the power, or he has both the will and the power. If he has the will but not the power, he is a weakling, and this is not characteristic of God. If he has the power but not the will, he is grudging, and this is a trait equally foreign to God. If he has neither the will nor the power, he is both grudging and weak, and is therefore not divine. If he has both the will and the power (and this is the sole circumstance appropriate to God), what is the source of evils, or why does God not dispel them?'

*

'Men are superior to all animals.'*

*

'This shall not be,* I swear. A harsh ordeal looms.
What purpose had I, grovelling with fawning words,
Save to achieve my end?

66 Enough reasoning is surely in evidence here, as she personally plans sacrilegious destruction. The verse that follows,

Be of firm purpose, and events will then conspire,

reflects her crafty logic, and plants the seeds of all the ensuing ills:

This day he has misguidedly consigned to me
The keys to unlock my fury's spate, to bring him low;
This spells for me some grieving, but for him harsh pain,
Encompassing my exile, but for him black death.

Doubtless the brute beasts do not possess this faculty of reason which you Stoics claim has been bestowed by divine benevolence
67 on mankind alone! So do you now realize how blessed this gift is which the gods have implanted in us? It was this same Medea who, in fleeing from her father and her native land,

Just as her sire* pressed close to hold her fast,
Cut down the boy, then tore him limb from limb.

> His corpse she strewed all o'er the countryside,
> So while the father gathered his son's parts
> (Thus cruel grief should hinder his pursuit),
> She could make good her flight, escape unscathed
> By murder of her kin.

So Medea was not short of reason, as well as wickedness!

68   'Another example is that notorious figure* who prepared a feast of death for his brother; does he too not exploit his reason, as his thoughts turn this way and that?

> More monstrous the misdeed which I must mount
> To crush and to constrain his cruel heart.

And we cannot leave unmentioned Thyestes himself, for whom

> 'Twas not enough to entice a wife to sin.

The observations of Atreus on this are just and to the point:

> I count this matter most profound,
> Profound too is the hazard run
> When royal matrons are befouled,
> Their stock defiled, their lineage stained.

How craftily that deed was done, for Thyestes sought the kingship by way of adultery! Atreus continues:

> Note this as well: the Father of the gods
> Had sent to me, to fortify my rule,
> A prodigy, a lamb whose golden fleece
> Shone out conspicuous from out the flock.
> Thyestes brazenly once stole that lamb,
> Using my wife as accomplice in the deed.

69   'This villainy which he employed was clearly buttressed by the utmost use of reason. It is not merely the stage that abounds in such crimes; even more, our daily life is studded with examples almost as outrageous. The households of each of us, the lawcourts, the senate, the voting-booths, allied communities, the provinces—all have experience of how reason lies behind right conduct, but also behind evil-doing. Right conduct is practised rarely and by the few, whereas the second is constantly performed by a host of people. It would therefore have been better if the immortal gods had granted us no use of reason whatever,

rather than to have it bestowed with such a baleful outcome. Just as it is better not to serve wine to the sick* on any account (for its effect is rarely beneficial, and very often harmful) rather than to risk manifest disaster in the hope of an uncertain cure, so it would perhaps have been better for the human race not to have received at all the combination of swift thought, incisiveness, and cleverness which we call reason (for it is harmful to the many and beneficial only to the few), rather than to be given it in such generous and abundant measure.

70   'My conclusion is that if the gods with their intelligence and will *have* shown concern for human welfare by bestowing gifts on men, they have served the interests only of those on whom they bestowed right reason, and these are very few, if indeed they exist at all. But we cannot accept that the immortal gods have shown regard merely for the few, so it follows that they have consulted no-one's interests.

   'You Stoics confront this argument usually in this manner. You say that the fact that many abuse the gods' kindnesses does not demonstrate that the gods have not made the best possible provision for us. After all, many people squander their inheritances, but this does not mean that they receive no kindness from their fathers. No one of course would deny this, but is there any similarity if we compare the two cases? It is true that Deianira did not intend to harm Hercules* when she presented him with the shirt dipped in the Centaur's blood; and contrariwise, the soldier who with his sword lanced the abscess of Jason of Pherae* which the physicians had failed to heal did not intend to do him a good turn. The truth is that many do good when they seek to do harm, and they do harm when they seek to do good. So the presentation of a gift does not reflect the motive of the donor, not does it prove his benevolence if the recipient makes good use of it.

71   'But is there any act of lust or greed or crime which is undertaken without preliminary design, or carried out without feeling or thought, in other words without reason? Every belief is based on reason; if true, it is right reason, but if false the reasoning is defective. But God gives us only reason, assuming that in fact he does; whether it is good or bad depends on ourselves. When

reason is bestowed upon a person by the gods' gift, it is not analogous to a bequest left to us, for if they had wished to harm us what better could they have bestowed on mankind? If reason does not underlie injustice, lack of restraint and cowardice, from what seeds would these vices sprout?

'Just now we mentioned Medea and Atreus as individuals of the heroic age who pondered their sacrilegious crimes by the calculation and balance-sheet of reason. But are not the light-hearted scenes of comedy also dependent on reason, considerably and constantly? Certainly the young fellow in *Eunuch** argues cleverly enough:

> What then am I to do?
> She shut me out, she calls me back; shall I go in?
> No, not if she goes on bended knees!

'Then too the boy in *The Youthful Comrades*,* just like the Academics, does not hesitate to carry the battle against received opinion with the weapon of reason, when he says that "when you're up to the eyes in love and debt", it is sweet,

> If your father's a miser, and a boor to boot,
> Who's hard on his children, and shows you no affection,
> No interest in your welfare . . .

He offers some modest justification for this unlikely assertion:

> You must cheat him of his profit, or appropriate a debt
> By forging a letter; send a confidential slave
> To put him in a panic; from that pinch-penny pater
> Extort all you can, and take pleasure in squandering it!

He further argues that a genial and generous father is a nuisance to a son who has a girl-friend:

> There's no way I can cheat him, nor rob him of a penny;
> There's no wile or contrivance I can try to put across him.
> My father's so compliant that he frustrates all my tricks.

I ask you: could any of these ruses or contrivances or deceits or tricks have been engineered without the use of reason? What a splendid gift of the gods this is to be sure, allowing Phormio* to declare:

> Bring on the old chap. My plans are all ready!

74   'But let us quit the theatre and make our way to the courts, where the presiding praetor is taking his seat. What case is under scrutiny? Why, to establish who set fire to the record-office.* What crime could be more underhand than that? Yet it was a Roman knight of distinction, Quintus Sosius, who pleaded guilty to the charge. Who then forged the public accounts,* for this was perpetrated as well? Why, Lucius Alenus, by copying the handwriting of six senior clerks; was there ever a craftier fellow than that? Pass judgement on other trials, like the matter of the gold from Toulouse* in the Jugurthan conspiracy; or go back in time to the trial of Tubulus* for accepting a bribe when acting as juryman; or a more recent case, the indictment of unchastity brought by Peducaeus.* Then there are the current cases* on charges of assassination, poisoning and peculation, and forging of wills brought under the recent law.

'Behind that familiar indictment,* "I say that the theft was carried out with your support and prompting", there lies the use of reason. Reason is responsible for all those cases of fraud in the matter of guardianships, unpaid commissions, partnerships, deposits on trust, and those other court-cases which arise out of breach of faith in purchase, or sale, or hire, or lease. Reason has caused the imposition of public jurisdiction over private suits by the law of Plaetorius,* and prosecution for malicious fraud promulgated by our friend Gaius Aquillius,* who has swept every kind of deception into that net of his. Aquillius indeed believes that a malicious fraud has been netted when there has been pretence of doing one thing and actual performance of something else.

75   'So do we really believe that the immortal gods sowed this monstrous crop of evils? Well then, if the gods gave reason to men, they also gave them malice, for malice is the crafty and deceitful intention of doing harm; and similarly they gave them cheating, and crime, and the other forms of wrong behaviour, none of which can be undertaken and perpetrated without the use of reason. Like the old woman on the stage,* who prays

Would that the pine-tree lengths in Pelion's glade
Had never crashed to earth beneath the axe,

so our lament is: would that the gods had not bestowed this cunning on the human race, for those who use it well are few and far between, and they themselves often fall victim to those who use it wickedly. As for those who employ it unscrupulously, they are beyond counting. It thus becomes clear that this god-sent gift of reason was bestowed not to benefit men, but to beguile them.

76   'But you repeatedly insist* that we men, and not the gods, are the culprits in this respect. This is like the doctor laying the blame on the severity of the disease, or the helmsman pleading the violence of the storm. Of course, doctors and helmsmen are only human, but they would look silly making such excuses, for the bystander would rejoin: "But who would have employed you if the circumstances were different?" We can press the argument against God even more forcefully: "You claim that men's vices are at fault, but you should have granted them the reasoning which precluded vices and sinning." How then is there possibility of mistake by the gods? When we humans make bequests and hope that we have made suitable arrangements in them, we can be mistaken; but how could a god make an error? Are we to cite as example the Sun when he let his son Phaethon go aloft* in his chariot? Or Neptune, when he granted his son Theseus the gratification of three wishes, as a result of which he destroyed Hippolytus?*

77   'Such stories are manufactured by the poets, whereas we seek to be philosophers dispensing facts and not fables. Yet even those gods in poetry, had they known that their concessions would prove destructive to their sons, would have been regarded as misguided in their generosity. If the favourite saying of Aristo of Chios* is true, that philosophers harm those pupils who misinterpret their laudable doctrines (for he admitted that students could emerge from the school of Aristippus* as profligates, and from the school of Zeno* with bitter tongues), then if those disciples were likely to be debased on leaving because they misinterpreted the discourses of the philosophers, it would certainly be preferable for the philosophers to say nothing rather than to

78   harm their listeners. Similarly, if men abuse the reason which the immortal gods have bestowed with good intentions, and

exploit it for deceit and malice, it would have been better for such reason to be withheld rather than bestowed on the human race. Just as the physician would be seriously at fault if he knew that the invalid for whom he prescribed wine would drink it neat and expire on the spot, so that Providence of yours is blameworthy for bestowing reason on those who she knew would use it unreasonably and wickedly. Perhaps, however, you Stoics claim that she did not know. I could wish that this were true, but you will not be so presumptuous, for I am well aware of the value which you put upon her name.

79 'But we can now conclude this topic. If, as all philosophers agree, foolishness is a greater evil than all ills imposed by fortune or sustained by the body put together, and yet no one gains wisdom,* we are all in the depths of despond. But you Stoics still claim that the immortal gods have the greatest concern for our welfare. However, just as it is an idle distinction whether no man *is* in rude health or *can be* in rude health, so I recognize no difference between "no one *is* wise" and "no-one *can be* wise." But I have laboured the point too long, for it is quite obvious. Telamon* expresses succinctly the argument that gods give no thought to the human race:

> If gods did care, the good would prosper, and the bad
> Would suffer; that's not the way of things.

'If the gods did care for the welfare of the human race, they should have made all men good; or at any rate they should have taken thought for the virtuous. Why then did the Carthaginians in Spain bring down those most valiant and virtuous men the two Scipios? Why had Fabius Maximus to escort his son, an ex–consul, to the grave? Why did Hannibal slay Marcellus? Why did Aemilius Paulus perish at Cannae? Why was the corpse of Regulus exposed to the cruelty of the Carthaginians? Why was Africanus* not protected by the walls of his own house?

'But these and other numerous instances are ancient history; let us review those closer at hand. Why is my uncle Publius Rutilius, that most innocent and learned of men, in exile? Why was my friend Drusus killed in his own home? Why was that exemplar of restraint and wisdom, the *pontifex maximus* Quintus Scaevola,

slaughtered in front of the statue of Vesta? Why were numerous
leaders of the state earlier slain by Cinna? Why was Gaius
Marius, that traitor supreme, empowered to order the death of
Quintus Catulus,* a man of absolutely outstanding distinction?
81   Daylight would desert me if I sought to recount the catalogue of
good men overtaken by misfortune, and equally if I were to
recall the evil men who prospered. For example, why did Marius
enjoy seven consulships* and die as an old man in his own bed?
Why did Cinna, the cruellest creature alive, play the king for so
long?* You object that he did pay the penalty. But it would
surely have been better if he had been prevented and hindered
from executing all those outstanding men, rather than himself
paying the penalty in the end. Quintus Varius,* that most objec-
tionable of characters, met his death by execution after severe torture; seeing that he met his fate because he had disposed of
Drusus by the sword, and Metellus by poison, it would have
been better if their lives had been spared rather than that Varius
should have paid the penalty for his wickedness.

'Dionysius lasted for thirty-eight years as tyrant of the richest
82   and most flourishing of cities; earlier, Pisistratus* lorded it for
heaven knows how long in the city which is the flower of Greece.
Still, you will say, Phalaris and Apollodorus* both paid the
price; that is true, but only after they had tortured and murdered
many. Pirates are often executed in large numbers, but we
cannot gainsay that the captives who have met harsh deaths at
their hands outnumber them. We have it on record that Anaxarchus,* a follower of Democritus, was butchered by the
tyrant of Cyprus, and that Zeno of Elea* was tortured to death.
Need I mention Socrates, whose death when I read Plato's
account* moves me to tears? So you surely see that if the gods
do take note of human affairs, they pass judgement without dis-
tinguishing the deserving from the rest.

83   'The Cynic philosopher Diogenes* used to say that Harpalus,
who in his time was regarded as a successful brigand, was a
living testimony against the gods, because he survived so trium-
phantly all that time. I mentioned Dionysius* a moment ago.
Once when he had plundered the shrine of Proserpina at Locri,
he was sailing over to Syracuse, and when the most favourable

wind kept him on course, he remarked with a grin: 'My friends, do you observe what a pleasant sail the immortal gods grant to perpetrators of sacrilege?' He was a smart fellow, with a shrewd and perceptive outlook, and he continued to hold the same opinion. When he put in with his fleet at the Peloponnese, and made his way to the shrine of Jupiter at Olympia, he removed from the god the heavy cloak of gold with which the tyrant Gelon* had adorned the statue from Carthaginian spoils. He even went so far as to joke as he did this, saying that the golden cloak was oppressive in summer and cold in winter; he threw a woollen garment over the statue, remarking that this was suitable clothing all the year round. It was Dionysius, too, who ordered the removal of the golden beard from the statue of Aesculapius at Epidaurus, on the pretext that it was inappropriate for a son to sport a beard when his father in all the shrines was clean-shaven.

84 'The tyrant also ordered that tables made of silver should be removed from all the temples. He said that since they bore the inscription traditional from ancient Greece, "the property of the kindly gods", he wished to avail himself of that kindness. Further, he had no hesitation in removing the miniature statues of Victory, which were made of gold, and the cups and crowns which reposed in the outstretched hands of the statues; he claimed that he was not robbing them, but accepting them as offerings, for when we prayed for blessings from deities, and they proffered those blessings as gifts, it was crazy to refuse to accept them. The story goes that he also laid out in the forum those spoils which I mentioned were plundered from the shrines, and put them up for auction; once he had extracted the money, he proclaimed that anyone possessing an object from a sacred shrine was to restore it by a fixed date to where it belonged. He thus compounded his impiety to the gods with injustice to men.

'What was the outcome? Olympian Jupiter failed to strike him down with a thunderbolt; Aesculapius did not cause him to waste away in a wretched and protracted illness. He died in his own bed;* he was laid upon a royal pyre; the dominion which he had himself acquired by crime he bequeathed to his son as if it were a just and lawful inheritance.

85 'I broach this topic with reluctance, since my discourse seems

to lend authority to misbehaviour. That would be a justifiable assumption, if without recourse to any appeal to heaven our very awareness of virtue and of the vices did not carry such considerable weight. Once that awareness is removed, the whole moral edifice collapses. Just as a household or a state appears to be ordered without a sense of reason and discipline if rewards are not offered for just behaviour and punishments for misdemeanours, so there is certainly no divine governance in the universe, in so far as it is directed towards men, if no distinction is made in it between persons who are good and those who are evil.

86   ' "But the gods ignore trivialities,* and do not scrutinize small estates and tiny vineyards; Jupiter has no need to take notice if someone is blighted by frost or hail, for even in kingdoms kings do not bother their heads over every petty detail." This is how you Stoics argue. Was it, then, Publius Rutilius'* farm at Formiae which was the substance of my complaint a moment ago, and not his loss of citizen's rights? Yet the whole world believes that material benefits like vineyards, cornfields, olive-groves, their fertile crops and fruits, and in short all perquisites and profits in life come from the gods, but no one has ever attributed virtue to God's beneficence.

87   'This attitude is surely justified, for we ourselves rightly gain praise for virtue, and we rightly take pride in it. This would not be the case if we obtained it as a gift from God, and if it did not emanate from ourselves. On the other hand, if we gain distinctions or family property, or if we obtain some other unlooked-for blessing, or shrug off some misfortune, we then thank the gods, and we believe that nothing has accrued to our own praise. Did anyone, I ask, ever thank the gods for being a good person? People call Jupiter "Greatest and Best" because they have gained wealth or distinction or safety, not because he makes us just or moderate or wise, but because he makes us safe

88   and secure, rich and well endowed. No one ever vowed a tithe to Hercules* on condition that he became wise. True, the story goes that Pythagoras,* on making some discovery in geometry, sacrificed an ox to the Muses, but I do not believe it, because he refused to slay a victim even to Apollo at Delos, so as to avoid besmirching his altar with blood.

'But to return to the main point: the belief universally held is that men must seek from God the blessings of fortune, but that the source of wisdom must lie in ourselves. We can consecrate shrines to Mind and Virtue and Faith, but these are qualities which we see resident in ourselves; access to hope, safety, wealth, and victory we must seek from the gods.

'So, as Diogenes claimed, the successes and prosperity of the wicked wholly refute the notion of the gods' force and power. 89 You object that on occasion good men achieve successes; indeed, we latch on to these, and without any justification attribute them to the immortal gods. The opposite was the case when Diagoras, whom they call the Atheist,* visited Samothrace, where a friend remarked to him: "You believe that the gods are indifferent to human affairs, but all these tablets with their portraits surely reveal to you the great number of those whose vows enabled them to escape the violence of a storm, so that they reached harbour safe and sound." "That is the case", rejoined Diagoras, "but there are no portraits in evidence of those who were shipwrecked and drowned at sea." This same Diagoras was once aboard ship when a storm blew up. The crew were fearful, and in their panic they told him that it served them right for allowing him to embark. He then pointed out to them several other vessels on the same route which were similarly in trouble, and he asked them whether they thought that there was a Diagoras aboard them as well. The fact is that one's character, and the kind of life which one has lived, has no bearing on one's good or evil fortune.

90 'What Balbus claims is that neither gods, nor indeed kings, pay heed to every detail. I fail to see the connection between the two. If kings take no action even in full knowledge, they are seriously culpable, but God cannot even make pretence of ignorance. What a remarkable apology you make for him, when you state that even if someone escapes punishment for a crime by death, the divine power ensures that such punishment is exacted from children, grandchildren, or their descendants! What a signal sense of justice the gods manifest! Would any state allow an individual to promulgate a law condemning a son or grandson, if a father or grandfather had transgressed?

> What limit,* in the house of Tantalus,
> To slaughter can be set? Will penalties
> Exacted for the death of Myrtilus
> Be ever sated by incurring punishment?

91   'Whether poets have corrupted Stoics, or Stoics have lent their authority to poets, I cannot readily say, for both groups recount marvels and monstrous deeds. The pain nursed by the man who was pierced by the iambics of Hipponax, or was punctured by the verses of Archilochus,* was not inflicted by God, but emanated from himself. When we contemplate the lust of Aegisthus or that of Paris, we do not seek its cause in God, for we can virtually hear the clamour of their guilt. When I see a host of sick people restored to health, I do not regard Aesculapius as their benefactor, but Hippocrates. The traditional regimen of the Lacedaemonians at Sparta I refuse to attribute to Apollo rather than to Lycurgus. My contention is that Critolaus brought Corinth down, and Hasdrubal* Carthage; it was these two men, and not some angry god (for you Stoics affirm that God can never experience any anger whatsoever) who gouged out from their sea-coasts those idyllic eyes.

92   'Still, God could at least have relieved and preserved those great and glorious cities, for you yourselves often claim that there is nothing which God cannot perform, and effortlessly at that. Just as our limbs are moved spontaneously at the behest of mind and will, so, you claim, all things are fashioned, moved and transformed by the gods' power. You contend that this conclusion is based not on the superstition of an old wife's tale, but on scientific and rational grounds,* for the stuff which comprises and encloses all things is wholly flexible and changeable, so that from it there is nothing which cannot be fashioned and transformed even in a trice. It is divine Providence, you say,* which fashions and orders the whole of matter, and she can accordingly achieve her will, no matter the direction in which she goes. The conclusion must be that she does not know her own powers, or that she gives no thought to human affairs, or that she cannot decide what is best for us.

93   'Your riposte is that Providence does not concern herself with individuals.* This does not surprise me, for she does not take

thought even for cities—and if not for cities, then not for peoples and nations either! If Providence is going to spurn these as well, it is hardly surprising that she holds the entire human race in contempt. But how can you Stoics argue that the gods do not attend to every aspect, yet simultaneously claim that dreams are distributed and allotted to men* by the immortals—I raise this question with you, Balbus, because you Stoics maintain that dreams portend the truth—and that also we should bind ourselves with vows?* Vows, of course, are utterances of individuals, so the divine mind must hearken to individuals, and your school must therefore realize that Providence is not so fully occupied as you thought. Even if we grant that she is fully stretched in turning round the heavens, protecting the earth, and controlling the sea, why does she allow the multitude of deities* to relax in idleness? Why does she not appoint some of these unoccupied gods to preside over human affairs? After all, Balbus, you have detailed countless numbers of them!

'This is about all I have to say about the nature of the gods. My purpose has been not to deny their existence, but to make you realize how hard it is to understand it, and how problematic are the explanations offered.'

94 'These were Cotta's final remarks. Lucilius rejoined: 'This has been quite an impassioned attack, Cotta, which you have made, on the thesis which the Stoics have established concerning the gods' providence in the most reverent and sagacious terms. But since dusk is now falling, you must grant us some other day to counter these arguments of yours; for I must engage with you in defence of our altars and hearths, our temples and shrines of the gods, and the walls of our city, which you priests declare are sacred; indeed, you circumscribe our city more conscientiously with religious observance than with the walls themselves. I think that it would be sacrilegious for me to forsake these sacred buildings, as long as I have a breath left in my body.'

95 Cotta then observed: 'For my part, Balbus, I long to be refuted. I preferred to expound the arguments which I presented rather than to justify them, and I am sure that I can be readily worsted at your hands.'

'That's for sure,' interjected Velleius. 'Why, Balbus thinks that even dreams are sent to us by Jupiter! But those very dreams are not so trivial as the Stoics' version of the nature of the gods.'

Following the discussion, we went our different ways. Cotta's argument seemed to Velleius to be the more truthful, but in my eyes Balbus' case seemed to come more closely to a semblance of the truth.*

Explanatory Notes

(*Numbers in the left-hand margin refer to sections of the text.*)

1 *Brutus*: this is the Marcus Iunius Brutus who planned the assassination of Julius Caesar in March 44. He was a considerable intellectual; as a former pupil of Antiochus, he claimed allegiance, like Cicero himself, to the Academic school. Cicero's close friendship with him is attested by their voluminous correspondence, only a fraction of which has survived, and by Cicero's dedication to him of *De finibus* and *Tusculans*.

2 *almost all of us*: reading *fere* for the corrupt *sese* of the MSS, obelized by Ax.

Protagoras: our knowledge of him comes chiefly from the dialogue of Plato bearing his name. Two of his statements have gained him immortality. Eusebius (*Praep. Evang.* 14. 3. 7) has preserved one sentence of his from his treatise *On the gods*: 'So far as gods are concerned, I cannot know whether they exist or not, nor what they are like in appearance; for many factors impede our knowledge—obscurity and the shortness of life.' Plato, *Theaetetus* 151e, attributes to him the statement that 'Man is the measure of all things, of things that are that they are, and of things that are not that they are not'—a statement which excludes any appeal to divine revelation about the gods' existence.

Diagoras . . . Theodorus: Diagoras, a lyric poet of the late fifth century, was said to have lost his faith in the existence of gods when a man who broke his oath remained unpunished by them. See further 3. 84, and L. Woodbury, *Phoenix* (1965), 178 ff. Theodorus of Cyrene was an adherent of the Cyrenaic school in the late fourth and early third centuries, and a pupil of Aristippus (on whom, see 3. 77 nn.). For Theodorus, see Diogenes Laertius 2. 98 ff.

3 *there are and have been philosophers*, etc.: Cicero now briefly visualizes the difficulties which the Epicurean theology raises for Roman religious practice, and indirectly for the coherence of Roman

society. This observation is a challenge to contemporary Epicureans, who include Cicero's friend Atticus and other acquaintances mentioned in his correspondence (*Fam.* 15. 19).

4 *mentioned in the present work*: for these Stoic arguments, see 2. 151–68.

Carneades: the President of the New or Third Academy from a date before 155 to 137–6 is the philosopher who exercises greatest influence on Cicero, as is clear from *De finibus, Tusculans*, and above all *Academica*. See Introduction, p. xxxvi.

5 *well-disposed critics ... malicious backbiters*: when he settled to compose this treatise, Cicero had already published *Hortensius, Academica, De finibus*, and *Tusculans*. He here reflects on the reactions aroused by them.

6 *a school of thought ... long left behind*: he refers not to the demise of the Academy, but to its more positive orientation under its head Antiochus of Ascalon, with his ecumenical attitude to Stoics and Peripatetics (Introduction, p. xxxvi).

philosophers outstanding in their field: it is striking that the philosophers mentioned in this section do not include his Epicurean teachers, Phaedrus and Zeno of Sidon; those mentioned are Stoics or Academics. The Stoic Diodotus lived in Cicero's house from 84 to 59, and Posidonius, another Stoic, taught him at Rhodes. Philo, head of the Academy, came to Rome from Athens as a refugee from Mithridates in 88, and Cicero sat at his feet; Antiochus, his successor at the Academy, was Cicero's teacher in Athens ('I loved the man', says Cicero, 'and he loved me.' *Acad.* 2. 113.)

7 *the political situation*: Cicero had on principle supported the senatorial party under Pompey in the Civil War, and though Caesar treated him generously subsequently, he was excluded from the life of politics. In 46 Caesar was appointed dictator for ten years, and in 44 for life.

8 *I have stirred the enthusiasm of many ... to write*: this claim is repeated in *De officiis* 2. 2. but it is not known to whom he refers; perhaps Brutus, or Varro (*Acad.* 1. 9).

9 *the savage and crippling blow*: this was the death of his daughter Tullia in childbirth a year earlier (*Fam.* 4 5f., *Att.* 12. 14f.). Cicero had divorced his wife Terentia in 46, and married the youthful Publilia for her money, only to divorce her in turn in

45; but these events did not occasion him as much distress as the death of his daughter.

10 *'the master said so'*: the criticism of the Pythagoreans reflects also on the Epicureans, who likewise quote their founder's *Canon* and *Kuriai Doxai* in justification of their views.

11 *the four books of my Academica*: this work, the second in the sequence written in 46–44, was devoted to epistemology. It was originally written in two books entitled *Catulus* and *Lucullus*, but was later rewritten with new spokesmen in four books. The two versions go under the titles of *Academica Priora* and *Academica Posteriora*; by a quirk of fate, the second half of *Priora* and the first quarter of *Posteriora* only have survived. Book 1 (from the *Posteriora*) discusses the notion of the probable resumed in § 12 here, and Book 2 (*Lucullus*, the second book of *Priora*), the problem of scepticism as reviewed by successive Academics.

12 *I have discussed this matter . . . elsewhere*: see *Acad.* 2 103 ff.

13 *The Youthful Comrades*: this play was written by Caecilius Statius, a member of the Gallic tribe the Insubrians inhabiting the region of Milan. He came to Rome as a prisoner in the 190s, and like Terence adapted Menander for the Roman stage. Cicero (*Att.* 7. 3. 10) criticizes his Latinity; my translation reflects the laboured nature of the original.

14 *auspices over which I myself preside*: Cicero had held the office of augur since 53 BC.

15 *a most rigorous and careful discussion*: the dialogue is imaginary. In a letter to Varro (*Fam.* 9. 8), Cicero warns his friend that he will find himself involved in the *Academica* in a conversation which never took place! The dramatic date of this dialogue is 76 BC (see Introduction, p. xxxviii), when Cicero was still a relatively unknown figure, during the *Feriae Latinae*, a movable feast, which the consuls arranged between April and July. The depiction of time and place is in imitation of Plato's practice in his dialogues.

Cotta . . . Velleius . . . Balbus: see Introduction, p. xxxviii f.

16 *Marcus Piso*: Marcus Pupius Piso Calpurnianus (consul 61) became a political enemy of Cicero in the 60s, but had died by 44 when this dialogue was composed. He would have represented the Peripatetics, the school founded at Athens by Aristotle; he is introduced as spokesman for the school in *De finibus* 5. Cicero

excluded this school from the dialogue because its importance centred primarily on logic and ethics, and Pupius's theological views would not have offered so distinctive a contrast as that between the other three.

Stoics are at one with Peripatetics: significantly enough, Balbus interprets this with reference to ethics, the main focus of interest of all the schools. Peripatetics and Stoics were agreed that virtue was to be sought (though Aristotle himself made intellectual contemplation the highest end), but for Stoics it was the only good, whereas the Peripatetics classified health, wealth, nobility, and high position as lesser goods. For Stoics, such advantages were 'things indifferent', but when pressed they conceded that they were preferable to their opposites of sickness, poverty, etc., and they accordingly established categories of 'things preferred' and 'things not preferred'. Antiochus reasonably suggested that the Peripatetics' 'lesser goods' were identical with the Stoics' 'things preferred'; Balbus insists that the honourable (that is, virtue) cannot be identified with the advantageous, as the Peripatetics do by calling both 'goods'.

17 *taught . . . to know nothing*: a humorous allusion to the scepticism of the Academics.

18 *with the breezy confidence*, etc.: this scathing presentation of Velleius is an index to Cicero's aversion from the pontificating tendencies of the Epicureans, and more fundamentally from their ethical tenets.

the Epicurean intermundia: for the Epicurean doctrine that the gods inhabit the *intermundia*, or empty spaces between the worlds, see Introduction, p. xxxii.

the craftsman-god in Plato's Timaeus: Cicero himself translated this dialogue; the celebrated myth in it (89d–92e) recounts how the *demiourgos* created an orderly universe out of existing matter.

19 *tools and levers and scaffolding*: Cicero makes Velleius take Plato's creation-myth literally, ignoring the preliminary comment at *Timaeus* 28c: 'To find the maker and father of the universe is a hard task, and when you have found him, it is impossible to speak of him before all the people.' Such poetic myths make an easy target when interpreted literally; hence these knockabout jokes from Velleius. For Plato's discussion of the four elements, see *Timaeus* 32c and following.

those solids of five shapes: according to Pythagorean theory adopted by Plato, the four elements are represented by geometrical shapes; earth by particles in the shape of a cube, fire by a triangular pyramid, air by an octahedron, and water by an ikosahedron (twenty-sided). These are selected as the only possible regular rectilinear solids (all the faces being identical in size and shape) which can be enclosed in a sphere with all their corners touching the surface; see I. M. Crombie, *An Explanation of Plato's Doctrines* (London, 1962), ii. 197 ff.

to strike the mind and to produce sensations: the theory of perception outlined in the *Timaeus* posits a cone of light formed between the object seen and the eye. Particles from the object impinge on the eye, which transmits the shock to the mind.

20 *What thing has some sort of beginning but no end?* Velleius's logic is strong; it can be met only by Plato's claim (*Timaeus* 32c) that the creation is made eternal by the will of the Creator.

If your Stoic Pronoia, Lucilius, is identical with this: Velleius here turns to Lucilius Balbus to ask if the Stoic deity also created an eternal universe. He is uncertain because most Stoics postulate a cyclical process of destruction and regeneration, though Panaetius dissented.

21 *what it must have been in extent*: Velleius argues that we can comprehend the notion of eternity before creation by thinking of it as spatial extension back from the moment of creation.

22 *like some aedile . . . with decorative figures*: the aediles at Rome supervised public buildings, and mounted public shows. There is a pun on *signa* ('decorative figures') here; the word means both 'statues' as erected by the aediles, and 'stars' as created by Pronoia.

23 *as you Stoics usually claim*: see 2. 133 ff.

merely for the wise? . . . for the benefit of the few: the Stoics argued that a small minority (Hercules, Socrates, the Cynic Diogenes are cited as examples) were able to attain the status of wise men by embracing virtue, which they defined as 'living according to nature'. God, suggests Velleius, has wasted his time in creating the world for mankind if so few appreciate the gift.

they . . . failed to see into what shape . . . intelligent mind could be installed: both Plato and the Stoics posit a sentient world endowed with mind. The Timaeus myth describes how the world obtains its soul, and for the Stoics the soul of the universe is identical with Pronoia. Epicureans argue that since reason is embraced within the human form alone, intelligent mind can pass only into that form, which the gods share with men.

24 *I shall treat this matter*: see § 48.

25 *Now I shall recount the older views*: it is important to grasp two features of this review of philosophy prior to the Hellenistic period. Cicero endeavours to visualize the tenets from the standpoint of an Epicurean's notion of gods as untroubled and perfect beings in human shape. Second, since he is personally hostile to the Epicurean school, he is not averse to summarizing their views in a simplistic and misleading way. These inaccuracies or oversimplifications can be measured by comparing the thumbnail accounts of individual philosophers with the texts in Kirk–Raven–Schofield.

Thales: the statement that 'god was the mind that fashioned all things from water' misleads; Thales will have argued not that mind was an external agent working on the water, but an immanent and dynamic force within it.

Anaximander: he posited that the first principle was the *apeiron* or 'boundless', but this probably means 'indefinite' in the sense of intermediate between fire and air, or between air and water. This intermediate matter, from which worlds emerge and into which they disappear, is itself alive and eternal; Velleius' criticism is in this sense misplaced.

26 *Anaximenes*: the claim that the air which he posited as first principle is created cannot be correct, since like other Ionians Anaximenes believed that matter is eternal.

Anaxagoras: astonishingly, Velleius omits Heraclitus and his theory that fire is the first principle. Anaxagoras is chronologically and logically out of place here; he should have followed Parmenides, against whose teaching his views are formulated. Moreover, Velleius appears wrongly to posit Anaxagoras' Nous (Mind) as a transcendent rather than immanent force; he is presenting the objection, familiar to all students of natural theology: how can a non-material, non-sensory deity impinge on the world of sense?

27 *Alcmaeon of Croton*: Cicero has derived this account of the Pythagorean's theology (perhaps indirectly) from Aristotle's *De*

anima 405a. Since the Epicureans believed that both the heavenly bodies and the soul were compounded of atoms, they believed that they would eventually break up. Alcmaeon inferred their immortality from their capacity for perpetual self-movement. By the 'soul', he means the world-soul, alive and eternal.

27–8 Velleius here mounts four familiar Epicurean arguments against the Pythagorean doctrine of the world-soul, from which our individual souls are abstracted: God is dismembered, God must be miserable, men must be omniscient, and God as incorporeal mind has no contact with the earth. Since the Stoics take over this doctrine of the world-soul, the argument is directed against them as well.

Xenophanes: he is best known for attacking anthropomorphism ('If cattle and horses and lions had hands, they would depict the gods like cattle and horses'). He posits instead a single god 'greatest among gods and men, not like men in form and thought, remaining motionless in the same place, shaking all things by the thought of his mind' (frs. 23, 26). Velleius reproduces Aristotle's interpretation that this is a god coextensive with the world.

Parmenides: his description of the universe (recounted in a poem in hexameters) is obscure. He speaks of concentric rings of light and darkness, thin and thick rings of air, with a fiery circle round the solid centre. However, this is in the second part of his poem, called *The Way of Seeming*, which he rejects as a false view (he prefaces it with 'Here I end my trustworthy discourse . . . henceforward learn the beliefs of mortal men.'). The charges that he deifies war, disharmony, and desire may also he misplaced, since they too presumably appeared in *The Way of Seeming*.

in another philosopher: Alcmaeon (cf. § 27).

29 *Empedocles*: see the Glossary. Traditionally regarded as an associate of Parmenides, he differed from him in positing four eternally distinct substances, fire, air, water, and earth, and gave them symbolic names of deities. Velleius fails to mention Empedocles' thesis that two agents, Love and Strife, unite and separate the elements; the suggestion that the elements are born and destroyed runs wholly counter to Empedocles' view.

Protagoras: see § 2 n.

Democritus: ('our perception' translates the reading of the MSS, *sententiam*, in preference to the emendation *scientiam*.)

The celebrated atomist philosopher argued that objects composed of atoms give off 'images' (*eidola*) which strike the senses and enter the mind; 'the world of nature' refers to his doctrine of atoms; and 'our perception and understanding' refers to the reception of the images by the senses and the mind. But Velleius ludicrously oversimplifies by claiming that for Democritus these are gods, whereas he probably called the physical process *theion* or 'divine' in the sense of 'spontaneous' or 'uncaused'.

Diogenes of Apollonia: not the famous Cynic philosopher, but a follower of Anaximenes (see § 26), who posited air as the first element, which he endowed with divine intelligence.

30 *Plato*: for the citation from the *Timaeus*, see § 19 n.; the quotation from the *Laws* (7. 821) totally misrepresents Plato's own view, for in that passage he is presenting the common notion of Athenians which he proceeds to contradict, here and elsewhere (*Laws* 9. 966) arguing that astronomy should be studied as a work of piety. There is justification for the claim that Plato's god is incorporeal; as for his lacking pleasure, Plato attacks the notion that gods enjoy pleasure (*Philebus* 33b), which for Epicureans is the highest good. It is true that in his *Timaeus* Plato makes the stars gods, owing their immortality to the will of the *Demiourgos*; and in the *Laws*, Ouranos (heaven) is the supreme deity, and the stars are the adornments of the gods. It is possible to make these views consistent by identifying Ouranos with Demiourgos as labels for the creative Mind; but Plato's pronouncements are poetic and speculative, not to be subjected to the literal interpretation employed by Velleius.

31 *Xenophon*: the range of writings of Plato's fellow-pupil under Socrates includes four books of *Memorabilia*, a defence of the master's teaching. Velleius here freely adapts *Memorabilia* 4. 3. 13 f., as when he claims that the soul is called a god, whereas it 'partakes of the divine nature' in Xenophon.

32 *Antisthenes*: after associating with Plato and Xenophon as disciple of Socrates, he founded the Cynic school, which was concerned more with ethics than with physics. Cicero may have gleaned this quotation from his friend the Epicurean Philodemus.

Speusippus: the nephew and successor of Plato as head of the Academy; no other testimony exists for the view expounded here, which is reminiscent of Anaxagoras' doctrine of *Nous*.

33 *Aristotle*: (In translating 'in dissenting', I retain *dissentiens* against
the emendation *non dissentiens*, because Aristotle introduces radically different notions of God.) The four views assigned to him
here are: (i) divinity assigned wholly to Mind; this is Anaxagoras' *Nous*, which Plato adopted; (ii) the world is god; this probably distorts Aristotle's view that the heavenly bodies are
rational beings; (iii) some other person is in charge of the world;
this is Aristotle's first Mover, himself unmoved, the object of
desire which rouses the first heaven to movement (see *Metaphysics*
11); (iv) the heat of the heavens is god; this is the *aether*, the quint-
essence, the fifth element, the upper fiery region of the stars.
When Velleius adds that a moving god cannot be untroubled
and blissful, he uses epithets by which Epicureans denote the
nature of their gods' existence.

34 *Xenocrates*: the work on the gods of this fellow-student of Aristotle
and later head of the Academy (339–314) is wholly lost; the con-
ferment of divinity on the planets, sun, moon, and fixed stars is a
restatement of Plato's doctrine.

Heraclides: this minor figure of the Academy is adduced as further
evidence of the Platonists' identification of divinity with the physical world. The notion of a pervasive Mind, investing the world
with eternal movement and life, is implicitly contrasted with the
Epicurean notion of anthropomorphic gods.

35 *Theophrastus*: Aristotle's successor as head of the Lyceum in 322
wrote a work in three books called *Concerning Gods*; the description here indicates that he follows the Platonist–Aristotelian concept of astral divinity.

Strato: this Peripatetic from Lampsacus, who was head of the
Lyceum *c.*287–269, was an unusual figure in his school for his
interest in physics. A similar statement to the views expressed
here is found in Cicero's *Academica* 2. 121.

36 *the philosophers of your school*: since the Stoics are one of Velleius'
two main opponents in the dialogue, he devotes extended criticism to them, selecting for attack six prominent spokesmen of
the rival school.

Zeno of Citium in Cyprus, founder of the Stoic school, came to
Athens in 313, and lectured in the Painted Stoa, close to the
agora. The Stoics use the term 'law of nature', which they derive
from Heraclitus, as an alternative title for Pronoia, Destiny or

Logos, the range of labels used to present the Stoic god, which is the fiery *pneuma* directing the course of the world. The combination of fire and air which is *pneuma* is identical with Aristotle's *aether*, the upper air. The stars are begotten from that purest *aether* (see 2. 39), so they are part of the *pneuma*; years, months and seasons are divine through their association with the movement of the stars, which make manifest the government of the Stoic god.

Hesiod's Theogony: this poem (*c.*700 BC) incorporates myths about the origins of gods, heroes and the world. The Stoics rationalize the myths by suggesting that the deities symbolize the operations of *pneuma* in the various spheres of nature and of human activity.

37 *Aristo*: of Chios, friend and pupil of Zeno, was preoccupied chiefly with ethics, if the fragments (gathered by Von Arnim, *Stoicorum Veterum Fragmenta* 1. 103 ff.) are any guide. He presumably preached the orthodox Stoic doctrine about the *pneuma* as world-soul.

Cleanthes of Assos in the Troad, followed Zeno as head of the Stoic school. Velleius' survey of his views of god merely adumbrates the central Stoic notion of the *pneuma* as the fiery aether animating the universe, often called Reason or Logos and symbolized by the Graeco-Roman deities ('gods have a particular shape').

as having left its . . . imprint on us: Velleius seems deliberately to use the imagery which the Stoics themselves employed in their theory of knowledge. Perceptions leave their imprint like a seal on wax, says Velleius, yet the perception of gods which is impressed on our minds makes no appearance in Cleanthes' account.

38 *Persaeus*: a minor Stoic figure, introduces Euhemerism into Stoic theology (though it is doubtful if he had met or read Euhemerus of Messene). This accusation by Velleius (Cicero seems to have garnered it from his Epicurean friend Philodemus) probably arose from the veneration which Stoics accorded to their tiny band of patron saints (on whom, see 2. 62). Ironically enough, Epicureans like Lucretius similarly venerated Epicurus as a god-like figure (see § 43).

39 *Chrysippus*: here we reach the greatest single name in Stoicism, the third head of the Stoa after Zeno and Cleanthes, often called 'The Second Founder' because he composed a whole corpus of writings on logic, physics and ethics. He accordingly attracts Velleius' most vicious criticism. The first nine kinds of deity attributed to him (reason, the soul and mind of nature, the world, the effusion of the world-soul, the guiding principle, the all-embracing nature of things, Fate and Necessity, fire and aether, all things in flux and flow) can all be subsumed under the single concept of Pronoia/*pneuma* and the world which it animates; the tenth appends Persaeus' Euhemerism. Since Stoic physics lays down that individual souls at death join the world-soul, the notion that some individuals attain immortality is an innovation; it is echoed by Balbus later at 2. 62. It is often assumed that this incorporation of the deification of human persons does not emerge in Stoicism till the first century AD, when Platonist elements enter, as in Seneca's letters; this passage suggests that it appears in early Stoicism.

40 *Jupiter is the aether . . . the air . . . is . . . Neptune, . . . the earth . . . Ceres*: in this Stoic rationalization, the Olympian deities represent the *pneuma* in the various spheres, Jupiter in the sky, Neptune in the seas (for the notion that the waters are infused with air, cf. Pliny, *NH* 2. 4, 9. 6), Ceres is the earth (she was identified with Demeter, wrongly interpreted as equivalent to Ge-meter, 'Mother Earth').

41 *Orpheus, Musaeus*: these are hazy names of legend. For Orpheus, see § 107 n.; Musaeus is said to have been his disciple. The mystery-religion associated with Orpheus seems to have been close to Pythagoreanism; different poets wrote under his name.

Diogenes of Babylon: he succeeded Chrysippus as head of the Stoa. Philodemus mentions him as the author of a work on Athena/Minerva, in which he represented the goddess as symbolic of the activity of the *pneuma* in the fields of art and learning.

42 *poets*: Velleius seeks to contrast implicitly this depraved behaviour ascribed to the gods by the poets with the Epicurean deities, models of tranquillity and civilized conduct.

43 *the Magi . . . the Egyptians*: the Magi were the priests of the Medes, professing Zoroastrian dualism and precursors of the cult of Mithras. With them and with the Egyptians' worship of animal

deities (and perhaps a hint of the barbaric myth of Isis and Osiris) he associates the superstition of popular cults at Rome.

Epicurus terms this prolepsis: in § 44 Cicero claimed to have coined the Latin word *anticipatio* to render this Greek concept. Thereby he distorts (whether intentionally or not is disputed) the true sense of *prolepsis*. Epicureans argue that following the repeated impact of images on the senses or the mind, we grasp a general conception of an object (as in this case of the gods); this is what *prolepsis* implies. Cicero's rendering appears to interpret it as previous knowledge of objects before their images have impacted on the senses, in other words a knowledge which predates sense-experience.

the divine treatise of Epicurus: this work, *Rule and Judgement*, which discussed the Epicurean theory of knowledge, has not survived. We are dependent upon Epicurus' *Principal Doctrines* and his *Letter to Herodotus* for reconstruction of the theory.

44 *we must use neologisms*: referring to the coining of *anticipatio* in § 43.

45 *the dictum expounded by Epicurus*: this is a direct citation of Epicurus, *Principal Doctrines* 1.

46 *primary concepts*: the evidences afforded by nature before reviewed by the reason.

47 *whose views differ according to the moment*: a jocular criticism of the Academics' doctrine of probability, by which judgements may vary according to circumstances.

49 *not corporeal, but quasi–corporeal*, etc.: the Epicureans believed that the gods, like everything else, are atomic compounds, but they are composed of atoms so fine that they differ in kind from the atoms which constitute the human frame.

perceptible not to the senses, but to the mind: unlike mundane objects which give off images composed of atoms which strike the senses, the images of gods are so fine that they bypass the senses and impinge directly on the mind.

or in measurable identity: the phrase *ad numerum* has given rise to much controversy; for the sense of 'individual identity' of the gods, see Rist, *Epicurus*, App. E; Long, *Hellenistic Philosophy*, 46 f.

50 *an exact balance . . . isonomia*: no attempt is made by Velleius to defend this doctrine, perhaps because it was such a familiar fea-

ture in Presocratics like Heraclitus and Empedocles. For the views expressed here, see Rist, *Epicurus*, 144 ff. Cicero introduces the doctrine here to indicate that in Epicureanism the gods are infinite in number.

51 It is surprising that in this account of the life of the Epicurean gods, no mention is made of their locale. It is strange, too, that Velleius refers to 'god' in the singular, perhaps to contrast the leisurely existence of the individual Epicurean deity with the ceaseless activity of the Stoic god next described.

He takes pleasure in his own wisdom and virtue: this is the Aristotelian view of god absorbed in his own excellence.

53 *having recourse to a* deus ex machina: the thought is borrowed from Plato, *Cratylus* 425d. Euripides in particular was criticized for ending nine of his eighteen plays in this way; for example, in his *Medea* the heroine, after killing her children and Jason's new bride, escapes by winged car from the housetop.

54 *unbounded tracts of space*: the Epicureans taught that the void encompassing innumerable worlds is infinite; cf. Lucretius 1. 958 ff. The implication is that it would have been beyond the powers of a craftsman-god to create on such a scale.

55 *The outcome of an eternal verity and a chain of causation*: Velleius is criticizing the Stoic argument that statements about the future must be either true or false, and that the future is accordingly determined.

mantike: the basis of the theory of divination is that all parts of the creation are in harmony with each other, reflecting the divine dispensation. If disharmony appears in one aspect (e.g. in an animal's entrails) it signifies disharmony in the world at large, and portends disaster. Cicero's treatise *On Divination* strongly criticizes the theory from the Academic viewpoint.

soothsayers, augurs, etc.: soothsayers (*haruspices*) inspected animals' entrails; augurs, the flight of birds; the others are more general expressions for prophets of the future. The Romans inherited these techniques of prophecy from the Etruscans; Stoics were able to reconcile them with their doctrine of fate.

57 *with his customary bonhomie*: Cicero contrasts Velleius' bellicose demeanour (§18) with Cotta's greater urbanity. Cotta then takes the characteristic Academic stance by promising a Socratic

scrutiny of Epicurean falsehood rather than a positive exposition of his own.

58 *Lucius Crassus*: some editors delete this name, since it is missing from most early MSS, and because Crassus, the most celebrated orator of Cicero's youth, was allegedly ignorant of philosophy. But he was the friend of Velleius (*De or.* 3. 78), and the Latin demands a name at this point; Crassus' flattery of his friend need not be based on deep philosophical knowledge.

59 *During my time in Athens I often attended Zeno's lectures*: Cotta had been a member of the moderate party in the Roman senate led by Drusus; when Drusus was murdered in the disorders of 91 BC, Cotta and other supporters were hounded into exile. So in all likelihood he did hear Zeno lecture at Athens in the early eighties. This Zeno was the Epicurean from Sidon (born *c.*150), whom Cicero himself heard lecture at Athens in 78 (cf. *Fin.* 1. 16) so that the comments passed on him here reflect Cicero's own assessment.

Philo: Philo of Larissa, head of the Fourth Academy at Athens (*c.*109–88 BC), came to Rome as a refugee during the First Mithridatic War. Cicero heard his lectures at Rome in 81 BC.

60 *Simonides . . . Hiero*: Simonides of Ceos (*c.*556–468 BC) was celebrated as a composer of hymns, dirges, and elegies. He was a favoured figure at the court of Hiero I of Syracuse (478–467/6). This story may be apocryphal; in Tertullian the same conversation is ascribed to Thales and Croesus (*Apol.* 46. 8).

61 *though I am a pontifex*, etc.: of the four main colleges of priests at Rome, the sixteen *pontifices* took precedence over the augurs, the *decemviri sacrorum* (the college was increased to fifteen by 51 BC) who supervised the Sibylline books, and the *epulones*, who organized religious feasts. Cotta was elected *pontifex* soon after his return to Rome in 82 BC; tenure of this priesthood reflected his high stature in the state.

62 *persons of all communities . . . believe it to be so*: see § 43. The argument for the existence of gods *ex consensu gentium* was widely maintained in antiquity; where atheism is noted, it is usually ascribed to uneducated barbarians as here, or to ignoramuses; Plato, *Laws* 886a, remarks that there are many young atheists, but no old ones.

63 *Diagoras . . . Theodorus . . . Protagoras*: see 1. 2 nn.

To quote Lucilius: Lucilius, often called the father of Roman satire, died in 102 BC. In one of his satires (see Warmington, iii. 1138 ff.), a meeting of the Gods' Council discusses the death of the perjurer Lupus, on whom see also Horace, *Sat.* 2. 1. 68. For Tubulus Hostilius as murderer and briber of juries, see the texts in Pease's edition, and cf. 3. 74. Papirius Carbo (consul 120) was notorious as the advocate who defended Opimius, assassin of Gaius Gracchus; the allegation that he murdered Scipio Aemilianus is probably unfounded. All three characters mentioned by Lucilius are thus depicted as public villains. The phrase 'sons of Neptune' describing them is proverbial for 'the most fierce monstrosities' (Gellius 15. 21) and is the antonym of 'son of Jupiter', a man of virtue.

65 The supplement in brackets, or similar formulation, is added by editors. But possibly the addition is unnecessary, and Cotta, imitating Velleius, is arguing by syllogism: 'There is nothing which lacks a body; everywhere is occupied by bodies; therefore there can be no void.'

66 *the cryptic utterances of the natural philosophers . . . seem more probable*: like a true Academic, Cotta claims only probability and not truth. By 'natural philosophers' he means Aristotle, who in *Physics* 4. 6 ff. argues that void does not exist, and in *Physics* 6. 1 that matter is infinitely divisible.

Democritus . . . Leucippus: the separate contributions of the two great atomist philosophers, pupil and teacher, cannot be distinguished; see Kirk–Raven–Schofield, ch. 17. Lucretius 2. 333 ff. offers a similar description of the shape of the atoms.

by some sort of accidental collision: Cotta is wrong to attribute this view to the Greek atomists; in fact in § 69 he absolves Democritus of this doctrine. The notion of accidental swerve (*clinamen*) was introduced by Epicurus to support his ethical teaching; it allowed him to combat the Stoic doctrine of necessity.

67 *without the direction of nature or reason*: Cotta here exploits Stoic cosmological theory, for these terms are often used for the Stoic *pneuma*.

68 *it follows that they are not eternal*: this argument, that only simple and not composite substances can be eternal, is a familiar feature in earlier philosophy. The Epicureans argued that in the purer region of the *intermundia*, the finer atoms of which the gods are

allegedly composed are not liable to separate; but the argument is frail.

as you argued a moment ago: see § 20.

69 Cotta now presents three alleged instances of absurd Epicurean tenets; the swerve of the atoms, the denial of the disjunctive proposition, and the infallibility of the senses.

it swerved: the theory of the swerve (*clinamen*) of the atoms is Epicurus' attempt to correct the thesis of Democritus that the heavier atoms overtake the lighter in their downward path, resulting in an impact which initiates movement in all directions. Since all atoms of whatever weight descend at the same rate (see Cicero, *Fin.* 1. 19, Diogenes Laertius 10. 61), a different explanation is necessary to defend the doctrine of free will against Stoic determinism.

70 *viability to defend his thesis*: that is, the thesis that the atoms latch on to each other to create material objects.

confronting the logicians: ancient philosophers combined logic and dialectic as the first branch of philosophy, the science of reasoning, which embraces also epistemology. In the science of logic, the disjunctive proposition is what is often nowadays called 'the law of the excluded middle'; given two conflicting propositions, one or other must be true. The Epicureans adopted Aristotle's solution (*De interpretatione* 9), that necessity is present only if the two prepositions are combined; if taken separately, the statements 'Epicurus will be alive tomorrow/Epicurus will not be alive tomorrow' are not necessary. Again Epicurus is concerned here to combat the notion of Stoic necessity.

Arcesilaus used to hammer away at Zeno: Arcesilaus, founder of the Second Academy, here attacks not the Epicurean Zeno but the founder of the Stoics of the same name, who argued that sense-perceptions give us certain knowledge in some things, but that in others we must suspend judgement. Epicurus claimed that all sense-perceptions are reliable, but that our judgement of them may be distorted, a view inherited from Aristotle (*De anima* 3. 3).

was he too clever: the text is uncertain; I translate *nimis callide*.

71 *one augur can look another in the eye without grinning*: the author of this *mot* was the elder Cato (Cicero, *Div.* 2. 51). Augurs were able to suspend public business when it suited them, by claiming unpropitious signs from heaven, while simultaneously regarding these

religious practices, inherited from the Etruscans, with some contempt. Cicero recounts the *mot* with relish as an augur himself.

72 *not a whiff of the Academy or the Lyceum*: Cotta's allegation that Epicurus made no attempt to study the doctrines of the schools founded by Plato and Aristotle is ill-founded; see Rist, *Epicurus*, 1 ff.

Xenocrates: see § 34 n.

Pamphilus: this teacher is otherwise unknown.

His father Neocles had gone there: when Samos was seized by the Athenian general Timotheus in 366, the Athenian Neocles was one of the party of settlers who migrated there. According to Diogenes Laertius, Epicurus had three brothers. He lived on Samos until he was eighteen in 323, when he went to Athens to perform his military service.

73 *Epicurus shows extraordinary contempt for this Platonist*: Cicero is probably alluding to Epicurus' treatise *On Nature*, of which only fragments survive. Book 14 (there were 37 in all) appears to have contained an attack on Platonist physics, and may have included disparagement of Pamphilus.

caught red-handed in the case of Nausiphanes: this is because his boast of never having had a teacher (§ 72) is found to be untrue. Nausiphanes of Teos may have followed Democritus in preaching a doctrine of determinism, in contrast to the Epicurean theory of the chance swerve of the atoms.

74 *as Pythagoras used to do from outsiders*: for Pythagoras' secretive behaviour, see W. K. C. Guthrie, *History of Greek Philosophy*, i (Cambridge, 1962), 150 ff.

as Heraclitus did: he was notorious for his obscure sayings; Cicero (*Fin.* 2. 15) calls him *skoteinos*, 'the dark'.

75 *the Venus of Cos*: this was the famous painting of the fourth-century artist Apelles of Colophon, which depicted Aphrodite–Venus rising from the sea-foam. It was removed by Augustus from Cos to the temple of Divus Iulius at Rome.

76 The arguments here are a resumé of Velleius' statements in §§ 43, 47 f.

77 *some strategy of philosophers*: the allusion may be to Aristotle, *Metaphysics* 1074b.

an eagle or lion or dolphin: Cicero selects creatures from the three domains of air, land, and sea.

[*It is likely . . . to resemble men*]: some commentators regard this sentence as an intrusive gloss; others think that some words have fallen out before it.

78 *the bull which bore off Europa*: this is the famous myth of how Jupiter in the guise of a bull charmed and bore off Europa from Phoenicia to Crete; it is frequently depicted in art and literature, as at Horace, *Odes* 3. 27.

the famous merman Triton: a painting found at Herculaneum depicts him with sea-creatures for legs. Compare the description of Apollonius Rhodius 4. 1608 ff.

79 *national servicemen*: at the age of 18, Athenians were called up to defend the Attic frontiers in platoons of about fifteen; see § 72 n. for Epicurus' national service.

I know why you're grinning: Cotta appears to have an eye for handsome boys.

Alcaeus: this is the famous lyric poet (*fl. c.*600) from Mitylene on Lesbos, whose partiality for young boys is mentioned elsewhere by Cicero (*Tusc.* 4. 71) and also by Horace (*Odes* 1. 32). The Latin here forms part of a hexameter, and is probably a quotation from a satirist.

Quintus Catulus, etc.: the son, fellow-pontiff with Cotta and consul in 78, supported Cicero in the suppression of the Catilinarian conspiracy. The father (consul in 102 and a highly respected member of the Optimates) was proscribed by Marius in 87, and committed suicide. He was one of a group of versifiers before Catullus who adapted Hellenistic motifs to their erotic poetry; see G. Luck, *The Latin Love-Elegy* (London, 1959), 39 ff. His relevance here is as a Roman counterpart to Alcaeus, a poet in love with a boy with a physical defect.

your fellow-townsman Roscius: Roscius, like Velleius, was a native of Lanuvium. He was the most celebrated actor in the time of Cicero, who speaks highly of him (*Orator* 1. 130, etc.).

80 *the Academy must be flourishing in heaven*: the point of the joke is that the Academics advanced four arguments to establish that nothing can be known for certain, the third of which is the argument from indistinguishable resemblances: if there is no difference

between *a* and *b*, it is impossible to recognize *a* and to fail to recognize *b* (see *Acad.* 2. 81).

82 *many shrines plundered*: conspicuous examples of such sacrilege were the looting by Marcellus at Syracuse, that by Pleminius at Locri, and that by Fulvius Nobilior at Ambracia (Livy 26. 30. 8 ff., 29. 18. 1 ff., 38. 43. 6 ff.); more recently the troops of Sulla, and the praetor Verres in Sicily, had become bywords for such rapine (Sallust, *Cat.* 11. 6; Cicero, *Verr.* 2. 4. 1).

crocodile or ibis or cat: see the extended discussion of Egyptian religion at Herodotus 2. 35 ff.—for the crocodile, 2. 69; the ibis, 2. 75; the cat (the cat-cemetery in the ancient city of Bubastis), 2. 67. Cicero (*Tusc.* 5. 78) repeats the statement of Herodotus 2. 65 that it was a capital offence to kill these animals.

Apis: for the holy calf of Memphis, see Herodotus 2. 38.

Sospita . . . Juno: she is called 'your' Sospita because there was at Lanuvium a celebrated shrine of Juno the Saviour, the guardian deity of childbirth. The Vatican museum contains a statue which corresponds exactly with her description here. There was a famous statue of Juno at Argos by the fifth-century sculptor Polyclitus; she held a pomegranate, symbol of fertility, and a sceptre, with a cuckoo above (Pausanias 2. 17). Juno had other roles besides that of guardian of childbirth, and she appears at Rome with other appurtenances (Latte, 166 ff.).

Jupiter Ammon: Ammon was an Egyptian god with a well-known shrine in the oasis of Siwa. He was identified by the Romans with Jupiter by syncresis.

83 *Alcamenes*: this noted fifth-century sculptor was a pupil of Phidias. In later tradition, Hephaestus–Vulcan was depicted as lame because he was cast down from heaven by Zeus, and landed on Lemnos, where he had a smithy (see 3. 55).

84 *Vulcan does not bear the same name*: see 3. 55 for various Vulcans, including the Egyptian.

our pontifical registers: Augustine (*CD* 4. 8) by contrast claims that these 'huge rolls' could scarcely contain all the names and functions of the deities.

85 *some people think*: at 1. 123, the Stoic Posidonius is quoted to this effect.

The Principal Doctrines: Epicurus left a catechism of forty maxims—the Ten Commandments, so to say, of Epicureanism. The first, quoted here, enunciates the Epicurean ideal of *ataraxia* or lack of disturbance.

86 *Metrodorus*: he is the most famous pupil of Epicurus; see §§ 93, 113.

inwardly scared of things which in reality do not worry ordinary people over-much: the Epicureans laid great stress on the anxieties induced by fear of the gods in this life and of divine vengeance in Hades after death. See e.g. Lucretius 1. 110 and 146 ff. Cicero elsewhere maintains that the Epicureans exaggerate these fears (cf. *Tusc.* 1. 10 and 48), and Cotta here argues that Epicurus visits his own fears on the world at large.

87 *The sun accomplishes its course*: though Aristarchus of Samos had propounded the notion of a heliocentric universe in the third century BC, the authority of Aristotle prevailed, and Roman philosophers unanimously adhere to the doctrine of a geocentric universe.

Epicurus, you can have seen nothing comparable to this: the argument runs that many things in our experience are without parallel, and that therefore there may be rational beings in non-human shape.

88 *the non-existence of the courses of sun, moon, and planets*: (the Latin does not have 'the courses of', but such an addition is demanded by the sense.) The argument is directed at the Epicurean epistemology, by which certain knowledge is attainable only through the senses.

imagining that you were born on Seriphus: this tiny island in the Cyclades was proverbial for its backwardness. See the famous story of Themistocles and the Seriphian at Plato, *Rep.* 329e–330a, repeated by Cato in Cicero's *De senectute* 8.

97 *To press this argument*, etc.: I follow those scholars who, after Bake (*Mnemosyne* (1853), 414), transpose part of § 97 to this place in the text between § 88 and § 89.

beasts found in the Indian Ocean or in India: literally 'in the Red Sea and in India'. Both Greeks and Romans apply the term Red Sea to the Indian Ocean and to the Persian Gulf, as well as to the Red Sea. The additional mention of India here suggests that the Indian Ocean is in Cotta's mind; the 'beasts' are presumably whales, monsters of the deep comparable in size with elephants on land.

89 *the technique of the logicians*: at § 48, Velleius compresses his argument that the gods have human shape into the mould of the chain-argument or *sorites*; this was a practice favoured by Stoics rather than by Epicureans.

90 *the gods have always existed*: though Epicureans argued that the gods are composite creatures formed from atoms, the evidence of Hippolytus and Philodemus suggests that they believed that the gods existed 'from eternity'. See Rist, *Epicurus*, 152 f.

91 *at a Roman's possessing such wide knowledge*: Cicero pats himself obliquely on the back.

93 *Metrodorus and Hermarchus*: it is said that Metrodorus would have followed his friend Epicurus as head of the Garden had he not died first; Hermarchus succeeded instead. They joined with Epicurus in attacking Pythagoras for equating all things with number, Plato for his notion of the demiurge initiating motion in the universe, and Empedocles for positing that love and strife combine and separate the four elements. All these views of purposive creation are at odds with the Epicurean doctrine of the fusion and separation of the atoms by chance.

Leontium: the Epicureans admitted women into their school. Leontium is said to have been the mistress of Epicurus. She attacked Theophrastus, successor of Aristotle as head of the Lyceum, presumably for the Peripatetic doctrine of God the unmoved Mover.

Zeno . . . Albucius . . . Phaedrus: for Zeno, see § 59 n.; Albucius was a Roman, who after being condemned for extortion as praetor in Sardinia, was exiled to Athens, where he became an Epicurean philosopher of note. Phaedrus, head of the Epicurean school, was still alive at the dramatic date of this dialogue (76 BC), but Cotta is referring to the time he heard him lecture in Athens in the 80s.

Epicurus buffeted Aristotle, etc.: Cicero is critical of the uninhibited language of philosophical controversy at Athens (cf. *Fin.* 2. 80). For such alleged abuse by Epicurus, see also Diogenes Laertius 10. 9. Phaedo is the young friend of Socrates who lent his name to Plato's dialogue on the immortality of the soul; he later retired to Elis, and established a school of philosophy there. Timocrates is said to have been a hot-tempered youth who dissented from Epicurus' views about the means of happiness; see § 113. For Democritus and Nausiphanes, see §§ 29, 73 nn.

Apollodorus, Sillis: a contemporary Stoic named Apollodorus is a more likely target than the Epicurean Apollodorus, Zeno's own teacher. Sillis is unknown; even the form of the name is uncertain.

Socrates ... an Attic trifler ... referred to Chrysippus as Chrysippa: Zeno's use of the Latin word *scurra* to describe Socrates was presumably for the amusement of Roman pupils like Cotta (and later, Cicero and Atticus); the precise sense may be 'trifler', or perhaps 'know-all'; see P. B. Corbett, *The Scurra* (Edinburgh, 1986), 3 f., 27 ff. For Chrysippus, see § 39 n.; ancient critics suggest that his prolixity led to his being regarded as a garrulous old lady.

94 *all the physical cares and concerns*: Cotta becomes tediously repetitive; cf. § 92.

95 *beatitas or ... beatitudo*: Roman pioneers in philosophy had sometimes to coin neologisms to express Greek concepts. Cicero here wonders how to render Greek *eudaimonia*, for which earlier he used *beata vita*. Of the two neologisms launched here, *beatitudo* catches on, but *beatitas* fades out.

96 *in virtue than in appearance*: Cotta uses Stoic arguments to rebut the Epicurean claims, whereas at 3. 38 he roundly rejects the Stoic notion that God has need of the cardinal virtues.

97 *as Ennius remarks*: the citation is from a lost satire.

98 The thesis that gods have human shape because reason and intelligence are found only in humans is now rebutted by the argument that human intelligence is the result of environmental factors which the gods have not experienced.

100 *You directed withering criticism*: see § 53.

what great and outstanding work do you adduce ...: Cotta knows perfectly well that the Epicureans believe that the gods have no part in the creation or the guidance of the universe; hence his anticipation of Velleius' reply which sidesteps the question.

101 *ibises dispose of ... snakes ... from the African desert*: Herodotus 2. 75 (cf. also 3. 107 ff.) is the source of this account that the ibis confronts flying snakes and kills them, though in his version they hail from Arabia, where they are said to guard the frankincense; cf. also Pliny, *NH* 10. 75.

Egyptian rats and crocodiles and cats: the ichneumon or Egyptian rat similarly attacks snakes (Aristotle, *Hist. Anim.* 9. 6) and destroys crocodiles' eggs (a dubious benefit in the eyes of crocodile-worshippers). Crocodiles were thought to form a line of defence preventing invaders from crossing the Nile. The cat was favoured as destroyer of reptiles (Diodorus 1. 87).

103 *where is his residence*, etc.: an important omission from Velleius' earlier apologia is the physical abode of the gods, which Epicureans argue is in the *intermundia*, the spaces between the worlds. Cotta now demands enlightenment on this issue.

some are thought to be born even in fire: this claim derives from Aristotle's *Generation of Animals* (3. 9, 5. 19), with specific reference to the salamander which 'exstinguishes the fire by walking through it'.

105 *no substance or . . . measurable identity*: see § 49 for Velleius' formulation, criticized here by Cotta.

a hippocentaur: half-horse and half-man, it is regularly cited as a non-existent creature of the imagination; cf. Plato, *Phaedrus* 229d, Cicero, *Tusc.* 1. 90, etc.

106 *I seem to behold Tiberius Gracchus*: in 133 BC, when Tiberius Gracchus sought to promulgate his agrarian law, it was vetoed by his fellow-tribune M. Octavius. Thereupon Gracchus proposed to the *comitia tributa*, meeting as often on the Capitol, that Octavius be deposed from office. Cotta adduces the incident to criticize the Epicurean theory of knowledge, according to which images of the participants still strike the mind over fifty years later. Epicureans would have responded that such images are constantly present in the air, so that the mind can intercept those it wishes; see Rist, *Epicurus*, 24.

107 *from Democritus*: see § 29.

Homer and Archilochus, etc.: Cotta assembles from the remote past pairs of Greek poets, Roman kings, and Greek philosophers, and appends to them the non-existent(?) figure of Orpheus (the citation of Aristotle is from his lost *De philosophia*). For the probable Epicurean response, that not all images emanate from actual objects, see Rist, *Epicurus*, 24.

the Orphic poem now current: this will be the *Rhapsodic Theogony*; on the poem and its putative author, the Pythagorean Cercops, see W. K. C. Guthrie, *Orpheus and Greek Religion* (London, 1952), ch. 4.

108 *different images of the same person*, etc.: this list of objections to the
Epicurean theory of sense-impressions was a familiar feature of
philosophical dispute. The first objection, that the same images
appear to different individuals in different guises, was answered
by the claim that our senses do not deceive us, but our judgements
of them may. On the problem of non-existent, composite creatures like the six-headed, twelve-footed Scylla, living opposite
the whirlpool Charybdis, or the Chimaera, part-lion, part-goat,
part-serpent slain by Bellerophon, the Epicurean Lucretius (4.
372) explains that images of different creatures merge in our
minds. Lucretius likewise explains (4. 779 ff.) that images strike
us even in our sleep because they hover in the air perpetually.

109 For these citations of Epicurean views, see §§ 49–50. On *isonomia*,
see § 50 n.; *aequilibritas* is another Ciceronian coining.

110 *Let us now consider blessedness*: Cotta now attacks Velleius' statements in §§ 45–8.

111 *any good . . . detached from luxurious and lewd pleasures*: there is no
doubt that Epicurus' work *Peri Telous* did lay such emphasis on
physical pleasures; see Diogenes Laertius 10. 6, Athenaeus 7.
280a. Hence Cicero's strong antipathy to Epicurean ethics as
reflected at *Tusc*. 3. 41, *Fin*. 2. 29, etc.

112 *Juventas or Ganymede*: Juventas is the Roman title of Hebe, the
female counterpart of Ganymede as cupbearer of Zeus; cf.
Homer, *Il*. 4. 2, etc.

113 *to use Epicurus' word*: Cf. Athenaeus 12. 546, Cicero, *Tusc*. 3. 47, etc,
our teacher Philo: cf. § 6 n.

       Metrodorus . . . Timocrates: see 1. 93 nn.

115 *reverence and devotion*: Velleius has presented the argument for these
at § 45.

       Tiberius Coruncanius or Publius Scaevola: Coruncanius is cited
because he was the first plebeian *pontifex maximus* (252 BC) and
celebrated for his religious fervour; P. Mucius Scaevola (*pontifex
maximus* 131 BC) was famed for his knowledge of religious law
and ceremonial.

       not by violence, as Xerxes did: for Xerxes' burning of Greek temples,
see Herodotus 8. 109. Cicero elsewhere (*Leg*. 2. 10) reports the
tradition that he did this to prevent deities being confined
within walls, when the whole world was their temple.

117 *You free men from superstition*: Cicero doubtless thinks of the magnificent image at Lucretius 1. 62 ff., in which Epicurus is depicted as a warrior overcoming the foe superstition.

Diagoras or Theodorus . . . Protagoras: see 1. 2 nn.

118 For this notion that astute thinkers harnessed belief in divine sanctions to promote order and harmony in the state, cf. Plato, *Laws* 10. 889e; Livy 1. 19. 4, etc.

Prodicus of Ceos: (not Cos, as Rackham, or Chios, as McGregor, but the island off Attica). This sophist, contemporary with Socrates, is quoted by Sextus Empiricus (*Math.* 9. 18) to the effect that ancients deified sun, moon, rivers, fountains, etc., because of their benefit to man.

119 *Euhemerus*: Euhemerus of Messene (*fl.* 300 BC) wrote a travel-story, 'The Sacred Scripture', in which he describes a monument on the island of Panchaea which depicted Uranus, Cronus, and Zeus as earthly kings. He thus lent his name to the doctrine that departed heroes were deified (see § 38).

Ennius . . . translated him: Ennius of Rudiae (239–169 BC) is better known as the father of Roman literature through his *Annales* and his *Tragedies*, but he also wrote a *Euhemerus* based on *The Sacred Scripture*, in which remarkably enough he incorporated the Roman Jupiter as one of the heroes-turned-gods.

Eleusis . . . Samothrace . . . Lemnos: these are centres of mystery-religions. At Eleusis near Athens the cult of Demeter was practised (Cicero and his Epicurean friend Atticus were initiated there; see *Leg.* 2. 36). On Samothrace and Lemnos, the islands in the northern Aegean, the deities worshipped were the Cabiri, probably Phrygian in origin, but the ritual was increasingly identified with those of Demeter and Dionysus; see W. K. C. Guthrie in *OCD* s.v. Cabiri. Of the two poetic citations, the first, an iambic trimeter, is untraced; the second (anapaestic dimeter followed by paroemiac) is speculatively attributed to the *Philoctetes* of the early dramatist Accius.

120 *Democritus*: see § 29 n. Cotta here separates into contradictory parts Democritus' doctrine of images as recounted later by Sextus Empiricus (9. 19 and 42 ff.), according to which there are particles of divine force which form vast beings of long but not everlasting life, some of which are beneficent and others

malevolent. They are visible and audible, and when these images enter our consciousness we identify them as gods.

more appropriate to Democritus' native city: Democritus came from Abdera in Thrace, a town which in Roman times was regarded as a backwater of stupidity; cf. Juvenal 10. 50.

121 *the attitude of the Stoics*: this praise of Stoicism for its superior doctrine of friendship is disingenuous, for Epicureans laid great store by friendship at the human level (cf. *Principal Doctrines* 27: 'Of the things which wisdom acquires for the blessedness of life as a whole, by far the greatest is the possession of friendship'). At the level of divine benevolence, Cotta could have argued that the Stoic divinity was more helpful to the human race, but not in any personal sense.

122 *it will cease to be friendship*: Aristotle (*NE* 1155b) recognizes three levels of friendship: utility, pleasure, and goodness; Cotta here rejects the first, and espouses the Stoics' belief that 'friendship exists only between the virtuous' (Diogenes Laertius 7. 124). Cicero develops the theme of friendship at greater length in his *De amicitia*.

123 *Posidonius*: See §6 n. The Stoic philosopher and historian (*c.*135–*c.*50 BC) had studied under Panaetius at Athens, and later settled at Rhodes, where Cicero encountered him in 78. When Cotta claims acquaintance with him for himself and for Velleius and Balbus, he perhaps recalls the occasion of the visit of Posidonius to Rome in 87. (Cicero may have forgotten that Cotta was in exile at that time.) The work of Posidonius on the gods mentioned here must have been an important source for Cicero's discussion in the two following books, but surprisingly it is cited only once (2. 88).

Book 2

1 For the importance of rhetorical presentation in the philosophical dialogues, see Introduction, p. xxxvii.

circle of listeners: judicial hearings at Rome were regularly attended by a crowd of onlookers.

2 *Cotta . . . priest*: for Cotta's appointment as *pontifex*, see Introduction, p. xxiv.

my opening remarks: see 1. 60.

3 *our school divides this whole question... into four parts*: Cicero probably draws on Posidonius, *On the Gods*, a work in five books of which the fifth was a repudiation of Epicurean theology. The first four will have covered systematically the topics listed here.

4 *Ennius*: the first citation is from his play *Thyestes* (fr. 351 Warmington), the second from his *Annals* (fr. 448W). In the passage between the two I read *nutu* ('by his nod') for *motu* in Ax.

5 *securely lodged in succeeding generations*: the argument *ex consensu gentium* for the existence of gods, frequently invoked by the Stoics, is resumed at 2. 12.

the hippocentaur or the Chimaera: Balbus deliberately reinforces Cotta's arguments at 1. 105 and 108.

afraid of those monsters in the nether world: again echoing Cotta; see 1. 86 and n.

6 *Lake Regillus*: Livy 2. 19 f. records how Rome struggled against the Latin League and prevailed in 496 BC in this historic battle. Livy does not record the intervention of Castor and Pollux, though Postumius is said to have vowed a shrine to Castor. Plutarch (*Aemilius Paulus* 25) recounts a legend that the two deities reported the victory at Rome.

victory over Perseus: at Pydna in 168 BC Aemilius Paulus finally prevailed over Perseus, King of Macedon, in the Third Macedonian War (Livy 44. 40. 3 ff.).

our young contemporary: this Vatinius was the lieutenant of Caesar, whom Cicero impeached in 56 but was compelled to defend in 54. He was still in his 'teens at the dramatic date of this dialogue (76 BC).

his magistracy at Reate: this Sabine town was still a prefecture in 168 BC; the urban praetor sent his representative annually to preside over the law-courts. Plutarch (*Aemilius Paulus* 25) merely states that the rumour of the victory at Pydna reached Rome on the fourth day after the battle.

the Locrians ... at the river Sagra: this battle in Bruttium (legendary details recorded in Justin 20. 3) is dated about 560 BC, a few years before Pythagoras' arrival in Croton began to reinvigorate the city.

7 *the stories of Mopsus*, etc.: Mopsus may be the seer who accompanied the Argonauts and died en route (Apollonius Rhodius 4.

1502 ff.), or Teiresias' grandson who caused the death of Calchas. Teiresias, the blind Theban seer, is best known for his prominence in Greek Tragedy (*The Seven against Thebes* of Aeschylus, *Oedipus Rex* of Sophocles, *Bacchae* of Euripides). Amphiaraus of Argos was induced by his wife Eriphyle to join the expedition against Thebes; after being repelled, he was swallowed by a cleft in the ground, which became an oracular shrine. Calchas was the celebrated Greek diviner at Troy (*Iliad* 1. 69 ff.). The Trojan Helenus, son of Priam, gave prophetic advice to Hector (*Iliad* 6. 76, 7. 44).

Publius Claudius . . . Lucius Junius: they were consuls in 249 BC. Claudius Pulcher was defeated by the Carthaginian Adherbal off Drepana in Sicily, and Junius Pullus' ships a few days later were wrecked off Pachynus, the south-eastern promontory of Sicily. Roman historians regularly attributed such disasters to neglect of divine warnings. These anecdotes both appear in the first book of Valerius Maximus, under the heading *Neglect of Religion*.

8 *Coelius . . . Gaius Flaminius*: Coelius Antipater in the late second century composed a monograph on the Hannibalic War which was a main source for Livy. The claim that Flaminius when consul in 217 suffered disaster at Lake Trasimene because of his sacrilegious behaviour is echoed in Livy 21. 63, 22. 3. 11 ff.

9 *Attus Navius*: Cicero nods here through relying on a hazy memory. In his *De divinatione* 1. 31 (cf. 2. 80) he tells the story differently: Attus Navius an augur promised the Lares the largest bunch of grapes in his vineyard if he located his runaway pig. When he found it, he used his augur's staff to ascertain where the largest bunch of grapes was to be found. This augur was said to have lived not in the reign of Tullus Hostilius, third king of Rome, but in that of the fifth king Tarquinius Priscus.

flashing spear-points: this prodigy, repeatedly reported in the historians (e.g. Livy 33. 26. 8, 43. 13. 6; Tacitus, *Annals* 15. 7), is explained by some as attributable to electrical phosphorescence.

when men are summoned: I render Schoemann's *nulla* (sc. *auspicia*) *cum viri vocantur*.

10 *certain commanders*: the family of the Decii are meant. Publius Decius Mus is said to have sacrificed himself in 340 BC in the Latin War (cf. Livy 8. 9. 6, where the formal prayer is cited).

His son of the same name emulated his father in 295 at the battle of Sentinum against Etruscans and Gauls (Livy 10. 28. 12 ff.). Cicero (*Tusc.* 1. 89, *Fin.* 2. 61) claims that the grandson acted similarly at the battle of Asculum against Pyrrhus in 279, but this accretion to the family-history is unhistorical.

10–11 *events . . . in the consulship of Publius Scipio and Gaius Figulus*: the presiding officer in the elections of 162 BC was the father of Tiberius and Gaius Gracchus. Etruscan soothsayers at this time were increasingly encroaching on the role traditionally exercised by the decemvirs, the priests charged with the custody and scrutiny of the Sibylline books (cf. Livy 32. 1. 14; 42. 20. 2, etc.); hence Gracchus' indignation. Following the elections he retired to his province of Sardinia, from where he penned his admission that the proceedings had been defective. He had quitted the city limits because he required the open space of the Scipionic gardens to mark out the quarters of the sky, and he had omitted to take the auspices when crossing back into the city limits.

13 *Cleanthes*: 1. 37 n. The four reasons for belief in God were probably mediated to Cicero through Posidonius; the first and fourth had appeared in Aristotle's lost *De philosophia* (Sextus Empiricus 9. 20).

14 *the war which Octavius raised*: In 87 BC the support lent to Marius by the consul Cinna was challenged by his fellow-consul Cn. Octavius, a supporter of Sulla, who was engaged overseas against Mithridates. In the ensuing disturbance Octavius lost his life.

Tuditanus and Aquilius . . . Publius Africanus: C. Sempronius Tuditanus and M'. Aquilius were consuls in 129 BC, the year in which P. Scipio Africanus Aemilianus died suddenly. He had been a leading activist against the reforms of the Gracchi. This led to the (probably unjust) suspicion that his wife Sempronia, being the sister of Tiberius and Gaius Gracchus, had murdered him.

16 *Chrysippus*: for this, the greatest figure in Stoicism, see 1. 39 n. The argument propounded here anticipates Anselm's 'ontological' argument ('God is that than which nothing greater can be imagined'), which was formulated earlier in Aristotle's lost *De philosophia*.

17 *all things . . . higher are better*: the notion appears in Aristotle, *De caelo* 2. 5, and Cicero alludes to it elsewhere at *Tusc.* 1. 43, *Rep.* 6. 17.

having inhabitants who are dimmer-witted because of the denser atmo-
sphere: elsewhere (*De fato* 7), Cicero contrasts the Athenians,
whose clearer climate makes them sharper-witted, with the
Thebans, fat and strong (and accordingly slower on the uptake)
because of their cloudy skies.

18 *in the pages of Xenophon*: see his *Memorabilia*, 1. 4. 8.

the source of the moisture and the heat, etc.: the notion that the human
body derives its heat, breath, water, and solidity of flesh from
the four elements passes from Hippocrates to Plato (*Timaeus* 42),
and later becomes a commonplace in Stoic thought (Epictetus
3. 13; Marcus Aurelius 4. 4).

19 *a single divine, all-pervading, spiritual force*: Balbus refers to the Stoic
pneuma; see Introduction, p. xxxiv.

20 *more briefly and sparingly, as Zeno used to do*: for Zeno, see 1. 36 n. The
citations that follow, reflecting his exploitation of the Aristotelian syllogism, are useful because citations of his work elsewhere
are rare.

21 *condensed by Zeno like this*: Sextus Empiricus (9. 104) preserves the
Greek of this observation, together with approximations to the
quotations in 2. 22 below (see 9. 85, 9. 77).

22 The obvious objection to Zeno's arguments here is that a transcendent God can be the creator of both a non-sentient universe
and of sentient creatures within it.

23 *Earlier I stated*: see 2. 4.

arguments drawn from physics: Heraclitus, positing fire as the first
element, is the ultimate inspiration here; Aristotle develops the
arguments in *De anima* 2. 8 and elsewhere.

24 *Cleanthes*: see 2. 13 n.

26 ff. On the Stoic notions of the creative effects of fire and heat in
what follows, see S. Sambursky, *Physics of the Stoics* (London,
1959), ch. 1, 'The Dynamic Continuum'.

29 *in beasts something similar to the mind . . . in the case of trees and plants . . .*
in their roots: Aristotle again lies behind this; see *Hist. Anim.* 8. 1;
Part. Anim. 4. 7.

hegemonikon: for the sense of this word when applied to human
beings ('personality') see Rist, *Stoic Philosophy*, 24 ff. Here it is
used for the *pneuma* in the more general sense, the force that activates the whole of nature.

32 *Plato, the god . . . among philosophers*: Balbus cites Plato's *Timaeus* 89a. Though early Stoics were critical of Plato, the later more eclectic leaders, Panaetius and Posidonius, venerated him and called him divine. Cicero, who translated the *Timaeus*, likewise calls him *deus* elsewhere (*Att.* 4. 16. 3). Balbus accords him the title here as a pleasantry in his discussion of divinity, much as he calls Scipio Aemilianus 'a second sun' in the discussion of twin suns at 2. 14.

33–4 This gradation goes back to Aristotle's *De anima* 2. 3, which distinguishes between the soul of the plant as propagator and nurturer, that of the brute beast as possessing also sensation, pleasure and memory, that of the human person who additionally has reason, and finally God, the highest form of being and perfection of mind.

35 Cicero exploits these examples of the vine, the brute beast, and the artist, as each attaining in their different ways their level of perfection, also at *Fin.* 4. 32 ff.

37 *Chrysippus*: though he was a leading Stoic (1. 39 n.), the doctrine expounded here on the final end of animals and of man goes back to Aristotle, as Cicero indicates at *Fin.* 2. 40, a passage which echoes this one.

39 *nothing is better than excellence*: *virtus* is being used in the more general sense of excellence here rather than in the exclusively moral sense of virtue.

we must assign that same divinity to the stars: the Stoic doctrine that the stars are divine and endowed with intelligence and sensation, goes back to Plato and Aristotle (see 1. 30 and 33 nn.), and ultimately to Babylonian and Egyptian thought.

40 *is nurtured by moisture from the Ocean*: this doctrine, a commonplace in pre-Socratic thought, is condemned by Aristotle (*Meteorol.* 2. 2), who emphasizes that such exhalations from the sea descend again as rain.

42 *Aristotle regards it as nonsensical*: this citation is presumed to come from the lost *De philosophia*; Aristotle takes over the notion from Plato (e.g. *Timaeus* 40).

43 *an indication of no mere natural process*: *natura* is used here not in the technical Stoic sense as an alternative title of the fiery *pneuma*, but in a more derogatory general sense of mindless matter.

44 *We must praise Aristotle*: this citation is probably a continuation of
    the passage from the lost *De philosophia* quoted in 2. 42.

    depriving them of any stewardship or activity: this suggestion that the
    Epicurean theology is virtually atheism was argued by Posido-
    nius; see 1. 123.

45 *My remaining task*: Balbus promised at the outset to deal only with
    the two questions of the existence of gods and their nature (2. 3),
    but Cotta's request there that he deal also with the providential
    order of the universe and the gods' care for the human race is
    later met (2. 73 ff.).

    philosophers similarly naïve: the Epicureans are again the target.

    the universe first and foremost: implicit here is Balbus's intention to
    pronounce the heavenly bodies likewise as alive and divine; he
    does this at §§ 49 ff., following the aside which distracts him.

47 *the actual things which the universe creates*: these are detailed at 2. 57 ff.

48 *you natural philosophers*: the Epicureans prided themselves on being
    heirs to the atomist theories of Democritus, and their opponents
    regularly accord them this title in irony; see 1. 77, 1. 83, etc.

49 *his criterion . . . was his own palate . . . Ennius' 'palate of the sky'*: this
    laboured joke associates the Epicurean doctrine of pleasure
    (here interpreted as gormandizing) as the highest good with the
    use of the word *palatum* (normally the roof of the mouth) for the
    vault of the sky. The phrase of Ennius cited here, echoing a
    Greek idiom (see Varro in Augustine, *CD* 7. 8), is of uncertain
    provenance.

    two types of heavenly bodies: the distinction is between the fixed stars
    and the planets; it was believed that the second both moved
    around with the first, and also revolved round the earth under
    their own impetus.

    in two revolutions: that is, revolving with the heavens, but also inde-
    pendently round the earth (on the misguided assumption of a
    geocentric universe).

    some 365¼ daily circuits: some two years before the composition of
    this dialogue, Julius Caesar had reformed the calendar on this
    basis by inserting an extra day between 23 and 24 February
    every fourth year.

    by adjusting its course: but winter comes to the northern hemisphere
    when the south pole faces the sun, and vice versa.

50 *the equivalent of the winter and summer solstices*: that is, the furthest points northward and southward in the moon's monthly revolution.

the many effluences: it was popularly supposed that dew released from the moon galvanized both plant and animal life.

51 *'those which stray'*: this is the literal meaning of 'planets' in Greek.

the Great Year: the earliest extant reference to this concept, which probably goes back to the Pythagoreans, is in Plato, *Timaeus* 39, where its length is reckoned as 10,000 years. Cicero elsewhere (*Hortensius*, fr. 26) cites the figure of 12,954 years, and other estimates are advanced by other writers.

52–3 These calculations of the times taken by these circuits of the planets go back through Aristotle to the celebrated mathematician and astronomer Eudoxus of Cnidos (*c*.390–340 BC). Figures for the first three correspond roughly with modern calculations of the periods of revolution round the sun, but the figures for Mercury and Venus (which take 88 and 224.7 days respectively for their journey round the sun) are the time they take to complete the circuit of the Zodiac, which is approximately the same as for the sun itself, namely one year.

53 *one sign's length . . . two signs' distance*: the sun's yearly course is divided into twelve sectors, each represented by a sign of the zodiac; hence the gap is said to be never more than 30 or 60 degrees respectively.

55 *the fixed stars have their own spheres*: most pre-Socratics believed that the stars were embedded in the sky and revolved with it, but some thought that they were borne along by the swirl of the aether. Balbus here seems to argue that each star has its independent impetus, though this does not accord with the teaching of the Stoic Chrysippus.

56 *below the moon*: the moon was widely regarded as the boundary between the unchanging celestial region and the sublunary realm of corruption and change. The treatises of Plutarch offer instructive evidence of this; the terrestrial demons dwell on the moon, and descend from it to order the destinies of men. See especially *De genio Socratis* 591c; *De facie in orbe lunae* 943c–944d. Knowledge that the earth's orbit lies between those of Venus and Mars was a closed book to Romans, who accepted unquestioningly the notion of a geocentric world.

57 *Zeno*: 1. 36 n.

58 *not only creative, but in fact the creator*: the Latin word for creator, *arti-fex*, is literally 'craftsman', evoking Plato's *demiourgos* in the *Timaeus* (see 1. 22 n.).

   which the Greeks call hormai: for the Stoic notion of *hormai* as 'impulses of the soul', see Rist, *Stoic Philosophy*, 39 ff.

   'Providence' (for its name in Greek is Pronoia): Introduction, p. xxxiv.

59 *his shadowy, inactive gods*: see 1. 75.

60 *that tag of Terence*: see *Eunuch*, 732.

61 The Roman practice of deifying abstractions may have arisen in part from earlier titles of deities, and in part from the influence of Greek cults. Thus Faith and Freedom may be derived from cult-titles of Jupiter; the military qualities of Honour and Virtue were attributes of Mars; and Wealth (*Ops*) had a connection with Consus. The temple to Faith on the Capitol may have been built by Atilius Caiatinus in his censorship in 247, but he is known from other evidence to have dedicated a shrine to Hope (Cicero, *Leg.* 2. 28), so that *Spes* should perhaps be read for *Fides* here. The temple to Mind dates back to 215; Aemilius Scaurus (d. 90–89 BC) must have restored both temples to Faith and to Mind shortly before his death. There were three temples at Rome dedicated jointly to Virtue and Honour; that near the *porta Capena* was originally dedicated to Honour alone by Fabius Maximus Verrucosus in 234, but was later enlarged and dedicated to both deities at the instance of Marcellus following his successes in the Second Punic War. Safety, Concord, Victory reflect the influence of Greek abstract deities; likewise Desire and Pleasure, appended by Balbus to allow him to launch further criticism of Epicurean ethical theory. For Lubentina ('Sexual Joy') as a cult-title of Venus, see Varro, *LL* 6. 47.

62 *men who conferred outstanding benefits*, etc.: for Euhemerism, see 1. 38 and 119 nn.

   Hercules, etc.: Hercules became the patron saint of Stoics, his numerous labours in overcoming prodigious foes being equated with the pursuit of virtue. For Castor and Pollux as protective deities of Rome, see 2. 6 n. Aesculapius, the Latinized form of Asclepius, the Greek god of healing, was introduced into Rome during a pestilence in 293 BC. Liber son of Semele is the Roman title of Dionysus, donor of viticulture; he is contrasted here with

Liber the Italian god of fertility, one of the triad of Ceres, Liber, and Libera worshipped on the Aventine from 493 BC (they correspond with the Greek triad Demeter, Kore, and Iacchus). For the apotheosis of Romulus under the name Quirinus (originally the Sabine deity of the Quirinal hill prior to the foundation of Rome), see Cicero, *Rep.* 2. 20, *Leg.* 1. 3.

63 *Zeno . . . Cleanthes . . . Chrysippus*: see 1. 36, 37, 39 nn.; as Stoics, they regarded the gods of Greek religion as personified forces of nature.

63–4 *an ancient belief*, etc.: for the fable that the sky-god Ouranos (= Caelus) was mutilated by Kronos (= Saturn), see Hesiod, *Theog.* 159 ff.; for Saturn enchained by Jupiter, see Plato, *Euthyphro* 6a, etc. The Stoics, especially Chrysippus, devoted close attention to etymologies, but their conclusions were woefully unscientific. The derivation of Kronos from Chronos (Greek for Time) was a widespread misconception in the ancient world. The suggested derivations of Saturn, Jupiter, and Jove that follow are fanciful (in Latin usage, Iuppiter is found in the nominative and vocative cases only, the Latin for Jove being used for the other four cases).

64 *'Father of gods and men'*: 2. 4 n.

65 *Ennius, as I mentioned earlier*: for the first quotation that follows, see 2. 4 n. There is uncertainty about the reading and sense of the second quotation; I follow Warmington's rendering in *Remains of Old Latin*, i, *Ennius, Tragedies* fr. 388. For the Greek of the fragment of Euripides, see fr. 941 Nauck, here probably translated by Cicero himself.

66 *Juno . . . gets her name from the verb to help*: this spurious derivation is offered also by Varro, *LL* 5. 67; even more improbable is the suggested derivation of Neptunus from *nare*.

66–7 *the fables established a division*: see Homer, *Il.* 15. 187.

Portunus: he is the god of harbours; I therefore read and translate in what follows *portu* ('harbour') rather than *porta* ('gate'), the MSS reading retained by Ax. The etymologies that follow of Neptune, Dis, Ceres, Demeter, Mavors, Minerva, and Janus are all bogus. Vesta and the Greek Hestia are interrelated, but it is wrong to suggest that the first is 'borrowed' from the second.

68–9 Penates does derive from *penus*, store or larder; Apollo is indeed Greek in origin. The suggested etymology of *sol* is fanciful, but *luna* is certainly cognate with *lux* and *lucere*; Diana and *dies* are likewise connected etymologically.

69　*Timaeus* of Tauromenium in Sicily (*c.*356–260 BC) while exiled in Athens wrote a history of Sicily down to his own day in 38 books. Polybius devotes his book 12 to polemic against his unscientific approach, his superstition and his florid style; Cicero on the other hand praises his learning. Plutarch (*Alex.* 3) attributes this joke, which he condemns as frigid, not to Timaeus but to Hegesias of Magnesia, who wrote a *History of Alexander*.

　　Venus . . . venire: the etymology is absurd.

70　*the Titans, and . . . the Giants*: the Titans, led by Kronos, warred with Zeus; see Hesiod, *Theog.* 137 f., 154 ff. For the struggle of gods with the Giants, in which the Giants were repelled to earth, see Apollodorus 1. 6. 1.

71　*distinguished superstition from religion*: Varro, cited by Augustine (*CD* 6. 9), states that superstitious individuals fear the gods as enemies, but religious people love them as parents. See Introduction, p. xxvi f.

72　*were called superstitious*: *superstitiosus* does derive from *superstes*, but Balbus' explanation is less probable than that of Lactantius (4. 28), who suggests that surviving children used to worship their parents' images as if they were divine.

　　religious: philologists are divided whether *religio* is derived from *relegere*, as Balbus claims, or from *religare*, 'to bind fast', an etymology which Cicero himself supports elsewhere (e.g. *De domo* 105 f.). The derivations that follow are all correct.

73　*My next task*: this is the third of the four general headings which Balbus promised to discuss at the outset (see 2. 3).

　　yesterday: here and at 3. 18 Cicero indicates that his imaginary dialogue is spread over three days, just as the five books of *Tusculans* extend over five days. For Pronoia as the fortune-telling hag, see 1. 18.

74　'*the Council . . . of the Areopagus*': according to Aristotle, the Council of the Areopagus in early times virtually controlled the Athenian state, but in 462/1 Ephialtes severely restricted its political and judicial powers, though it remained the court for homicide, wounding, and arson; see the *OCD*.

75 *sentient nature*: Stoics usually identify 'nature' with the fiery Pronoia which activates all things; here, however, Balbus distinguishes between 'sentient nature' and the divine *pneuma* to which it owes its sentience; see § 77.

76 *Democritus... introducing 'phantoms'... Epicurus with his 'appearances'*; Cf. 1. 29, 1. 49 nn.

79 *Mind, Faith*, etc.: on these abstractions as deities, see 2. 61 n.

81 *Some philosophers ... Others again*: the implicit contrast is between those who propound a mechanical universe (see e.g. the Peripatetic Strato at 1. 35) and the Stoic notion of an intelligent universe.

   the thrust of a seed: this was a favourite Stoic example of nature's creative powers; see 2. 58 above, and Cicero, *De senectute* 52.

83 *air... shares with us our faculties*, etc.: for the Stoic theories of light-waves and sound-waves, see Sambursky, 22 f.

84 *All that is borne*, etc.: the obvious reference here is to the four elements, of which earth and water move downwards, and air and fire upwards.

88 *Posidonius*: 1. 123 n. Nothing further is known of Posidonius' orrery, but already Archimedes in the third century BC had fashioned one at Syracuse. Claudius Marcellus in his plunder of that city brought it to Rome, and kept it in his house. Cf. Cicero, *Tusc.* 1. 63; *Rep.* 1. 14.

   to Scythia or to Britain: these countries are chosen for their remoteness east and west from the centre of civilization. Britain, recently in the news from Caesar's forays in 55 and 54 BC, is repeatedly joined with the epithet 'furthest' in Catullus, Virgil, and Horace.

89 *Accius*: an Umbrian (170–*c*.90 BC), he was chiefly celebrated as a tragedian who modelled many of his plays on those of the three great Greek tragedians. This citation is from his *Medea* (frs. 381–95 Warmington).

   played by Silvanus: Silvanus here represents by syncretism the Greek god Pan, whose piping is a familiar motif in pastoral poetry.

91 *Pacuvius* (*c*.220–*c*.130 BC) came from Brundisium, and was famed as a painter but more especially as a tragic poet; Cicero considered him the best of Latin tragedians. The first line quoted here is usually assigned to his *Chryses* (frs. 110 f. Warmington); the

second cannot be definitely placed (*Uncertain Fragments*, fr. 14 Warmington).

93 *the twenty-one letters of the alphabet*: in Latin, i/j forms one letter, and u/v likewise; in Cicero's day there was no w, y, or z.

94 *colour or quality . . . or feeling*: 'quality' (*qualitas* means 'suchness') is one of the many words which we owe to Cicero's coining. It seems likely that he here remembers the long discussion in Lucretius 2. 730 ff., where arguments are presented for atoms being without colour; these are followed (842 ff.) by the claim that they do not possess qualities of heat, sound, taste, smell, and that they lack sensation (865 ff.).

95 This long extract is from Aristotle's *De philosophia*, from which Cicero has already quoted at 1. 33, 2. 42 and 44; the treatise has not survived.

96 *when the volcano erupted at Aetna*: the volcanic mountain overlooking Catana in Sicily had most recently erupted shortly before Caesar's death in 44 BC; Servius (on Vergil, *Georgics* 1. 472) reports that the disturbance was felt as far away as Rhegium.

97 *a clock*: Balbus thinks here of a water-clock rather than a sun-dial.

102 In this extended hymn on the glories of creation (98 ff.), Balbus becomes repetitive; for the sun's journeys, cf. 2. 49 above. Lucretius 5. 614 ff. describes how the sun passes 'from the summer quarters of the sky to the winter tropic of Capricorn, and then returns to the summer tropic of Cancer' (Bailey).

103 *the moon . . . more than half the size of the earth*: in fact the moon's diameter is little more than a quarter of that of the earth. Cleomedes, the astronomer of the second century AD, probably citing the Stoic Posidonius, states that the breadth of the earth's shadow is twice the moon's diameter.

now accelerating, etc.: more repetition; cf. 2. 51 above.

104 *a vast number of fixed stars*: Pliny, *NH* 2. 24, states that by his day astronomers had identified sixteen hundred of them.

some lines of Aratus: about two-thirds of Cicero's rendering of the *Phaenomena* of Aratus survives (469 lines, together with fragments of another 130, against 732 in the original Greek; cf. W. W. Ewbank, *The Poems of Cicero* (London, 1933)). Aratus of Soli in Cilicia composed his poem on astronomy at Alexandria about

275 BC; it was based on a prose-treatise by Eudoxus, the fourth-century astronomer.

when you were still a stripling: the dramatic date of this dialogue is 76 BC, when Cicero was 30. These limp translations of his date to about a decade earlier.

So here goes: in this long poetic section, the ostensible purpose is to demonstrate the workings of the divine intelligence by depicting the glory of the heavens, but Cicero exploits the theme to advertise his translation of Aratus' *Phaenomena*. He includes no fewer than forty-eight of the stars or constellations mentioned in the Greek poem, a translation of which appears in the Loeb series by G. R. Mair (1921).

105 *the two constellations of the Bears*: Ursa Major is more popularly known as The Plough or The Wagon; the title of 'The Seven Oxen' mentioned here may refer to the plough-formation. The Greeks called Ursa Minor 'Cynosure' or 'Dog's Tail', and Ursa Maior 'Helice' or 'Circling'. Aratus indicates that the Phoenicians navigated by the Lesser Bear, the Greeks by the Greater Bear.

106 *The . . . Dragon*: so called because it creeps across the northern hemisphere.

108 *Where rising and setting equally claim their place*: that is, on the surface of the sea at the horizon.

the Grieving Man: the Greek has 'toiling', not 'grieving'. The Greek name for the constellation, Engonasin, means 'On the Knees', and is usually explained as representing Hercules struggling with the dragon of the Hesperides. It is now called Hercules.

the Crown: the constellation of the Northern Crown is interpreted by Aratus as representing the hair of Ariadne, transported to heaven after being visited on Naxos by the god Dionysus.

the Serpent-holder: Aesculapius, the god of healing, whose symbol was a serpent, was in mythology raised to the stars after being slain by a thunderbolt for resurrecting the dead.

109 *the Seven Stars*: the Septentriones are the seven stars of the constellation of the Great Bear.

Arctophylax: the name literally means 'Guardian of the Bear'.

110 *Arcturus*: this is the brightest star in the constellation Arctophylax or Boötes.

Virgo: she holds an ear of corn probably because harvesting took place under this sixth sign of the zodiac, into which the sun enters in mid-August to mid-September. The brightest star in the constellation is still called Spica ('ear of corn').

the Twins . . . the Crab . . . Leo: these are the third, fourth, and fifth signs of the zodiac. The twins were thought to represent Castor and Pollux; the Crab (into which the sun moves in mid-June) was probably so called because thereafter the sun begins to move backward; Leo represents the violence of the sun in July–August.

The Charioteer . . . Helice . . . Capra: Capra, the She-goat (representing Amalthea, the she-goat which nurtured Jupiter on Mt. Ida) is a star in the constellation of The Charioteer (Auriga). It is now called Capella. For Helice, see 2. 105.

The Kids are two stars in the constellation Auriga.

The hornèd Bull: Taurus is the second sign of the zodiac.

111 *Hyades*: Romans after Cicero unanimously derive the name for these two stars in the constellation Taurus from *huein*, to rain, to lend them the title of 'Water-bringers', and not from *hues* ('pigs'); but in fact the derivation from *hues* is probably the correct one, since the constellations generally bear the names of living creatures.

Cepheus . . . Cassiepia . . . Andromeda: these commemorate the Ethiopian parents, Cepheus and Cassiepia, of Andromeda. When chained to a rock, she was rescued by Perseus, who had earlier slain Medusa the Gorgon. From her blood when he beheaded her sprang the Horse, the winged Pegasus. See Ovid, *Met.* 4. 663 ff.

the Ram: Aries, the first sign of the zodiac, got its name from the ram with the golden fleece on which Phrixus and his sister Helle escaped to Colchis.

the Fish: Pisces is the twelfth sign of the zodiac, and therefore adjacent to the first, the Ram. Perhaps the twelfth month (February–March) was the start of the fishing season.

112 *The Pleiades*: they were known to the Romans as Vergiliae, and today as the Seven Sisters, representing the seven daughters of Atlas. Their rising in May and their setting in late October mark the beginning and end of the sailing season.

the Lyre: this was envisaged as representing the lyre first fashioned by Mercury (see Horace, *Odes* 1. 10. 5).

The winged Bird: in mythology Cygnus, king of Liguria, turned into a swan and was raised to the sky by Jupiter (Manilius 1. 337).

Aquarius: the eleventh sign of the zodiac, heralding the rainy season; cf. Horace, *Sat.* 1. 1. 36.

Capricorn . . . within his zone, clothed in enduring light by Titan: Capricorn is the tenth sign of the zodiac, entered by the sun (here Titan, because the sun was begotten by the Titan Hyperion) in December–January. It may have got its name ('Horned Goat') because the sun begins to climb the heavens at about the winter solstice (so Macrobius, *Sat.* 1. 17).

113 *The Scorpion . . . Drawing the bent Bow*: the Scorpion, the eighth sign of the zodiac, draws after it the bow of Sagittarius the Archer, the ninth sign of the zodiac.

the Eagle: Aquila was translated to heaven because it was the favourite bird of Jupiter.

the Dolphin: the constellation represents the dolphin which rescued Arion.

Orion: in mythology, 'the giant hunter' (Homer, *Od.* 11. 572) pursued the daughters of Atlas (see the Pleiades in 2. 112); hunter and hunted were transformed into constellations by Jupiter.

114 *The Dog-star*: Sirius, the brightest star in the heavens, lying southeast of Orion, rises in August the hottest month; hence the expression 'dog days'.

The Hare: many constellations bear their names because the primitive hunters compared them with their quarries.

Argo: this constellation is called after the ship in which Jason sailed in search of the golden fleece; cf. 2. 89.

River's banks: Aratus states that it represents the Eridanus, the Greek name for the Po in northern Italy.

The Altar: the name, Thuterion in Greek, goes back to Eudoxus (see 2. 104 n.).

the Centaur: the constellation allegedly resembles the head and trunk of a man poised on the body and legs of a horse.

Hydra: the Lernaean hydra slain by Hercules as one of his twelve labours is said to have lent its name to the constellation.

the Wine-bowl: the constellation Cratera, resembling the mixing-bowl used for wine.

The feathered Crow: the Crow or Raven (*Corvus*) lies below and behind the Hydra; hence 'to peck her tail'.

Procyon: the Greek word means 'Before the Dog'.

116 *the sea ... never spills over*: this does not discount the possibility of local flooding. Balbus, in common with his Roman contemporaries, visualizes the earth as bounded on east and west by the ocean, and he claims that it will never be deluged by a universal flood.

117 *as I ... said earlier*: see 2. 47 f.

118 *they used to concede that Panaetius registered doubts*: Cicero is recalling the lectures which he heard as a student. Panaetius of Rhodes (*c.*185–109 BC) divided his mature years between Rome, where he was a member of Scipio Aemilianus' circle, and Athens, where he became head of the Stoic school in 129. He espoused the Aristotelian doctrine of the eternity of the world, and thus rejected the Stoic notion of the cyclic destruction and regeneration of the universe. See Rist, *Stoic Philosophy*, 175 f.

the entire universe will go up in flames: this Stoic doctrine is taken over from Heraclitus, who argued that fire is the first principle (see Kirk–Raven–Schofield, ch. 6). The Stoics adapted the Pythagorean theory of the Great Year (2. 51 n.) to their doctrine of cyclic destruction.

119 *those which are said to wander*: Balbus has already discussed the planets at some length at 2. 52 f.

obey the injunction of the sun: referring to Mercury's and Venus' proximity to the sun on its yearly circuit; cf. 2. 52–3 n.

120 *if they are planted close to cabbage-stems*, etc.: similar observations are found in Varro (*RR* 1. 16) and Pliny (*NH* 20. 34).

123 *Elephants are equipped even with hands*: Latin has no word to describe the elephant's trunk; the alternative to *manus* is to use the Greek *proboscis*, as in Pliny, *NH* 8. 10.

while others keep watch: it seems likely that in this passage where there is a hiatus in the text, Cicero has in mind Aristotle, *Hist. Anim.* 9. 39, where the different snaring techniques of spiders are described. The lost section probably depicted the spider concealed in a recess, ready to pounce upon unwary insects.

124 *ducks' eggs . . . under hens*: Pliny, *NH* 10. 55 has substantially the same account.

In my reading, etc.: This account of the predatory habits of the spoonbill is found also in Pliny, *NH* 10. 40.

According to the written account, this same bird: etc.: see Aristotle, *Hist. Anim.* 9. 10.

125 *sea-frogs*: Cicero gives a simplified version of the stratagem described by Aristotle in *Hist. Anim.* 9. 37.

The kite and the crow: see Aristotle, *Hist. Anim.* 9. 1.

cranes . . . fly in triangular formation: this observation does not appear in *Hist. Anim.*, but the lore is so widespread later (see e.g, Aelian, *Hist. Anim.* 3. 13; Plutarch, *Mor.* 967b) that it may have appeared in Aristotle's lost *De philosophia*.

126 *dogs cure their sickness by vomiting, and Egyptian ibises by purging their bowels*: Aristotle's *Hist. Anim.* 9. 6 is the source for the dog-lore. Plutarch, *Moralia* 994c recounts similarly the behaviour of the ibis.

126–7 *panthers . . . wild goats . . . does*: Aristotle, loc. cit., reports these case-histories though Cicero's version of the last differs slightly from Aristotle's.

127 *lions their tread*: the Teubner edition has *cursu*, which I translate. At *Moralia* 966a, Plutarch describes how lions walk 'with paws clenched' to avoid leaving a trail for the hunter to follow.

cuttlefish . . . stingray: cf. Aristotle, *Hist. Anim.* 9. 37.

129 *Tortoises and crocodiles*: Cicero diverges from the version in Aristotle's *Hist. Anim.* 5. 33, which claims that both creatures sit on their eggs until they hatch out.

130 *the Nile . . . Euphrates . . . Indus*: Herodotus 2. 19. 2 states that the Nile rises at the summer solstice, and after a hundred days falls again; see the commentary of How and Wells for the accuracy of this statement. On the Euphrates (irrigation by canals), see Herodotus 1. 193. 2. For the Indus as the greatest of all rivers (the Nile and Volga are actually longer) see Arrian, *Anab.* 5. 4. Ancient geographers remark on the cereals which India produces, but they do not credit the Indus with sowing the seeds.

131 *the Etesian winds*: these trade-winds (Etesian means 'yearly') blow from various quarters in July–August (see e.g. Seneca, *Q. Nat.* 5. 10). The ancients generally regarded them as north-east winds,

but Livy (37. 23. 4) agrees with modern authorities in identifying them as predominantly from the north-west.

133 *for the benefit of the gods and the human race*: 'the gods' here refers to the elements in creation to which the Stoics ascribe intelligence and reason; see 2. 54.

135 *the gullet*: for *stomachus*, taken over from the Greek in this sense, see Aristotle, *Hist. Anim.* 1. 12.

136 *The windpipe, called 'rough'*: the trachea (the present-day term, which means 'rough' in Greek) is so called because unlike the common artery it has a series of rings to strengthen it. See in general G. E. R. Lloyd, *Greek Science after Aristotle* (London, 1973), 81 f.

by reason of its abundant heat: Cicero here takes over Aristotle's notion that food in the stomach undergoes a qualitative change through the body's heat, a theory later rejected by Erasistratus (*c*.260 BC).

137 This account of the digestive system is defective; for Erasistratus' more accurate explanation, see Lloyd (§ 136 n.), 80 f.

the middle intestine: this is a misunderstanding of Aristotle's Greek at *Hist. Anim.* 1. 16, where *mesenterion* is a membrane between the intestines.

the so-called 'gates' of the liver . . . the vein which is called 'hollow': the terms 'portal vein' and 'hollow vein' (*vena cava*) are still in use, the second being the great trunk vein which runs into the heart from above and below.

138 *the blood is distributed*: this account of the circulation of the blood suggests that it courses through the veins but not through the arteries; this is a misconception (see Lloyd (§ 136 n.), 82 ff.). Harvey in 1630 was the first to advance the correct explanation.

139 *they issue from the heart . . . to every part of the body*: Aristotle, *Hist. Anim.* 3. 5 is probably the ultimate source for this section, though he specifically denies that the sinews extend as far as the veins and arteries.

142 *which is called the pupil*: *pupula* means a little doll. It is used for the pupil of the eye because it reflects a small doll-like image; for the Greek equivalent, see Plato, *Alcibiades* 139a.

143 For the protection of the eyes by the lids and eyebrows, Cicero has drawn upon Aristotle, *Part. Anim.* 2. 15.

144 *hard and horny*: Cf. Aristotle, *De anima* 2. 8.

amplified by the tortoise-shell or horn: the lyre was equipped with a sounding-board. Mercury was said to have made the first lyre from tortoise-shell (cf. Horace, *Odes* 3. 11. 1 ff.) but horn was more commonly used.

145 f. *much superior to those of brute beasts*: clearly a bogus claim; for animals' superior scent, cf. Aristotle, *De anima* 2. 9. The arguments that follow are more relevant to man's aesthetic and moral sensibility than to his physical awareness.

147 *that your eloquence was granted to me*: Cicero makes Balbus acknowledge the contribution made by the Academics in the field of epistemology, which he discusses earlier in the *Academica*.

our ability to discern and understand external reality: the Academics disputed the Stoic claim that our senses and reason could establish objective truth; see e.g. *Academica* 2. 79 ff., 91 f.

148 *has united us . . . has weaned us*: Cicero echoes here his *De oratore* 1. 30 ff., esp. 33.

149 *formed in the seat of the intelligence*: I translate *a mente* thus to remind the reader that the Stoics posited the heart as the seat of the reason, and considered that the voice first issued from the heart.

compare the tongue to the plectrum, etc.: this Stoic conceit surfaces repeatedly in the writings of the Church Fathers; see e.g. Jerome, *De spiritu sancto* 35.

150 *for the exercise of numerous skills*: Lucretius 4. 830 ff. is at pains to rebut the Stoic claims that our hands and tongue were created specifically for practical use.

151 *the remarkably sharp senses of elephants*: Aristotle, *Hist. Anim.* 9. 46 earlier draws attention to these.

We put trees to use: reading, with Ax, *arborum confectione*.

153 *with which justice and the other virtues are closely linked*: for the Stoics, the virtues are inseparable; see F. H. Sandbach, *The Stoics* (London, 1975), 43.

only in their immortality: the Stoic notion that immortality is irrelevant to the good life is particularly strong in Seneca; see e.g. *Ep.* 73. 13.

154 *a city which houses both*: the image goes back to Posidonius (so Diogenes Laertius 7. 138), and repeatedly recurs in Cicero's philosophical writing; see e.g. *Fin.* 3. 64.

159 *men of the golden age*: the notion of an earlier idyllic existence begins in extant Greek literature with Hesiod's *Works and Days*, in which the golden age is successively followed by the silver, bronze, and iron ages. For the later development in Dicaearchus, the fourth-century pupil of Aristotle, see W. K. C. Guthrie, *In the Beginning* (London, 1957), ch. 4.

Then, on a sudden, etc.: these are lines from Cicero's translation of Aratus' *Phaenomena*, 129 ff. (see 2. 104 n.).

160 *Chrysippus*: see 1. 39 n.

life ... to serve as salt: the witticism was a Stoic commonplace, cited in almost identical terms by Cicero in his *Fin.* 5. 38, as well as by Varro and Plutarch later. Clement of Alexandria, *Stromata* 7. 34, attributes it to Cleanthes.

'*birds of flight*' *and* '*birds of utterance*': the eagle and the vulture are in the first group, the raven, crow, and owl in the second; see R. M. Ogilvie, *The Romans and their Gods* (London, 1969), 56.

161 *many cures for illnesses and wounds*: Pliny devotes an entire book of his *NH* (30) to such animal remedies.

162 *Carneades*: 1. 4 n.

163 *The haruspices ... the augurs*: the *haruspices* were Etruscans who originally confined themselves to examining entrails of sacrificial animals. But following the Second Punic War, they broadened their scope to interpret prodigies more generally. For the augurs' attention to birds, see 2. 160 n. For general discussion of divination, about which Cicero waxes sceptical in his *De divinatione*, see Ogilvie (§ 160 n.), ch. 4.

165 *Curius, Fabricius, and Coruncanius*: in the war with Pyrrhus of Epirus (280–275 BC) the consul M'. Curius Dentatus, already celebrated as a successful general, prevailed in 275 in the battle of Beneventum. C. Fabricius Luscinus, anecdotally famous for his sporting warning to Pyrrhus about the treachery of his physician, conducted abortive negotiations with Pyrrhus, and as consul in 278 regained cities and territories which had gone over to him. Ti. Coruncanius as consul in 280 frustrated Pyrrhus' attempts to join forces with Etruscan cities, and forced the

king to retreat to Tarentum. All three were, like Cicero himself, 'new men'.

Caiatinus, Duillius, Metellus, and Lutatius: A. Atilius Caiatinus as consul in 258 had successes against Hamilcar in Sicily and in 254 became the first Roman dictator to operate outside Italy. C. Duillius, by defeating Hannibal off Mylae in 260 gained the first naval triumph at Rome. L. Caecilius Metellus served as Caiatinus' Master of Horse in 254, and won an important battle over Hasdrubal near Panormus in 250; C. Lutatius Catulus won the culminating battle of the war off the Aegates Islands, and then negotiated the peace with Hamilcar in 241.

Maximus, Marcellus, and Africanus: these were the three great heroes of the Second Punic War. Q. Fabius Maximus Cunctator helped Rome to survive early disasters by his policy of attrition, and later recovered Tarentum. M. Claudius Marcellus, the hard man of the war, successfully resisted Hannibal in the open field near Nola, and later expelled the Carthaginians from Sicily, capturing Syracuse (214–211). P. Cornelius Scipio Africanus, after expelling the Carthaginians from Spain (210–206), was elected consul and led the successful operations in Africa (204–202).

Paulus, Gracchus and Cato: L. Aemilius Paulus' chief claim to fame was his conclusive victory over Perseus in the Third Macedonian War at Pydna in 168. Ti. Sempronius Gracchus, father of the Gracchi, achieved fame by his settlement of Spain in 180–179, and by his political eminence as consul (twice) and censor (169). The Elder Cato's all-round qualities as soldier, advocate, politician and author are celebrated in Livy's encomium at 39. 40. 4 ff.

Scipio and Laelius: P. Cornelius Scipio Aemilianus, son of Aemilius Paulus and adopted son of Africanus' son Publius, was chiefly famed for his concluding victory in the Third Punic War and his destruction of Carthage (146); he later captured and destroyed Numantia in Spain (133). C. Laelius, his legate at Carthage, was his intimate friend; because of this friendship, Cicero used his name as title for his treatise *De amicitia*.

166 *Ulysses and Diomedes, Agamemnon and Achilles*: in Homer, Athena is continually the protectress of Achilles and Diomedes in the *Iliad*, and of Ulysses/Odysseus in the *Odyssey*; Agamemnon does not obtain such habitual divine protection.

168 *as leading citizen and as priest*: Cotta became consul in 75, shortly after the dramatic date of this dialogue; for his election as pontifex earlier, see 1. 61 n.

Book 3

5 *I shall indeed defend them*: Cicero's choice of a *pontifex* as spokesman for the Academics deliberately dilutes the sceptical views of the school to take account of the historical and patriotic Roman outlook, in which the religious ritual is inextricably bound up with national identity. Cicero emphasizes the importance of these in his *Rep.* 2. 15 ff. (Romulus and the auspices), 2. 26 ff. (Numa and Roman ritual).

Tiberius Coruncanius, Publius Scipio, and Publius Scaevola: for the eminence of Coruncanius and Scaevola in the fields of religious law and ceremonial, see 1. 115 n. The Scipio mentioned here is Nasica Corculum (cf. 2. 10), who became pontifex maximus in 150; his learning in pontifical law was proverbial (see Cicero, *De or.* 2. 134, *Sen.* 50).

Zeno or Cleanthes or Chrysippus ... Gaius Laelius: the first three are the outstanding philosophers of the Stoic school (see 1. 36, 37, 39 nn.); Cotta wishes to distance himself wholly from the Stoic school. The Laelius praised here was mentioned at 2. 165; he obtained the sobriquet of 'Wise' for putting virtue before all else. As praetor in 145, he successfully opposed the proposal of the tribune C. Licinius Crassus to fill vacant priestly offices by popular election (see Cicero, *Amic.* 6 and 96), a speech which is probably referred to here.

the interpreters of the Sibyl or the diviners: the 'interpreters' are the keepers of the Sibylline Books, who by Cicero's day numbered fifteen (*quindecimviri sacris faciundis*); after consultation of the books, they recommended means of expiating the divine anger. For the gradual invasion by the *haruspices* (diviners) of their traditional role, see 2. 163 n.

Romulus by his auspices, and Numa by establishing our ritual: for the traditional accounts of how the auspices taken by Romulus initiated the foundation of Rome, and how Numa Pompilius, the second king of Rome, established Roman ritual, see Livy 1. 7 and 19 ff., with the commentary of R. M. Ogilvie.

8 *you Cotta, when speaking in court*: elsewhere Cicero (*Brutus* 201) categorizes Cotta as one of the two outstanding orators of his generation.

10 *the quotation which you cited*: cf. 2. 4.

11 *the judgement of idiots*: the Stoics made much of the argument *ex consensu gentium* (see 2. 5, 2. 12 ff.), but at the same time they were contemptuous of the ignorance of the masses. They confronted the dilemma by laying stress on 'the wise, the poets and philosophers' (Sextus Empiricus 9. 63 ff.) of every age who accepted the divine existence.

You object, etc.: cf. 2. 6.

the Via Salaria: it was so called because it was the route from the salt-mines near Ostia.

Homer . . . says are buried at Sparta: Cotta is citing *Iliad* 3. 243 ff., but at *Odyssey* 11. 301 ff., Homer says that after they were buried, Zeus allowed them to live on alternate days. The claim that Homer lived 'shortly after them', that is, immediately following the Trojan War, is of course spurious.

Marcus Cato, the senatorial leader: this is not true in the strict sense, since M. Aemilius Lepidus was *princeps senatus* between 179 and 152: Cato is being described as a leading figure in the general sense.

12 *what is susceptible to proof*: in 3. 29–34, Cotta in his role as Academic denies the immortality of the soul which Plato had defended in the *Phaedo* (69 ff.) and *Phaedrus* (245). Here Cotta speaks in his other persona as a Roman priest, and concedes what Balbus had argued at 2. 62, that certain benefactors venerated in Roman religion, like Hercules, Romulus and the Dioscuri, were rightly regarded as gods enjoying eternal life.

13 *the shrine dedicated to Castor and Pollux*: according to Livy (2. 42. 5), the temple was dedicated to Castor in 485 BC by Aulus Postumius, son of the dictator of the same name who had vowed it during the battle of Lake Regillus. On the arrival of the cult at Rome, see R. M. Ogilvie on Livy 2. 20. 12.

the decree . . . honouring Vatinius: cf. 2. 6 n.

a proverb: the circumstances surrounding its origin are explained in the Suda, s.v. ἀληθής.

{*On predictions and premonitions of the future*}: a short section of the text has been lost here. Comparison with 2. 6 ff. suggests that Cotta may have challenged Balbus' assertions about the evil consequences of the neglect of divination, and the contemporary scepticism about omens and prodigies.

14 *the ultimate consolation . . . hope*: the commonplace goes back to Hesiod, *Op*. 96.

   Who first demonstrated the fissure?, etc.: the objections that follow are mirrored in Cicero's *De divinatione* (2. 28 and 80), which incorporates the same sceptical attitude adopted by Cotta here.

   the augural staff: cf. 2. 9.

15 *physicians too are often wrong*: cf. 2. 12.

   the self-immolation of the Decii: cf. 2. 10 n.

   the utterances of a Faun: cf. 2. 6.

16 *Cleanthes believes*, etc.: see 2. 13 and n.

18 *that Chrysippus presented*: see 2. 16 and n. For the comparison with beautiful furniture, see 2. 17.

   syllogisms of Zeno: see 2. 21 f.

   all that you said two days ago: see 2. 73 n. It appears that Cicero presupposes a day's interval between the discourse of Balbus and this response of Cotta.

20 *to detach the mind from the . . . testimony of the eyes*: that is, to visualize gods in other than human shape.

21 This analogy of the city is logically fallacious, for whereas the universe is identical with the creation, the city is a mere part of the earth.

24 *more regular than . . . the Euripus*: the Euripus is the channel between the island of Euboea (Chalcis, its main city, commands the narrowest part of the strait) and the mainland of Attica. The currents there, so far from being regular, as Cotta breezily claims, were notorious for their unpredictability.

   that in the Sicilian strait: the straits of Messina between Italy and Sicily were in Cicero's time identified with the hazards of Scylla and Charybdis described by Homer, *Od*. 12. 73 f., 222 f. So this is a second dubious example of the 'regularity' in view of the hazards to shipping there (cf. Virgil, *Aen*. 5. 420 ff.).

   The greedy wave, etc.: Ennius, *Annals*, fr. 546 Warmington.

tertian and quartan fever: Pliny, *NH* 8. 50 discusses these intermittent bouts of fever which recur every third or fourth day (counting inclusively).

25 *Chrysippus*: for this philosopher, see 1. 39 n.; for the citations, 2. 16 f.

whose minds have hardened . . . like hands: the Latin word used here for 'practised' (*callidus*), literally means 'calloused'.

26 *Orion and the Dog-star*: Cotta uses these examples of inanimate stars because Balbus had cited them together at 2. 113 f.

as I shall show: the promise is not redeemed, unless a later passage has been lost.

27 *Socrates in the pages of Xenophon*: see 2. 18 n.

as Pythagoras believes: for the music of the spheres, see e.g. Plato, *Rep.* 617b; and in general, W. K. C. Guthrie, *A History of Greek Philosophy*, i (Cambridge, 1962), 246 f.

as Zeno has it: cf. 2. 57.

28 *association and interconnection by relationship*: referring to 2. 58.

the unique divine breath: the Stoic Pronoia/Providentia; see 2. 73 ff.

29 *Carneades*: for Cicero's Academic mentor, see 1. 4 n.

30–4 The arguments of Carneades that follow are directed against the doctrine of the eternity of Pronoia, which the Stoics claimed to be alive and sentient.

35 *Heraclitus . . . is reluctant to make his utterances comprehensible*: Heraclitus of Ephesus (on whom see Kirk–Raven–Schofield, ch.6) is said to have written *c.*500 BC a book 'On Nature', in three parts, on the universe, politics, and theology. It was written 'rather obscurely' (1. 74 n.) allegedly to prevent its being scorned by the common herd (Diogenes Laertius 9. 5). For the adaptation of his thesis that fire is the first principle by Stoic thinkers, see Long, *Hellenistic Philosophy*, 145 f., 155 f.

36 *why fire rather than breath?* In fact, from Chrysippus onwards the Stoics identified Pronoia not with pure fire but with a compound of fire and air; see Long (n. above), 155.

the same response: as at 3. 32 above.

37 *all fire needs sustenance*: cf. 2. 40 and 118.

Cleanthes: 1. 37 n. Cotta recalls the words of Balbus at 2. 40, and perhaps cites from an unidentified poet, since the Latin here falls into a hexameter.

38 *any divine nature . . . endowed with no virtue*: Cotta here challenges the view advanced by Balbus at 2. 30 ff. and 79, that the perfection of virtue lies in God. He here reviews the cardinal virtues (prudence, justice, courage and temperance) to argue, with Aristotle (*Nic. Eth.* 7. 11, 10. 81), that the gods have no concern with them. For the Stoics the virtues are one, in God and in man (cf. Cicero, *Leg.* 1. 25).

39 *the Syrians, who adore a fish*: the goddess Atargatis was represented with the face of a woman and the body of a fish; see Diodorus 2. 4.

the Egyptians: see 1. 43.

Alabandus . . . Tenes . . . Leucothea . . . Palaemon: Alabandus was the eponymous hero of Alabanda in Caria; Tenes from Tenedos (off the coast of the Troad; cf. Virgil, *Aen.* 2. 21 ff.) was according to Plutarch (*Mor.* 297e–f) killed by Achilles. Leucothea/Ino was the sea-goddess who supported Odysseus in shipwreck (Homer, *Od.* 5. 333 ff.); her son Melicertes was transformed into the deity Palaemon, whom the Romans identified with Portunus, god of harbours.

Hercules, Aesculapius, etc.: 2. 652 n.

40 *Behold the dazzling vault*, etc.: see 2. 4 and n.

She-goat . . . Crown: Cotta picks up these names of stars from Balbus' citations of Aratus (2. 105 ff.), which are prefaced by the claim that the stars are divine (2. 39 n.).

41 *advanced in status from humans to gods*: for the Euhemerism, see 1. 119 n.

as Accius puts it: 2. 89 n. This citation cannot be assigned to any certain play (Warmington ii, *Incerta* 14 f.).

Homer recounts: at *Od.* 11. 601 ff., Homer actually says that Hercules' ghost is in Hades, while the hero disports with the immortal gods.

those who scrutinize the secret and abstruse books: this may be a reference to the antiquarian researches of Varro (anachronistically, since they postdate the occasion of the dialogue). Varro claimed to have identified forty-three bearers of the name Hercules (so Servius on Virgil, *Aen.* 8. 564).

the Hercules who ... struggled with Apollo to seize the tripod: Hercules in his madness sought the advice of the Delphic oracle, but when the priestess offered no reply, he tussled with Apollo and bore off the tripod (Hyginus, *Fab.* 32).

the son of the Nile ... composed the Phrygian writings: for the Egyptian Heracles, see Herodotus 2. 43. There was a temple to him at the mouth of the Nile (Tacitus, *Ann.* 2. 60), the river which was said to have sired all the gods. One would have expected Phrygian writings to be ascribed to the Hercules from Mt. Ida, who is mentioned next.

the Digiti of Mt. Ida, to whom the folk of Cos sacrifice: the Ida connected with the Digiti or Dactyloi is usually that in Crete, but is occasionally the Phrygian mountain. Cf. Clement, *Stromata* 1. 15. 73, describing the Dactyloi as the first sages, who invented musical rhythms; he numbers a Heracles among them. I read *Coi* for the *cui* of the MSS and in Ax, because the people of Cos were worshippers of Heracles (cf. Plutarch, *Mor.* 304c–d).

son of Jupiter and Asteria: this Asteria was a Titan, sister of Leto/ Latona (Hesiod, *Theog.* 404 ff.) and mother of the Phrygian Heracles (Athenaeus 392a). Herodotus went to Tyre to investigate Heracles-worship there, and found temples dedicated to the Tyrian Heracles and to Heracles of Thasos (2. 44). Carthago is the personification of the city of Carthage ('New City'), traditionally said to have been founded from Tyre.

Belus: this is the Latinization of the Babylonian Baal, whose worship extended to India; see Pliny, *NH* 6. 16.

the one we know: the story of how Jupiter lay with Alcmena in the guise of her husband Amphitryo and sired Hercules was especially familiar to Romans through Plautus' play *Amphitryo*.

as I shall presently explain: see 3. 53.

43 *from those miniature sacrificial bowls ... described by Laelius*: the lesson inculcated by the bowls is that the gods welcome simple piety rather than offerings of ostentatious wealth; compare Horace, *Odes* 3. 23 and the tribute paid by Tertullian, *Apol.* 25. For Laelius' speech, see 3. 5 n.

Pans and Satyrs are not deities: Cotta means that they are not recognized as gods in the religion of the state, though they were popularly regarded as spirits of the wild; Cotta's argument is that the nymphs, since they were depicted as their sisters, should likewise be excluded.

temples . . . dedicated to nymphs: such a temple was a *cause célèbre* when set on fire by Clodius; see Cicero, *Pro Milone* 73.

Orcus . . . the rivers . . . Charon and Cerberus: Orcus, the ancient lord of the underworld, was increasingly identified with Dis/Pluto, but had no cult under his own name. The rivers of Hell are frequently personified, and occasionally deified, in Greek literature, but like the ferryman Charon and the three-headed dog Cerberus they had no role in Roman religious ritual.

44 *Saturn . . . worshipped in the lands of the west*: it is not clear whether Cotta refers to the worship of Cronos, the Greek deity with whom Saturn was identified, in the Islands of the Blest (cf. Hesiod, *Theog.* 167 ff.), or to the worship of Saturn, the ancient agricultural god of Italy as distinct from Greece. Saturn was never popular as a Roman deity, but he had a temple below the Capitoline hill, and the Saturnalia was a festival in his honour.

Caelus, Aether and Dies, etc.: Hesiod (*Theog.* 116 ff.) gives a slightly different genealogy: Erebus and Night are the parents of Aether and Dies (Day), but Night is the sole parent of most of the monsters in the catalogue that follows. Hyginus 1. 1 makes Caelus/Caelum one of the children of Aether and Dies. I translate *Morbus* (Sickness) for the obelized *Motus* in Ax.

45 *reservations about Hercules*, etc.: Balbus has in fact aired no such reservations. It seems likely that Cicero has made Balbus the mouthpiece for Posidonius' arguments defending the gods, and Cotta the mouthpiece for Carneades' destructive criticisms, but without adjusting the standpoints of the two sides.

Aristaeus . . . Theseus: Aristaeus was celebrated as the legendary innovator not only in olive-production (Cicero, *Verr.* 4. 128), but also in bee-keeping (Virgil, *Georgics* 4. 315 ff.). For his parents, Apollo and Cyrene, see Pindar, *Pyth.* 9. 65. For Theseus' descent from Neptune/Poseidon, see the *OCD* s.v. Neptune.

in civil law: cf. Gaius 1. 82.

the islanders of Astypalaea worship Achilles: this island in the Cyclades is close to Cos, where Achilles and his ancestors were also worshipped.

Orpheus and Rhesus: Orpheus (cf. 1. 41 and 107) was the son of the Muse Calliope (Virgil, *Ecl.* 4. 57); Rhesus was the son of the Strymon and a Muse (?Euterpe); see Euripides, *Rhesus* 279, 393 f.

46 *Balbus, you too*: cf. 2. 62, but there Balbus insists on immortality as well as human virtues as the criterion of divinity.

Hecate ... daughter of ... Asteria: for Asteria, 3. 42 n., for Hecate as her daughter, see Hesiod, *Theog.* 404 ff. Hecate had a celebrated shrine in Aegina (Pausanias 2. 30. 2); see E. R. Dodds, *The Greeks and the Irrational*[8] (Berkeley, 1973), 96.

they have a temple at Athens: Sophocles' *Oedipus Coloneus* is set in an enclosure sacred to the Furies on the fringe of Athens. The Furies (Erinyes in Greek) were called Eumenides ('Kindly Ones') in propitiatory address. For their development into ministers of vengeance, see Dodds (previous n.), 39.

the grove of Furina: according to Varro (*LL* 6. 19), few people in Cicero's day knew even the name of this ancient goddess, whose festival was on 25 July. Cotta mistakenly connects her name with the Furies; see Warde-Fowler, *Roman Festivals*, 187.

47 *Natio*: this is the sole mention of this goddess as minister of childbirth, a role usually allotted to Juno Lucina; see Latte, 52.

those abstract figures which you mentioned: see 2. 61.

Serapis and Isis: the cult of these Egyptians deities was introduced into Greece in the fourth century, and into Italy by the later second century. At this date the cult was still strongly discouraged by the Roman authorities; see Fordyce on Catullus 10. 26 f.

48 *Ino*: see 3. 39 n. Her father Cadmus was the legendary founder of Thebes in Boeotia.

Circe, Pasiphae, and Aeetes: Circe and Aeetes, both magicians, are described by Homer (*Od.* 10. 137 f.) as daughters of Perse and the Sun; for Pasiphae, wife of Minos, as daughter of the Sun, see Apollodorus 3. 7.

at Cercei: the promontory of Cercei/Circei (modern Monte Circello, half-way between Naples and Rome) became in post-Homeric legend the site of Circe's home, which in Homer is the island of Aeaea (*Od.* 10. 135). Strabo mentions the existence of a temple at Cercei (5. 3. 6).

Medea: the heroine of Euripides' play is associated with the previous three names in her role as magician. For her genealogy, and divine status in some Greek literary contexts, see *OCD*.

Absyrtus . . . called Aegialeus: the alternative name appears not only in Pacuvius (*Incert.* 80 Warmington), but also in Diodorus 4. 43 and Justin 42. 3.

49 *Amphiaraus and Trophonius*: for Amphiaraus, see 2. 7 n. Trophonius similarly had a shrine in Boeotia at which oracular responses were sought (cf. Herodotus 1. 46, 8. 134). Hence the mention of tax–collectors in this area, for both heroes were deified.

Erechtheus: this fabulous king of Athens gained victory over the invading Thracian Eumolpus by obeying the injunction of the Delphic oracle to sacrifice one of his daughters, whereupon the other two committed suicide to associate themselves with her.

Codrus: he is associated with Erechtheus in Cotta's mind because he too was a legendary Athenian king. In obedience to the Delphic oracle, he sacrificed his own life to save his country from the Dorian invaders.

50 *the Leonatic shrine, there called the Leocorion*: 'Leonatic' is presumably the Latinized form of Leocorion, which means 'shrine of the daughters of Leos'. He was one of the eponymous heroes of Athens, who is said to have sacrificed his daughter(s) to avert a plague; they became, like the Decii at Rome, symbols of self-immolation on behalf of the state. So Phocion called on Demosthenes to imitate them by delivering himself up (Diodorus 17. 15).

the Alabandans: 3. 39 n.

Stratonicus: on this Athenian musician and wit (*c.*410–360 BC), see *OCD*.

51 *on the heavens and the stars*: see especially 2. 68 for what follows. Lucifer ('Light-bearer') is another name for Venus as morning-star (see 2. 53).

Iris the rainbow: Iris, goddess of the rainbow and accordingly intermediary between gods and men, was the daughter of Thaumas the Titan, whose name means 'Wonder'.

to have given birth to the Centaurs: they were the offspring of Ixion and a cloud, which Zeus had shaped in the form of Hera to tempt him (Pindar, *Pyth.* 2. 21 ff.); hence the Centaurs became known as *Nubigenae*, born of a cloud.

the weather . . . deified: the temple was near the Porta Capena at Rome (Ovid, *Fasti* 6. 193); the Latin word (*Tempestates*) denotes the changing seasons.

sacrifice a victim to the waves: cf. e.g. Scipio Africanus' rite at Livy 29. 27. 5.

52 *Ceres . . . from gerere*: Cf. 2. 67.

terra . . . Tellus: on 15 April, in one of the oldest sacrificial rites in ancient Rome, pregnant cows were slain to Tellus in 'a series of acts all of which are connected with the fruits of the earth, their growth, ripening, and harvesting' (Warde-Fowler, *Roman Festivals* 71). A further festival honoured mother Earth and Ceres jointly on 24–26 January, the feast of the Paganalia (Warde-Fowler, 294 ff.). For the temple dedicated to Tellus at Rome in 268 BC, see Ovid, *Fasti* 1. 671.

Rivers and springs: the primitive animism which visualized spirit-presences in every aspect of nature was particularly marked in the case of running waters. Horace's Bandusian spring (*Odes* 3. 13), Pliny's Clitumnus (*Ep.* 8. 8), the shrine to Pontus at Rome (Cicero, *Leg.* 2. 56; C. Papirius Maso dedicated the shrine after his victory over the Corsicans in 231) afford obvious examples. The tutelary deity of the Tiber was Tiberinus (cf. Virgil, *Aen.* 8. 31 ff.); the other streams mentioned here are unknown.

53 *argue that these gods . . . have been advanced from human status into heaven*: the sections ensuing (§§53–60), follow awkwardly from what precedes. J. B. Mayor in his edition transposes these to before § 43, since the final words of § 42 promise to enumerate the different Jupiters which now follow. I reluctantly follow Ax in maintaining the traditional order.

the first two . . . in Arcadia: for Zeus' Arcadian origins, see A. B. Cook, *Zeus*, i (Cambridge, 1914), 151 ff. The connections made here with Aether and Caelus do not appear to have been noted elsewhere.

Minerva . . . the author and deviser of war: Minerva takes on the traits of the Greek Athena; for her role in warfare, see *OCD*, Athena.

Saturn's son from Crete: the Cretan origin of Zeus is the most widespread version, stemming from Hesiod, *Theog.* 453 ff. Saturn here is the Roman equivalent of Kronos (3. 44 n.). There were sanctuaries of Zeus in Crete at Mt. Dicte and Mt. Ida (3. 42 n.).

the Dioscuri: Cotta cites them and Aesculapius (3. 57) because Balbus has adduced them at 2. 62 as humans who deserved to become gods.

the first three, who are called 'kings': they obtain this cult-title as sons of 'king' Jupiter. The cult of Tritopatreus is associated especially with the prayers of the newly-married to have offspring. Eubouleus ('Good Counsel') is cited occasionally as a god of the underworld.

the second Dioscuri: Castor and Pollux are the generally recognized Dioscuri; see 2. 6, 3. 13 nn.

Alco, Melampus and Tmolus, sons of Atreus: though Cotta claims 'several authorities' for this statement, it is unsupported in extant literature. There is an Alco who is worshipped as one of the Cabiri (the deities worshipped at Lemnos and Samothrace), and Melampus is a celebrated soothsayer associated with the cult of Dionysus. Tmolus (a name found among Atreus' forbears) is a speculative emendation of a corruption in the text.

54 *the Muses*: Hesiod, *Theog.* 25 ff. is responsible for establishing the canonical number of Muses as nine, together with their names; other Greek authorities count them variously as three, four, seven, and eight. The Pierides, earlier a group distinct from the Muses in Hesiod, later become merged with them.

the Sun (Sol) got his name: c. 2. 68. The common tradition established by Hesiod, *Theog.* 371, makes Hyperion and Theia the parents. Heliopolis, lying 6 miles (8 km.) north-east of Cairo, was sacred to the sun-god Ra (cf. Herodotus 2. 3. 1). For the cult of the Sun at Rhodes, see *OCD* s.v. 'Rhodes, Cults and Legends'. The three 'founding fathers' are eponyms of the three chief cities of the island. For the connection with Colchis, see 3. 48 n. above.

55 *several Vulcans*: the usual tradition, descending from Homer, *Iliad* 1. 577 ff., is the third listed here, that he was the son of Jupiter and Juno. There was a conflation between Hephaestus' role in the Lemnos smithy with the volcanic activity in the Liparaean islands off Sicily, here called, as in Livy (21.51. 3), the Volcanian Islands; Maemalius is not otherwise known. For Hephaestus as Opas or Phthas, see Herodotus 3. 37. 2.

56 *Mercury*: the Roman god of trade inherited the functions of the
Greek Hermes, including that of guide of souls to Hades; his role
as lover of Proserpina, goddess of the dead, is found in Propertius,
2. 2. 11, and the identification with Trophonius mirrors this
aspect. Hermes was credited with introducing civilized life into
Egypt (Plato, *Phaedrus* 274c ff.), and this story of the flight from
Pheneus in Arcadia after slaying Argus may connect him with
the Egyptian goddess Isis, for Argus had persecuted Io, the *alter
ego* of Isis. For Theuth as the first Egyptian month, see Plutarch,
Isis and Osiris 378b.

57 *Aesculapius*: cf. 2. 62 n. The three figures cited here are local variants of Asclepius as worshipped in Arcadia. For Apollo and Cor-
onis as his parents, see Pindar, *Pyth*. 3. 8 ff., recounting how he
was struck down by Zeus for raising a dead man to life. For his
prominence in other regions of Greece, see. Guthrie, *The Greeks
and their Gods*, ch. 9. His burial-place, here given as Cynosura
near Sparta, or alternatively by the river Lusius in Arcadia
(where there was a temple to him; see Pausanias 5. 7), is elsewhere said to be Epidaurus.

the various Apollos: though in later times Apollo's worship was
centred at Delphi, the god was in origin an immigrant, perhaps
from the Hyperboreans ('the people of the far north') or alternatively from Lycia in Asia Minor; see Guthrie, *The Greeks and their
Gods*, 73 ff. The tradition that he was worshipped in Arcadia as
Nomio (personification of law) can be related more generally to
his role as law-giver; Guthrie, ch. 7.

58 *several Dianas*: for a broader survey of the presences of the goddess
in her Greek guise as Artemis, see Guthrie (as above), 99 ff. For
the obscure tradition that she was the mother of Eros/Cupid, see
Pausanias 9. 27. The 'more familiar' version, that she was the
daughter of Jupiter and Latona and twin of Apollo, stems from
Homer, Hesiod, and the Homeric Hymn to Apollo. The tradition
of descent from Upis and Glauce is obscure.

a host of gods called Dionysus: see Guthrie, ch. 6 for his widespread
cult. The connection made with Egypt recalls Herodotus' view
(2. 49) that his worship was introduced into Greece from there.
Nysa may be one of the Ocean nymphs charged with his rearing.
More popular is the view that the cult came from Thrace–Phry-
gia, as Euripides, *Bacchae* suggests; for the god's identification
with Thraco–Phrygian Sabazius, see Dodds, *The Greeks and the*

Irrational, 194. For the connection with the Cabiri, see *OCD* s.v. Cabiri. The 'triennial festival' was one held at Thebes when Dionysus returned from his two-year sojourn in Hades; according to Hyginus (167, 131) Nysus was the god's foster-father at Thebes. It is remarkable that Cotta does not mention the canonical story (from Hesiod, *Theog.* 940 ff.) that his parents were Zeus and Semele.

59 *Venus*: the first three Venuses cited here are variants of the cult of Aphrodite in Greece. The story that she was sprung from the foam (*aphros* in Greek) becomes widespread after Hesiod, *Theog.* 188 ff. For her temple at Elis, see Pausanias 6. 25. Homer (*Il.* 5. 312, 370 f.) makes her the daughter of Zeus and Dione. There were shrines to Anteros (possibly 'Rival in Love', indicating his conception outside marriage) at Athens and Elis (Pausanias 1. 30, 6. 23). Astarte was the Semitic goddess of sexual passion, fiercely condemned at 2 Kings 23; she was associated with Adonis (also originally Semitic), first in Phoenicia, and later as Aphrodite in Cyprus.

Minervas: for Minerva/Athena as mother of Apollo, see § 55; as daughter of Jupiter, § 53. For the connection with Sais in Egypt, see Plato, *Timaeus* 21e; Plutarch, *Isis and Osiris* 354c, identifies her with Isis. The cult-title Kore (here Koria) means 'maiden-goddess'; for this and her regular title Pallas, see Guthrie, *The Greeks and their Gods*, 108. The story of her murdering her father Pallas appears also in the Christian writer Firmicus Maternus, *De errore profanarum religionum*, 16. She is invested with 'winged anklets' through her role in war, in which she is equated with winged Victory (cf. Euripides, *Ion* 1529).

60 *Cupid*: the suggested parentage of Cupid/Eros varies much more widely than this passage indicates; see Kleine Pauly, s.v. *Eros*. He is identified with Anteros in Plato, *Protagoras* 255d.

to the point from which this digression led us: the digression begins at 3. 39, illustrating the illogicalities inherent in the Stoic theology.

61 *Mind, Faith*, etc.: 2. 61 n. Cotta here envisages Fortuna not in her ancient Italian role as the bringer of fertility, but as the Greek Tyche, goddess of chance or luck, to whom shrines and altars abounded in Hellenistic Greece. See Dodds, *The Greeks and the Irrational*, 242, 259.

62 *rationalizing fables…pursuing…etymologies*: this section is a riposte to the claims of Balbus at 2. 63 ff.; see 2. 64 n.

Veiovis, or…Vulcan: no satisfactory derivation has been proposed for these. Veiovis/Vediovis is an ancient Italian deity who has three festivals in the Roman calendar on 1 January, 7 March, and 21 May. See Warde-Fowler, *Roman Festivals*, 121 ff.

63 *Zeno…Cleanthes…Chrysippus*: 1. 36, 37, 39 nn.

a shrine to Fever, and…one to Bereavement…an altar…to Ill-fortune: Valerius Maximus 2. 5. 6 records that there were three shrines to Fever at Rome, containing remedial objects which had been attached to invalids. Arnobius (4. 7) makes Orbona ('Bereavement') the patroness of parents whose children had died. Cicero (*Leg.* 2. 28) states as here that there was an altar to Mala Fortuna on the Esquiline.

64 *Neptune…Ceres*: see 2. 71.

65 Cotta's argumentation which seeks to refute Balbus' claim that the universe is governed by divine intelligence has been almost entirely lost. The first two brief citations here ('Such arguments . . .', and 'We cannot be induced . . .') are quotations from the treatise made by Lactantius, *Div. Inst.* 2. 3. 2, and Arnobius, *Adv. Nat.* 3. 6, respectively. The headings which follow indicate the topics taken up by Cotta in response to Balbus' arguments; Lactantius in his *Divine Institutes* Book 2 reviews them.

First of all, then: this paragraph is also derived from a citation by Lactantius, *Div. Inst.* 2. 9. 14.

and that snakes are begotten, etc.: this fragment of the treatise is cited by the Verona scholiast on Virgil, *Aen.* 5. 95. It is speculatively inserted here to support the argument that Providence did not create snakes, since they were formed naturally from human bodies. Plutarch, *Cleomenes* 39, reports that as the corpse of Cleomenes (king of Sparta 235–219 BC) hung on a gibbet, a snake wound itself round it, whereupon 'learned men' explained that snakes were begotten from the juices of the human marrow.

…why, if God has made all things, etc.: the following two paragraphs are citations of lost sections of the dialogue made by Lactantius in his *De ira Dei* 13. 9–12, 20–1.

Men are superior to all animals: this fragment has been preserved by the grammarian Diomedes (Keil, *Grammatici Latini*, i. 313. 10).

This shall not be, etc.: at this point, where the manuscripts of the treatise resume, Cotta is arguing that the gods' gift of reason to men does not prove their benevolence, for reason can bring disaster in its train. He exploits the tragedy of Medea to make the point. Euripides' famous play had been translated closely by Ennius, whose version Cicero quotes here. The passages (Euripides, *Medea* 365 ff.; Ennius, *Tragedies* 274 ff. Warmington) record Medea's satisfaction at having wrung from the tyrant Creon a day's grace before being harried into exile; she plans to use the delay to bring down her ex-husband Jason, his new bride, and Creon himself, the girl's father.

67 *Just as her sire*, etc.: this refers to an earlier episode in the Medea saga, not covered in the play of Euripides. In one version of this earlier episode (see Cicero, *Pro lege Manilia* 22), she fled with Jason and the golden fleece from Colchis, and when pursued by her father Aeetes, she slew her brother Apsyrtus and scattered his limbs in order to delay the pursuit. The quotation here is probably from the *Medea* of Accius (on which, see 2. 89 n.).

68 *that notorious figure*: this is Atreus. When his brother Thyestes seduced his wife Aerope and caused Atreus unwittingly to slay his own son Pleisthenes, Atreus planned spectacular vengeance by serving up to Thyestes the bodies of his sons in an Irish stew. The citations are from the play *Atreus* by Accius (frs. 169 ff. Warmington).

69 *it is better not to serve wine to the sick*: in Theophrastus, *Characters* 13, the presumptuous man is guilty of this misdemeanour.

70 *Deianira did not intend to harm Hercules*: when the Centaur Nessus tried to rape Deianira, her husband Hercules slew him with a poisoned arrow. Nessus on his death-bed gave Deianira some of his blood, pretending that it was a love-charm; when later she sought to regain the affections of Hercules, she presented him with a shirt dipped in the poisoned blood. This tragic sequence was the theme of Sophocles' *Trachiniae*, and was later recounted by Ovid, *Met.* 9. 101 ff.

lanced the abscess of Jason of Pherae: this is not the mythological Jason who journeyed for the golden fleece, but the tyrant of Pherae (*c.*385–370 BC). According to Pliny, *NH* 7. 51, he sustained the wound in battle; an alternative tradition (Seneca, *Benef.* 2. 18. 8) has it that it was an assassination attempt.

72 *the young fellow in* Eunuch: Terence's play opens with Phaedria expressing resentment at being excluded by the courtesan Thais.

the boy in The Youthful Comrades: for the play and the citations of Caecilius, see 1. 13 n. and Warmington i. 536 ff.

73 *Phormio*: in Terence's play of that name, Phormio (line 32) decides to confront old Demipho on behalf of the old man's son Antipho, with his arguments rehearsed.

74 *who set fire to the record-office*: such arson became a popular pursuit in first-century Rome; cf. Cicero's *Pro Archia* 8; *Pro Rabirio* 8; *Pro Milone* 73. Since the dramatic date of this treatise is 76 BC, only the first of these can be the occasion referred to here, and since the fire mentioned in the *Pro Archia* was in the course of the Social War, the identification is by no means certain, for Cotta implies that the arson which he mentions was the result of private enterprise rather than an incident in war. Sosius is not otherwise known.

forged the public accounts: it is not clear if this case is connected with the burning of the record-office. It has been suggested that Alenus is the *cognomen* of Sosius, but this is uncertain. There were six senior secretaries (*scribae quaestorii*) employed at the treasury.

the gold from Toulouse: in the course of the war against the Numidian rebel Jugurtha, Roman forces were operating also against the Cimbri in Gaul, where Tolosa (Toulouse), recently compelled to pay tribute, joined the resistance against Rome. The consul of 106 BC, Servilius Caepio, plundered the temples of that city of their gold; he was later indicted and went in exile to Smyrna.

the trial of Tubulus: for this notorious briber of juries, praetor in 142 BC, see 1. 74 n. and *CAH* ix², 521.

Peducaeus: In 113 Sextus Peducaeus, tribune of the people, carried through a bill to try three Vestal Virgins who were accused of unchastity; all were condemned. See *CAH* ix², 747.

the current cases: the dramatic date of the treatise (76 BC) follows shortly upon the reorganization of the courts by Sulla. The nine permanent courts handled cases of assassination, poisoning, peculation or misappropriation of public moneys, and forgery of wills, this last being administered by a new court.

that familiar indictment: for indictment on charges of aiding and abetting, see the *Digest*, 47. 2.

the law of Plaetorius: this law, to which Cicero again adverts in *De officiis* 3. 61, may have been passed about 200 BC to protect minors against the rapacity of money-lenders.

Gaius Aquillius: he was praetor with Cicero in 66 BC, and a celebrated jurist. If he put through this *actio doli* at that time (see *CAH* ix², 562), it would be anachronistic in a discussion of 76 BC. Cicero mentions it again in *De officiis* 3. 60 f.

75 *the old woman on the stage*: Cotta here cites the opening lines of the *Medea* of Euripides in the translation of Ennius; see Warmington, i. 312. The old woman is the nurse, who laments the building of the first ship, made from the trees of Mt. Pelion in Thessaly, which bore Jason on his expedition for the golden fleece, and led to his liaison with Medea.

76 *But you repeatedly insist*, etc.: Cotta repeats the repetition; see 3. 70.

the Sun when he let his son Phaethon go aloft: Phaethon was allowed to drive the chariot of the Sun for a single day, with disastrous results for the earth and for himself; see Ovid, *Met.* 2. 31 ff.

Neptune ... Theseus ... Hippolytus: Poseidon/Neptune had granted Theseus three wishes. He used one of them when the king's wife Phaedra falsely accused her stepson Hippolytus of attempted rape; Theseus sought his death, and he was killed when Poseidon prompted a sea-bull to cause Hippolytus's chariot-horses to panic. Euripides, *Hippolytus* and Ovid, *Metamorphoses* 15. 497 ff. recount the story; this incident and the Phaethon-myth are similarly combined by Cicero at *De officiis* 3. 94.

77 *Aristo of Chios*: cf. 1. 37 n.

Aristippus: it is not clear whether Cicero distinguished between Aristippus, the friend of Socrates, and the grandson of the same name, usually regarded as the founder of the Cyrenaic school which preached pleasure as the immediate end of all action. Cotta here suggests that some pupils interpreted the Cyrenaic doctrine too crudely. See in general Long, *Hellenistic Philosophy*, 8; more technically, Rist, *Epicurus*, 43.

the school of Zeno: this is the Stoic Zeno (3. 36 n.). Since the Stoics preached that no one can deprive a man of the sole good which

is virtue, he is therefore always happy, and Stoics should therefore not have 'bitter tongues'.

79 *yet no one gains wisdom*: for Zeno, the founder of Stoicism, the acquisition of virtue depended on training the reason to think cor-
rectly; wisdom, defined as knowledge of good and evil, became
synonymous with virtue. But the attainment of it was an unat-
tainable ideal in the eyes of the Stoic Chrysippus, except for
such Stoic patron saints as Hercules and Socrates. See Sandbach,
The Stoics, 44 ff.

Telamon: in the drama of Ennius, *Telamon* (Warmington, i.
337 ff.), the hero laments the death of his son Ajax in these and
the immediately preceding words ('I have always said, and will
say, that the race of gods exists in heaven, but I believe that they
do not concern themselves with the activities of men'). This
view reflects the doctrine of the Epicureans. The complaint that
good men suffer, and that evil men prosper, is a theme which pre-
occupies Augustine in the *City of God*, 20. 2, and Boethius in *The
Consolation of Philosophy*, 4. 6.

80 *the two Scipios . . . Fabius Maximus . . . Marcellus . . . Aemilius Paulus
. . . Regulus . . . Africanus*: Cotta takes these first examples of the
apparent indifference of the gods to the sufferings of good men
from the history of the Punic Wars. The two Scipios, father and
uncle of the great Africanus, were killed in 211 in Spain (Livy
25. 32 ff.). Fabius Maximus Cunctator in old age delivered the
funeral oration over his son, who was consul in 213 (Cicero, *Sen.*
12). Claudius Marcellus was killed at Venusia in 208 through
his own impetuosity (Livy 27. 27), and Aemilius Paulus was
killed at Cannae in 216 (Livy 22. 49). Atilius Regulus, defeated
by Xanthippus in the First Punic War, was later canonized by
the dubious tradition that he was tortured after voluntarily
returning to Carthaginian captivity (cf. Horace, *Odes* 3. 5). The
Africanus referred to by Cicero here is Scipio Aemilianus; on his
death, see 2. 14 n.

Rutilius . . . Drusus . . . Scaevola . . . Cinna . . . Marius . . . Catulus: Rutilius Rufus, while serving as legate in Asia in 94–93, incurred the
hostility of the equestrian tax–collectors, and on returning to
Rome was convicted by an equestrian jury on a trumped-up
charge of extortion. His nephew Drusus as plebeian tribune in
91 BC was assassinated after putting through radical proposals
aimed at diminishing the political influence of the equestrians,

and the enfranchising of the Italians. Scaevola (consul in 95, *pontifex maximus* in 89) was killed by the pro-Marian city praetor Brutus Damasippus in 82, when on the point of joining Sulla. Contrary to the hostile reports of Cicero here and elsewhere, Cinna (consul in successive years 87–84 BC) was a political moderate who as ally of Marius sought to restrain his excesses, and who after Marius's death sought to negotiate with Sulla. Marius and Catulus, earlier allies, became bitter enemies; Catulus committed suicide when impeached by Marius. For thumbnail sketches of all these individuals, see E. Badian's entries in *OCD*. These political judgements are not necessarily Cicero's, but contribute to his characterization of Cotta.

81 *Marius ... seven consulships*: Marius was consul in 107, then in successive years between 104 and 100, and finally in 86 with Cinna.

Cinna ... the king for so long: after being driven out of Rome and deposed from the consulship in 87, Cinna marched on the capital and captured it later that year. He then held the consulship for three further years (86–84), dominating the political scene until killed in a mutiny in 84 at Brundisium (Appian, *Bell. Civ.* 1. 78).

Varius: Varius Hybrida, plebeian tribune in 90, put through a law *de maiestate*, which punished those who had fomented the Social War. His role as murderer of Drusus and Metellus is not recorded elsewhere. Cotta waxes bitter against him because he himself was exiled as a result of the law. Cicero elsewhere (*Brutus* 305) states that Varius was later exiled under his own law, but without detail of his death.

81–2 *Dionysius ... Pisistratus*: Cotta cites the long dominion of Dionysius I, tyrant of Syracuse 405–367, and of Pisistratus, tyrant of Athens 561–527, as further proofs of the divine indifference to human welfare.

82 *Phalaris and Apollodorus*: the two are cited together for their cruelty by Polybius 7. 7. 2, and Seneca, *De ira* 2. 5. 1. Phalaris was tyrant of Agrigentum in Sicily, *c*.565–*c*.549. The notoriety which he won for roasting his victims alive in a brazen bull became proverbial as early as Pindar (*Pyth.* 1. 95 ff.). For his horrific fate, see Ovid, *Ibis* 439 f. Apollodorus's reign of terror in Cassandreia (earlier Potidaea) lasted from 279 to 276, when he was expelled by an agent of Antigonus Gonatas, who probably executed him (see Polyaenus, 4. 6. 18).

Anaxarchus: this philosopher from Abdera in Thrace accompanied Alexander on his expedition, but later fell into the hands of his enemy Nicocreon, king of Salamis in Cyprus. For his brutal death, see Diogenes Laertius, 9. 10. 58.

Zeno of Elea: this is the celebrated disciple of Parmenides; see Kirk–Raven–Schofield, ch. 11. His courageous death under torture is widely but variously reported; see Cicero, *Tusc.* 2. 52 with Dougan's n.

Socrates . . . Plato's account: see Plato's *Apology*, *Crito*, and *Phaedo*.

83　*Diogenes*: the founder of the Cynics (*c*.400–*c*.325 BC) is chiefly known for his aggressive stance on ethics (see the *OCD*) rather than for scepticism about the gods, and one wonders if there is confusion here as elsewhere (see 3. 89 n.) with Diagoras. If Cicero did indeed mean Diogenes, it is possible that he has confused Harpalus, the notorious Macedonian noble and friend of Alexander, with Scirpalus, the brigand who captured and sold Diogenes according to Diogenes Laertius (6. 74).

Dionysius: see 3. 81–2 n. The connection made with the temple of Proserpina at Locri may be a lapse of memory on Cicero's part, since Locri was the king's faithful ally; moreover, when Livy records the sacrilegious looting of Locri by Pleminius in the Second Punic War (29. 18), the earlier pillage by Pyrrhus is recalled, but no such brigandage by Dionysius. On the other hand Dionysius is known to have plundered the shrine at Croton, his conspicuous enemy; see J. G. Bury, *History of Greece*[3] (London, 1951), 659, 663. The visit by Dionysius to the Peloponnese is not elsewhere attested; here too Cicero may have erred, confusing the temple of Zeus at Olympia with one of the temples of Olympian Zeus at Syracuse, a more probable location for Carthaginian spoils left by Gelon. Likewise when Cotta speaks of the statue of Aesculapius at Epidaurus, he may have confused it with a statue of Epidaurian Aesculapius (distinguishable from other Aesculapii by the beard and enfolding snake) set in a Sicilian location. Apollo, the father of Aesculapius, is regularly depicted as beardless (see 1. 83 above).

the tyrant Gelon: after gaining power at Gela in Sicily, he seized Syracuse in 485, and made it the greatest Hellenic power of the age. He defeated the Carthaginians at the battle of Himera in 480.

84 *He died in his own bed*, etc.: the reports suggest that he died following celebrations at the successful mounting of his tragedy at Athens (Diodorus 15. 4; Pliny, *NH* 7. 53). Doctors finally administered poison (Nepos, *Dion*. 2; Plutarch, *Dion*. 6). Diodorus further records the magnificence of the funeral. He was succeeded by his son Dionysius II, whom Plato unsuccessfully sought to turn into a philosopher-king.

86 *But the gods ignore trivialities*: This takes up Balbus' claim at 2. 167.

Publius Rutilius: see § 80.

88 *a tithe to Hercules*: his cult was popular with merchants, who frequently made an offering of a tenth of the profits of an enterprise (see e.g. Plautus, *Bacchides* 663 f.). As the patron-saint of Stoics, he was the wise man to venerate.

Pythagoras: the story that on discovery of the theorem that bears his name he sacrificed an ox appears in the Neoplatonist Proclus; see Kirk–Raven–Schofield, ch. 7 *ad fin*. For his refusal to slay a victim to Apollo, a vegetarian god, see Diogenes Laertius 8. 13.

89 *Diagoras . . . the Atheist*: see 1. 2. The anecdote that follows is told of Diogenes, not Diagoras, in Diogenes Laertius 6. 59. Samothrace, as the seat of the mysteries of the Cabiri (who were frequently invoked by those in peril at sea), housed many such tablets.

90 *What limit*, etc.: these lines are from a lost play by Accius, perhaps the *Atreus* or the *Oenomaus*; see Warmington, ii. 570. Oenomaus, king of Pisa in Elis, specified that the successful suitor for the hand of his daughter Hippodamia must best him in a chariot-race; supported by Myrtilus his charioteer, he speared any competitor threatening to overtake him. Pelops, son of Tantalus and father of Atreus and Thyestes, suborned Myrtilus with the promise of half his kingdom, and duly won Hippodamia, but then drowned Myrtilus to avoid having to reward him. Myrtilus cursed Pelops and his descendants, and the violent deaths ensued. See Sophocles, *Electra* 504 ff.; Euripides, *Orestes* 982 ff.

91 *Hipponax . . . Archilochus*: Hipponax of Ephesus (*fl.* 540–37) invented the scazon or limping iambic as a vehicle for his bitter satire. Archilochus of Paros (probably mid-seventh century) was famed as the innovator of the iambic, exploited for attacks on contemporaries; see Horace, *Ars Poetica* 79.

Critolaus . . . Hasdrubal: the two are combined because their cities, Corinth and Carthage, were destroyed by Rome in the same year 146 BC. Critolaus was *strategos* of the Achaean League in 147; he raised the standard against the Romans, and the destruction of Corinth by Mummius followed. Hasdrubal was the Carthaginian commander in the Third Punic War, as a result of which Carthage was destroyed.

92 *not on . . . superstition . . . but on scientific and rational grounds*: see 2. 63 f.

divine Providence, you say . . .: see 2. 75.

93 *Providence does not concern herself with individuals*: but Balbus at 2. 164 f. states the opposite. But it is true that he goes on to say (2. 167) that the gods disregard minor issues.

dreams are distributed . . . to men: for the Stoic claim, see 2. 166 and Cicero, *De divinatione* 1. 39 ff.

bind ourselves with vows: vows were a characteristic feature of the bargaining nature of Roman religion ('If you, Jupiter, grant me this, I promise you that . . .'). Stoics sought to accommodate this to their philosophy; see Seneca, *QNat.* 2. 37.

the multitude of deities: as Balbus explains in 2. 59–71, the various divinities are the manifestations of the Stoic Pronoia in their various spheres. Throughout this treatise there is a characteristic ambivalence between this Stoic view of Roman gods considered as symbols of Pronoia, and the Platonist notion of gods as subordinates created by the Demiurge (see Plato's *Timaeus* 41a, *Symposium* 202e).

95 *a semblance of the truth*: though Cicero carefully phrases his response, so as to remain consistent with his stance as Academic, it is clear that he is attracted temperamentally to the Stoic position, which seeks a reconciliation with the religion of the state and accordingly lends justification to his patriotic traditionalism.

Index and Glossary of Names

(References to the text are by Book and Section numbers)

Abelard, Peter (1079–1142), Christian philosopher, Introd. IX

Absyrtus, brother of the magician Medea, 3. 48

Academica, Cicero's treatise on epistemology, Introd. VIII; 1. 11

Academy/Academics, school of philosophy established by Plato, and surviving till closed by Justinian in 529 AD, Introd. VII; 1. 1 and *passim*

Acantho, Rhodian mother of the Sun, 3. 54

Accius, L., Latin tragedian who composed free versions of the plays of Aeschylus, Sophocles, Euripides, and others
    Medea, 2. 89; uncertain play, 3. 41

Acheron, river in Epirus reputed to flow into Hades, 3. 43

Achilles, hero of Homer's *Iliad*, 2. 166

Adonis, handsome Cypriot youth beloved by Aphrodite, married to Astarte, 3. 59

Aeetes, magician and daughter of the Sun, 3. 48, 54

Aegialeus, alternative name of Absyrtus, 3. 48

Aegisthus, adulterous murderer of Agamemnon, 3. 91

Aemilius Paulus L. (consul 219, 216), killed at Cannae, 3. 86

Aemilius Paulus Macedonicus, L. (consul 182, 168), victor over Perseus in Third Macedonian War, 2. 6, 165

Aemilius Scaurus, M. (consul 115), restorer of temples, 2. 61

Aesculapius, Latinized form of Greek god of healing Asclepius, deified through services as human, 2. 62; 3. 39; sundry origins of, 3. 57;

mistaken for benefactor, 3. 91; statue at Epidaurus, 3. 83

Aetna, volcanic mountain in Sicily, 2. 96

Africa, 2. 165; 3. 24

Africanus *see* Cornelius

Agamemnon, king of Mycenae and Homeric hero, 2. 166

Agricola, Rudolf, humanist, Introd. IX

Alabanda, opulent city of Caria in Asia Minor, 3. 39, 50

Alabandus, eponymous hero of Alabanda, 3. 39, 50

Albertus Magnus (c.1200–1280), Dominican philosopher, Introd. IX

Albucius, T. (praetor c.105), Epicurean philosopher at Athens after condemnation for extortion in Sardinia, 1. 93

Alcaeus (b. c.620), lyric poet of Mytilene fond of boys, 1. 79

Alcamenes, fifth-century Greek sculptor, 1. 83

Alcmaeon of Croton, late sixth-century Pythagorean and physician, deifies stars, 1. 27

Alcmena, wife of Amphitryon and mother of Heracles by Zeus, 3. 42

Alco, son of Atreus, named as one of the Dioscuri, 3. 53

Alenus, L., forger of Roman public accounts, 3. 74

Alexander the Great, Introd. VII

Altar (Ara), constellation, 2. 114; 3. 40

Ambrose of Milan (c.339–397), leading Christian apologist, Introd. IX

Amphiaraus of Argos, husband of Eriphyle; having attacked Thebes, he was swallowed up by the ground, and became an oracle, 2. 7; 3. 49

Anaxagoras of Clazomenae (c.500–428),

first philosopher to practise at Athens; his doctrine of Mind (Nous), 1. 26

Anaxarchus of Abdera, fourth-century atomist philosopher and teacher of Pyrrho; executed by Nicocreon of Cyprus, 3. 82

Anaximander of Miletus (*c.*610–540), Ionian scientist positing the *apeiron* as first principle, 1. 25

Anaximenes of Miletus (*fl. c.*550), Ionian scientist positing air as first principle, 1. 26

Andromeda, constellation named after the daughter of Cepheus rescued by Perseus, 2. 111 f.

Anemo *fl.*, tributary of Tiber (?corruption of Almo), 3. 52

Anteros, divine son of Mars, 3. 59 f.

Antiochus of Ascalon (*c.*130–*c.*68), President of the Fifth Academy and friend of Cicero, Introd. I, II, VII; 1. 76

Antiope, mother of the Pierian Muses, 3. 54

Antisthenes of Athens (*c.*445–*c.*360), founder of the Cynics: *Physicus*, 1. 32

Aode, a Muse, 3. 54

Apis, Egyptian deity worshipped in the form of a bull, 1. 82

Apollo, Greek god of music, prophecy, medicine, cattle, archery, 1. 81, 83; 2. 68; 3. 42, 50, 55, 57, 59, 88, 91; plurality of Apollos, 3. 57

Apollodorus of Cassandreia (d. 276), cruel tyrant, 3. 82

Apollodorus, Stoic philosopher contemporary with Zeno of Sidon, 1. 93

Aquarius (constellation), 2. 112

Aquilius, M'. (consul 129), 2. 14

Aquillius Gallus, C. (praetor 66), Roman jurist, 3. 74

Aquinas, Thomas (1225–1274), Dominican philosopher and theologian, Introd. IX

Aratus of Soli (*c.*315–240), author of astronomical poem *Phaenomena*, Introd. I, IV; 2. 104 ff.

Arcadia/Arcadians, Greek provenance

of Jupiter and of Aesculapius, 3. 53, 57; worship Minerva as Koria, 3. 59

Arcesilaus of Pitane (316–242), founder of the Second Academy, Introd. IV, VII; 1. 11, 70

Arche, a Muse, 3. 54

Archilochus of Paros, seventh-century iambic and elegiac poet, 1. 107; 3. 91

Archimedes of Syracuse (*c.*287–212), mathematician and inventor, 2. 88

Arctophylax (constellation), 2. 109 f.

Arcturus, brightest star in the constellation of Boötes, 2. 110

Ardea, ancient city and port of Latium, 3. 47

Areopagus, 'Hill of Ares' at Athens, on which the Council, originally charged with virtual government of the city, had a restricted judicial function, 2. 74

Argo, constellation called after Jason's ship which journeyed for the Golden Fleece, 2. 114; 3. 40

Argonauts, sailors on the Argo, 2. 89

Argos, famed city in the Greek Peloponnese, 1. 82

Argus, fabulous creature with a hundred eyes, sent by Hera to supervise Io and later killed by Hermes, 3. 56

Aristippus, philosopher-associate of Socrates, or his grandson a Cyrenaic, 3. 77

Aristo of Chios, friend and pupil of Zeno the Stoic, 1. 37; 3. 77

Aristotle of Stagira (384–322), founder of the Peripatetics, Introd. I, IV, VIII, IX; 1. 93, 107; 2. 42, 44, 94 ff., 125
  On Philosophy, 1. 33
  Protrepticus, Introd. II
  Nicomachean Ethics, Introd. II

Aristus, brother of Antiochus the Academic, Introd. I

Arnobius, African convert to Christianity (*c.*295 AD) and apologist, Introd. IX

Arpinum, birthplace of Cicero, Introd. I

Arsinoe, mother of Aesculapius, 3. 57

Arsippus, father of Aesculapius, 3. 57

Astarte, Semitic goddess equated with Venus, 3. 59

Asteria, Titan sister of Latona and
    mother of Phrygian Hercules, 3. 42
Athens/Athenians, Cicero at, Introd. 1;
    Cotta at, 1. 59, 79; Protagoras
    banished from, 1. 73; statue of Vulcan
    at, 1. 83; Epicurus avoids offence at,
    1. 85; ruled by Council of Areopagus,
    2. 74; temple of Eumenides at, 3. 46;
    shrine of Erechtheus at, 3. 49 f.;
    Apollo tutelary deity at, 3. 55; 57; also
    2. 154, 165
Atilius Caiatinus, A. (consul 258, 254 BC),
    dedicated a Roman temple, 2. 61, 165
Atilius Regulus, M., captured in First
    Punic War and later again consigned
    to Carthage, 3. 80
Atreus, son of Pelops and brother of
    Thyestes, 3. 53, 68, 71
Atticus, T. Pomponius, Epicurean friend
    and correspondent of Cicero, Introd.
    I, II, IV, VIII
Attus Navius, Roman augur in reign of
    Tarquinius Priscus, 2. 9; 3. 14
augurs/augury, Introd. III; 2. 7 ff., 163
Augustine of Thagaste (354–430),
    Christian apologist, Introd. II, IX
        City of God, Introd. III, IX
Aurelius Cotta, C. (consul 75),
    Academic spokesman in dialogue,
    Introd. VIII and *passim*
auspices, 2. 7 ff.

Bacon, Roger (*c.*1214–92), Franciscan
    philosopher, Introd. IX
Baker, Robert, annotator of first
    translation of *Nature of the Gods*, 1
Balbus *see* Lucilius
Bears (constellations), 2. 105; Great Bear
    (Ursa Major), 2. 107; Lesser Bear
    (Ursa Minor), 2. 111
Belus, Latinization of Phoenician deity
    Baal, worshipped in India, 3. 42
Bereavement (Orbona), goddess
    worshipped at Rome, 3. 63
Bibulus *see* Calpurnius
Bird (Avis), constellation, 2. 112
Boeotia, tax-farmers in, 3. 49
Bonaventure (1221–74), Franciscan
    theologian, Introd. IX

Bow (Arcus), constellation, 2. 113
Britain, tides at, 3. 24; also 2. 88
Brooks, Francis, translator of *Nature of
    the Gods*, 1
Brutus, M. Iunius (85–42), assassin of
    Julius Caesar and friend of Cicero, 1. 1
Brutus (oratorical treatise), Introd. 1
Bull (Taurus), constellation, 2. 110;
    3. 40

Cabirus, father of god Dionysus, 3. 58
Cadmus, legendary founder of Boeotian
    Thebes and father of Ino, 3. 48
Caecilius Metellus, L. (consul 251), hero
    of First Punic War, 2. 165
Caesilius Metellus Numidicus, Q.
    (consul 109), enemy of Marius,
    poisoned by Varius Hybrida, 3. 81
Caecilius Natalis, interlocutor in
    Octavius of Minucius Felix, Introd. IX
Caelus, Latinized name of Greek sky-
    god Ouranos, 2. 63; 3. 44, 53, 55, 56,
    59, 62
Caiatinus *see* Atilius
Calchas, celebrated Greek priest and
    prophet at Troy, 2. 7
Callias, host at the *Symposium* of
    Xenophon, Introd. VIII
Calpurnius Bibulus, M. (consul 59),
    blocks Caesar's legislation, Introd. III
Calpurnius Piso Caesoninus, L. (consul
    58), Introd. IV
Comirus, Rhodian son of Helios (the
    Sun), 3. 54
Cannae, site of Roman defeat in 216 by
    Hannibal, 3. 80
Capitol at Rome, 1. 106; 3. 111
Capra (constellation), 2. 110
Capricorn (constellation), 2. 112
Carbo *see* Papirius
Carneades of Cyrene (214–129), founder
    of the Third Academy, Introd. II, IV,
    VII, IX; counters Stoic arguments, 1. 4;
    2. 162; 3. 44; practises negative
    dialectic, 1. 11; proves all life mortal,
    3. 29
Carthage/Carthaginians, scene of
    torture of Regulus, 3. 80; destruction
    of, 3. 91; personification of, 3. 42

Cassiepia (constellation), 2. 111

Castor, one of Dioscuri, fought on
  Roman side at Lake Regillus, 2. 6;
  3. 11 f.; deified as benefactor, 2. 62;
  3. 13; son of Jupiter and Leda, 3. 53

Catilinarian conspiracy, Introd. 1

Cato *see* Porcius

Catulus *see* Lutatius

Centaur (constellation evoking fabulous
  creature half-man, half-horse), 2. 114

Centaurs, born from a cloud, 3. 51;
  bloody shirt of, 3. 70

Cepheus (constellation with name of
  father of Andromeda), 2. 111

Cerberus, three-headed dog guarding
  entrance to Hades, 3. 43

Cercei, promontory between Rome and
  Naples, 3. 48

Cercops of Miletus, sixth-century poet
  and Pythagorean, 1. 107

Ceres, ancient Italian corn-goddess
  identified with Greek deity Demeter,
  Introd. VI; etymology of, 2. 67; 3. 52,
  62; identified with the earth, 1. 40;
  2. 71; 3. 64; corn so called, 2. 60;
  3. 41;mother of Liber and Libera,
  2. 62

Chains (Vincla), constellation, 2. 114

Chalcis, main town of Euboea, 3. 24

Charioteer (Auriga), constellation, 2. 110

Charon, ferryman in Hades, 3. 43

Chimaera, fabulous triple-bodied
  monster (lion-goat-serpent), 1. 108;
  2. 5

Chrysippus (*c.*280–207), third President
  of Stoa, Introd. IV, VI; posits
  multiplicity of gods, 1. 39; referred to
  as Chrysippa, 1. 93; argues that
  universe is God, 2.16, and perfect,
  2. 37 f., 3. 18, 25 f.; explains
  symbolism of myths, 2. 63 f., 3. 63;
  justifies existence of pigs,
  2. 160;rejected as authority on
  religion, 3. 5

Cinna *see* Cornelius

Circe, divine magician of Aeaea, later of
  Cercei, 3. 48, 54

Claudius Marcellus, M. (five times
  consul from 222), restores temple,

2. 61; slain by Hannibal, 3. 80; also
  2. 165

Claudius Pulcher, P. (consul 249),
  disastrous treatment of chickens, 2. 7

Claws (Chelae), constellation, 2. 114

Cleanthes of Assos (331–232), second
  head of Stoa, Introd. IV, VI; posits
  plurality of gods, 1. 37; gives four
  reasons for belief in gods, 2. 13 f.,
  3. 16 f.; demonstrates heat in body,
  2. 24; states that stars are fire, 2. 40;
  explains symbolism of myths, 2. 63;
  3. 63; rejected as religious authority,
  3. 5; explains restricted course of sun,
  3. 37

  Against Pleasure, 1. 37

Cleomenes, king of Sparta (235–219),
  3. 65

Clitomachus of Carthage (187–110),
  pupil of Carneades and later head of
  Academy, Introd. VII

Cludius, H. H., author of spurious
  Nature of the Gods IV, 1

Cocytus, river of Hades, 3. 43

Codrus, legendary Athenian king, 3. 49

Coelius Antipater, L., historian of
  Second Punic War, 2. 8

Colchis, region at east end of Euxine
  Sea, site of Golden Fleece and home of
  Medea, 3. 54

Columbanus (550–615), Irish monk,
  founder of Luxeuil and Bobbio,
  Introd. IX

Concord (deity), 2. 61, 79; 3. 47

Consolatio of Cicero addressed to himself,
  Introd. II

Corinth, Greek city destroyed in 146 BC,
  3. 41

Cornelii Scipiones (consuls 222, 218),
  brothers killed in Spanish operations,
  3. 80

Cornelius Cinna, L. (consul throughout
  87–84), ally of Marius, 3. 80 f.

Cornelius Lentulus Lupus, L. (consul
  156), attacked by satirist Lucilius,
  1. 63

Cornelius Scipio Africanus, P. (236–
  183), hero of Second Punic War,
  Introd. II; 2. 165

Cornelius Scipio Africanus Aemilianus,
P. (185–129), destroyer of Carthage
and Numantia, Introd. 11; death
presaged, 2. 14; cherished by the gods,
2. 165; but neglected by them at
death, 3. 80

Cornelius Scipio Nasica Corculum, P.
(consul 162), 2. 10; authority on
religion, 3. 5

Corsica, spoils from, 3. 52

Coruncanius, Ti. (consul 280), first
plebeian *pontifex maximus* and religious
authority, 1. 115; 3. 5; prominent
general in war with Pyrrhus, 2. 165

Corybas, father of Cretan Apollo, 3. 57

Coryphe, daughter of Oceanus and
mother of Minerva, 3. 59

Cos, Aegean island, 3. 42

Cotta, *see* Aurelius

Crab (Cancer), constellation, 2. 110

Crassus *see* Licinius

Cratippus of Pergamum, Peripatetic
contemporary of Cicero, Introd. 1, 11

Crete, wild goats in, 2. 126; provenance
of Jupiter, 3. 53; of Apollo, 3. 57

Critolaus, *strategos* of the Achaean
League at the destruction of Corinth,
3. 91

Croton, southern Italian city, 2. 6

Crow (Corvus), constellation, 2. 114

Crown (Corona), constellation, 2. 108;
3. 40

Cupid, boy-god of love identified with
Eros, 3. 58; plurality of Cupids, 3. 59 f.

Curius Dentatus, M'. (consul four times
from 290), victor at Beneventum,
2. 165

Cynosura, town near Sparta, 3. 57

Cynosure ('Dog's Tail'), constellation,
2. 105 f.

Cyprus, home of Venus, 3. 59; of the
tyrant Nicocreon, 3. 82

Decii, father (consul 340), son (consul
four times from 312), grandson
(consul 279), all said to have devoted
their lives to win Roman victories in
the field, 3. 15

Deianira, wife of Hercules, whom she

unwittingly killed with Nessus' shirt,
3. 70

Delos, site of Apollo's shrine which
Pythagoras refused to defile, 3. 88

Delphi, visited from Hyperboreans by
Apollo, 3. 57

Demeter, Greek goddess of corn, 2. 67

Democritus of Abdera (*c.*460–360),
atomist philosopher inspiring
Epicurus; his theory of images, 1. 29,
107; of atoms and void, 1. 66, 69;
teacher of Nausiphanes, 1. 73; of
Anaxarchus, 3. 82; belittled by
Epicurus, 1. 93; confused views on
gods, 1. 120

Desire (Cupido) as deity, 2. 61

Diagoras of Melos (late fifth century),
lyric poet branded as atheist, 1. 2, 63,
117; anecdotes about him, 3. 89

Diana, Italian goddess identified with
Greek Artemis; identified with moon,
2. 68; 3. 51; 'Light-bearer' and
'Universal Wanderer', 2. 68;
etymology, 2. 69; plurality of Dianas,
3. 58; mother of Cupid, 3. 60

Dicaearchus of Messana (late fourth
century), Peripatetic philosopher,
Introd. 1

Diderot, Denis (1713–84), French
encyclopaedist, Introd. ix

Dies (Day), deity and mother of Caelus,
3. 44; mother of Mercury, 3. 56;
mother of Venus. 3. 59

Digiti of Mt Ida, said to be the first
sages, 3. 62

Diodotus, Stoic resident in Cicero's
house, Introd. 1; 1. 6

Diogenes of Apollonia (*fl.* 440–430),
eclectic philosopher; 'makes air a
god', 1. 29

Diogenes of Babylon (*c.*240–152), Stoic
pupil of Chrysippus, later head of the
Stoa and teacher of Panaetius:
  On Minerva, 1. 41

Diogenes of Sinope (*c.*400–325), founder
of Cynic school, 3. 83, 88

Diogenes Laertius (third century AD),
author of compendium of
philosophers, Introd. v

Diomedes, Homeric hero, 2. 166

Dione, mother of Venus, 3. 59

Dionysius I, tyrant of Syracuse 405–367, 3. 81

Dionysus, god of ecstatic religion and wine, 3. 58; plurality of identities, 3. 58

Dioscuri, three different identities, 3. 53

Dis, deity of the earth, 2. 66; etymology, 2. 66

Dog-star (Canis), 2. 114; (Canicula), 3. 26

Dolphin (Delphinus), constellation, 2. 113

Drusus *see* Livius

Duillius, C. (consul 260), victor over Carthaginians at Mylae, 2. 165

Dyrrhachium, Introd. 1

Eagle (Aquila), constellation, 2. 113

Egypt/Egyptians, watered by the Nile, 2. 130; their deification of animals, 1. 43, 83 f., 101; 3. 39; the Egyptian Hercules, 3. 42; Egyptian Sun, lord of Heliopolis, 3. 54; Egyptian origin of Mercury, 3. 56; Egyptian Minerva 3. 59

Eleusis, town in Attica famed for mystery-religion, 1. 119

Elis, town in Greek Peloponnese with temple of Venus, 3. 59

Empedocles of Acragas (*c.*493–433), Presocratic philosopher and poet, positing the four elements as divine, 1. 29; contradicted by Epicurus, 1. 93

Engonasin ('On the Knees'), constellation, 2. 108

Ennius, Q., of Rudiae (239–169), Latin poet and dramatist; translated Euhemerus, 1. 119
 Annals, 2. 93
 Saturae, 1. 97
 Thyestes, 2. 4, 49, 65

Epicurus of Samos (341–270), founder of Epicurean sect, 1. 17 ff., 43 ff., 61; unlearned, 1. 71 f.: his atomist theory criticized, 1. 70; his theology criticized, 1. 71, 86 ff., 102 ff., 114 ff.; epistemology criticized, 1. 105 ff.;
 doctrine of pleasure criticized, 1. 113; draws on Democritus, 1. 120
 Letters to Herodotus and Menoeceus, Introd. vi
 Principal Doctrines (Kuriai Doxai), 1. 85
 Rule and Judgement, 1. 4, 43

Epidaurus, statue of Aesculapius at, 3. 83

Erechtheus, legendary king of Athens deified, 3. 49 f.

Esquiline, hill at Rome with altar to Ill-fortune, 3. 63

Etesian winds, capricious trade-winds bringing benefits, 2. 131

Etruscan soothsayers making true predictions, 2. 10 f.

Eubouleus, one of first set of Dioscuri, 3. 53

Euhemerus of Messene (*fl. c.*300), Cyrenaic who gave his name to the doctrine that gods were originally heroic mortals, 1. 119; cf. 3. 50

Eumenides ('Kindly Ones'), ancient goddesses originally earth-spirits, but from Aeschylus onward identified with Erinyes, subterranean deities of vengeance, 3. 46

Euphrates, massive river fertilizing Mesopotamia, 2. 130

Euripides (*c.*485–407), celebrated Greek tragedian, 2. 65

Euripus, channel between Attica and Euboea, 3. 24

Europa, Phoenician maiden carried off by Zeus in the form of a bull to Crete, 1. 78

Europe, 2. 160

Fabius Maximus Verrucosus, Q. (consul five times between 233 and 209), famed as 'Cunctator', in Second Punic War, 2. 61, 165; 3. 80

Fabricius Luscinus, C. (consul 278), outstanding leader in the war with Pyrrhus, 2. 165

Faith (Fides) as deity, 2. 61, 79; 3. 47, 61, 88

fauns, Italian rustic deities, 2. 6; 3. 15

Feriae Latinae (Latin Festival), Introd. VIII; 1. 15

Fever (Febris), deity, 3. 63

Figulus *see* Marcius

Fish (Pisces), constellation, 2. 111, 114

flamen Dialis (Priest of Jupiter), Introd. III

Flaminius, C. (consul 232, 217), fell at Trasimene in consequence of religious impiety, 2. 8

Fons ('Spring'), deified, 3. 52

Formiae, town in Latium, 3. 86

Fortune, Italian deity later conflated with Greek Tyche, goddess of chance, 3. 61

Francklin, Thomas, translator of *The Nature of the Gods*, l

Freedom (Libertas), deified, 2. 61

Furies, Latin equivalents of Erinyes, avenging spirits, 3. 46

Furina, Italian goddess (wrongly) identified with Furies, 3. 46

Ganymede, boy cup-bearer of Zeus, 1. 112

Gelon, tyrant of Gela and (from 485) of Syracuse, lord of all Sicily till death in 478, 3. 83

Giants, race of monstrous men who warred on Titans, 2. 70

Glauce, mother of Artemis/Diana, 3. 58

Gracchus *see* Sempronius

Great Year, 2. 51 f.

Grieving Man (constellation) *see* Engonasin

Guile (Dolus), deified, 3. 44

Hades, 3. 43

Hannibal, Carthaginian general in the Second Punic War, 3. 80

Hare (Lepus), constellation, 2. 114

Harmony (Concordia), deity, 3. 61

Harpalus, profligate treasurer of Alexander the Great, 3. 83

Hasdrubal, Carthaginian commander at fall of Carthage, 3. 91

Hecate, goddess of the underworld, 3. 46

heimarmene (fate), 1. 55

Helenus, son of Priam, Trojan prophet, 2. 7

Helike ('spiral'), constellation, 2. 105, 110

Heliopolis ('City of the Sun'), city north-west of Cairo, 3. 54

Heraclides of Pontus, temporary head of the Academy in Plato's absence (361–60), 1. 34

Heraclitus of Ephesus (*c*.500), who posited fire as the first principle, Introd. VI; obscure writer, 1. 74; 3. 35

Hercules, deified hero, 2. 62; 3. 39; plurality of identities, 3. 42; accidentally murdered by Deianira, 3. 70; recipient of tithes, 3. 83; also 3. 50

Hermarchus of Mytilene, successor of Epicurus as head of The Garden, 1. 93

Hesiod (*fl.* 700), epic poet: *Theogony*, 1. 36

Hesperus (Evening Star), 2. 53

Hestia, Greek goddess of the hearth identified with Vesta, 2. 67

Hiero I of Syracuse (d. 467–6), Sicilian tyrant whose court was thronged with literary figures, 1. 60

Hierocles, anti-Christian philosopher, Introd. IX

Hippocrates, physician contemporary with Sophocles, dubiously regarded as the father of medicine, 3. 91

Hipponax of Ephesus (*fl. c*.540), iambic poet notorious for fierce and colloquial abuse, 3. 91

Hippolytus, in mythology stepson of Phaedra; when her advances were rejected, she accused him to her husband Theseus of attempted rape. At Theseus' request Poseidon engineered his destruction, 3. 76

Hobbes, Thomas (1588–1679), English philosopher: *Leviathan*, Introd. IX

Homer, father of epic poetry, myths in, 1. 41; depiction of gods in, 2. 70; gods as guardians of heroes, 2. 166; burial of Dioscuri, 2. 11; also 1. 107 *Odyssey* (11. 600 ff.), 3. 42

Honour (Honos), deity, 2. 61; 3. 47, 61

Hope (Spes), deity, 3. 47, 61

Horse (Equus), constellation, 2. 11 ff.,
  114
Hortensius of Cicero, Introd. 11
Hortensius Hortalus, Q. (consul 69),
  Introd. 11
Hostilius Tubulus, L. (praetor 142),
  accepted bribes when judge, 1. 63;
  3. 74
Hume, David (1711–76), Scottish
  philosopher:
    Dialogues concerning Natural Religion,
    Introd. 1x
Hyades, constellation, 2. 111
Hydra, constellation, 2. 114
Hyperion, father of the Sun, 3. 54

Ialysus, son of the Rhodian Sun, 3. 54
Ida Mt., name of mountains near Troy
  and in Crete, 3. 42
Idyia, mother of Medea, 3. 48
Ill-fortune (Mala Fortuna), deity with
  altar on Esquiline, 3. 63
India, 3. 42
Indian Ocean, 1. 97
Indus *fl.*, 2. 130
Ino, wife of Cadmus, deified as
  Leucothea, 3. 39, 48
intermundia, Introd. v
Iris, divine personification of the
  rainbow, 3. 51
Isidore (*c.*560–636 AD), bishop of Seville:
    Etymologies, Introd. 1x
Isis, Egyptian goddess, 3. 47
isonomia (equilibrium), 1. 50, 109

Janus, deity of door and arch, and hence
  of beginnings, etymology of, 2. 67
Jason, tyrant of Pherae in Thessaly
  (385–370), 3. 70
Jerome (*c.*342–420), Christian apologist
  and biblical scholar, Introd. 1x
John of Salisbury, twelfth-century
  humanist, Introd. 1x
Jove, alternative title for Jupiter,
  etymology of, 2. 64
Jugurtha, 'conspiracy' of (112–105),
  Numidian insurrection, 3. 74
Julius Caesar, Introd. 1–11
Junius Pullus, L. (consul 249), his

disaster attributed to neglect of
  auspices, 2. 7
Juno, Roman goddess, allegorical
  interpretation of, 1. 36; 2. 66;
  recognizable in statuary, 1. 81, but
  differing in different places, 1. 82;
  mother of Vulcan, 3. 55; as Juno
  Lucina, goddess of childbirth, 2. 68
Jupiter, Introd. v1; allegorical
  interpretation of, 1. 36, 40; 2. 4, 65;
  3. 10 f., 40; father of Minerva, 1. 41;
  familiar depiction of, 1. 81, 83, 100,
  but Jupiter Ammon different, 1. 82;
  etymology of, 2. 64; plural identities,
  3. 42, 53 ff.; father of Apollo, 3. 57; of
  Diana, 3. 58; of Dionysus, 3. 58; of
  Venus, 3. 59; titles of, 3. 87; Olympian
  shrine of, 3. 83 f; also 3. 84
Jupiter, planet, 2. 52, 119
Juventas, female attendant on gods,
  Roman equivalent of Hebe, 1. 112

Kant, Immanuel (1724–1804), German
  philosopher, Introd. 1x
Kids (Haedi), constellation, 2. 110
Koria, Arcadian title of Minerva, 3. 55
Kronos, father of Zeus, Greek
  counterpart of Saturn, 3. 64
Kuriai Doxai, Introd. v

Lactantius, Christian apologist:
    Divine Institutes (303–313), Introd. 1x
Laelius, C. (consul 140), intimate of
  Scipio Aemilianus, Introd. 11; 2. 165
    Oration on religion, 3. 5, 43
Lares, Roman shrine of, 3. 63
Latona, Latin form of Leto, mother of
  Apollo, 3. 57; sister of Asteria, 3. 42
Leda, mother of Dioscuri; Zeus mated
  with her in form of a swan, 3. 53
Lefèvre, translator of *The Nature of the
  Gods*, Introd. 1x
Lemnos, Aegean island on which
  mystery-cult was practised, 1. 119;
  abode of Vulcan's smithy, 3. 55
Leo, constellation, 2. 110; 3. 40
Leocorion, shrine at Athens, 3. 50
Leontium, female adherent to
  Epicurean school, 1. 93

Leucippus, late fifth-century originator of atomist theory, 1. 66

Leucothea, name of Ino when transformed into a deity, 3. 39, 48

Liber, Italian god of fertility and of wine identified with Dionysus, 2. 60; distinguished from him, 2. 62; name used by metonymy for wine, 3. 41; one of the Dioscuri, 3. 53

Libera, Italian goddess of agriculture, 2. 62

Licinius Crassus, L. (consul 95), famed orator, Introd. VIII; 1. 58

Licinius Lucullus, L. (consul 74), Introd. II

Liguria, region of north-west Italy, 2. 61

Lindus, eponymous hero of ancient Rhodian city, 3. 54

Lion *see* Leo

Livius Drusus, M. (tribune 91), Introd. VIII; 3. 80 f.

Locke, John (1632–1704), English philosopher: *Essay concerning Human Understanding*, Introd. IX

Locris/Locrians, southern Italian city, 2. 6; 3. 11, 83

Love (Amor), deified, 3. 44

Lucifer (Morning Star), 2. 53; 3. 51

Lucilius, C. (d. 102–1), early Roman Satirist, 1. 63

Lucilius Balbus, Stoic interlocutor in dialogue, Introd. VIII and *passim*

Lucina *see* Juno

Lucretius Carus, T. (*c*.94–*c*.55), Epicurean author of *De rerum natura*, Introd. V

Lucullus *see* Licinius

Luna, mother of Dionysus, 3. 58

Lupus *see* Cornelius

Lusius *fl.*, river in Arcadia, 3. 57

Lutatius Catulus, Q. (consul 102), composer of light verse, 1. 79; driven to death by Marius, 3. 80

Lutatius Catulus, Q. (consul 78), son of the foregoing, 1. 79

Luxeuil, monastic foundation of Columbanus, Introd. IX

Lyceum, school of Peripatetics, 1. 72

Lyre (Fides), constellation, 2. 112

Lysithoe, mother of Hercules, 3. 42

Macedonia, Cicero in, Introd. 1

Maemalius, father of Vulcan, 3. 55

Magi, priests of the Medes, 1. 43

Maia, mother of Mercury, 3. 56

Manlius Torquatus, L. (praetor 50), Introd. II

Marcellus *see* Claudius

Marcius Figulus, C. (consul 162), 2. 10

Marius, C. (*c*.157–86), leader of Populares and foe of Sulla, 3. 80 f.

Mars, Italian god of war and agriculture, father of Anteros, 3. 59; etymology of Mavors, 2. 67; 3. 62

Mars, planet, 2. 53, 119

Maso *see* Papirius

Matuta, Mater, Italian goddess of growth identified with Greek Leucothea, 3. 48

Maximus *see* Fabius

McGregor, H. C. P., translator of *The Nature of the Gods*, 1

Medea of Colchis, mythological enchantress, 3. 48; exemplar of misuse of reason in killing her brother, 3. 67 f., 71

Melampus, one of third set of Dioscuri, 3. 53

Melete, one of first set of Muses, 3. 54

Mercury, planet, 2. 53

Mercury, plural identities of, 3. 56; father of Cupid, 3. 59

Mesopotamia, 2. 130

Metellus *see* Caecilius

Metrodorus of Lampsacus (331–278), leading Epicurean spokesman; clear expositor, 1. 86; critic of other philosophies, 1. 93; attacks his brother Timocrates, 1. 113

Mind (Mens) as deity, 2. 61, 79; 3. 47, 61, 88

Minerva, Italian goddess, counterpart of Athena, representations of, 1. 81, 83, 100; etymology of, 2. 67; 3. 62; daughter of Jupiter, 3. 53; mother of Athenian Apollo, 3. 55; plurality of identities, 3. 59

Minucius Felix (*fl.* 220 AD), Christian
apologist:
  Octavius, Introd. IX
Mitylene, Introd. I
Mnemosyne, mother of Muses, 3. 54
Money (Moneta) as deity, 3. 47
Montaigne, Michel de (1533–92),
  French philosopher, Introd. IX
Monte Cassino, Introd. IX
Montesquieu, French philosopher,
  Introd. IX
Mopsus, name of two prophets (here
  contaminated?), 2. 7
Mucius Scaevola, P. (consul 133),
  eminent religious authority, 1. 115; 3. 5
Mucius Scaevola, Q. (consul 95), the
  Pontifex, slain by Brutus Damasippus,
  3. 80
Musaeus, mythical singer related to
  Orpheus, 1. 41
Muses, plurality of identities, 3. 54;
  recipients of Pythagoras' sacrifice,
  3. 88
Myrtilus, charioteer of Oenomaus, 3. 90

Natio, goddess of childbirth, 3. 47
Nausiphanes, disciple of atomist
  Democritus, attacked by Epicurus,
  1. 73, 93
Neocles, father of Epicurus, 1. 72
Neptune, god of the sea, Introd. VI;
  3. 43, 52; symbolic meaning of, 1. 40;
  2. 66, 71; 3. 64; familiarity of
  portraiture, 1. 81, 83; etymology of,
  2. 66; bestows wishes on Theseus,
  3. 76; 'son of Neptune', 1. 63
Niccoli Niccolò, Introd. IX
Nile, *fl.*, fertilizes Egypt, 2. 130; father of
  Hercules, 3. 42; of Vulcan, 3. 54 f.; of
  Mercury, 3. 56; of Dionysus, 3. 58; of
  Minerva, 3. 59
Nodinus *fl.*, tributary of the Tiber, 3. 52
Nomio, Arcadian title of Apollo, 3. 57
Numa Pompilius, second king of Rome,
  1. 107; establishes Roman ritual, 3. 5,
  43
nymphs, 3. 43
Nysa, Ocean nymph(?), 3. 58
Nysus, father of Dionysus, 3. 58

Oceanus, deity of water, and son of Sky
  and Earth, 3. 48; father of Coryphe,
  3. 59
Octavius, M., fellow-tribune of Ti.
  Gracchus (133), 2. 106
Octavius Mamilius, Latin commander
  at Lake Regillus, 2. 6
Oeta, Mt., Thessalian site where
  Hercules was cremated, 3. 41
Olympia, site of the Olympic Games,
  2. 6; of temple of Zeus, 3. 83
Olympias, mother of Alexander the
  Great, 2. 69
Opas, Egyptian title for Vulcan, 3. 55
Orator of Cicero, Introd. I
Orbona *see* Bereavement
Orcus, god of Hades, 3. 43 f.
Orion, constellation, 2. 113; 3. 26
Orpheus, legendary Thracian singer,
  interpreted by Chrysippus, 1. 41;
  existence denied by Aristotle, 1. 107
Orphic rites, 3. 58
Owgan, H., translator of *The Nature of
  the Gods*, l

Pacuvius, M. (*c.*220–*c.*130), Latin
  tragedian, calls Medea's brother
  Aegialeus, 3. 48
  Chryses, 2. 91
Paetus *see* Papirius
Palaemon, deified son of Leucothea,
  3. 39
Palatine hill, 3. 63
Pallas, variant title of Athena/Minerva,
  3. 59
Pamphilus, disciple of Plato criticized by
  Epicurus, 1. 72 f.
Pan, Arcadian god, son of Hermes/
  Mercury, 3. 56; plurality of Pans, 3. 43
Panaetius of Rhodes (*c.*185–109), Stoic
  philosopher, Introd. VI; questions
  Stoic doctrine of cyclic destruction,
  2. 118
Papirius Carbo, C. (consul 120),
  depicted as villain, 1. 63
Papirius Maso, C. (consul 231),
  dedicates temple to Fons, 3. 52
Papirius Paetus, L., Epicurean friend of
  Cicero, Introd. I

Parmenides of Elea (b. *c*.515), Presocratic philosopher; his notion of God, 1. 28

Pasiphae, daughter of Perseis and the Sun, 3. 48

Paulus *see* Aemilius

Peducaeus, Sex. (tribune 113), indicts Vestal Virgins for unchastity, 3. 74

Pelion, Mt., provided timber for the Argo, 3. 75

Peloponnese visited by Dionysius, 3. 83

Pelops, father of Atreus, 3. 53

Penates, household gods, 2. 68

Penelope, mother of Pan, 3. 56

Peripatetics, school founded by Aristotle, Introd. VII; relation to Stoicism, 1. 16

Persaeus (*c*.306–243), pupil of Zeno the Stoic, deifies heroes and their discoveries, 1. 38

Perseis, daughter of Oceanus and consort of the Sun, 3. 48

Persephone, Greek counterpart of Proserpina, carried off to Hades by Dis; symbol of corn-seed, 3. 66

Perseus, king of Macedon (*c*.213–166), defeated in Third Macedonian War and imprisoned, 2. 6

Perseus, constellation called after slayer of Medusa and rescuer of Andromeda, 2. 112

Petrarch (1304–74), first Italian humanist, Introd. IX

Phaedo, pupil of Socrates, 1. 93

Phaedrus (*c*.140–70), quick-tempered Epicurean, 1. 93

Phaethon, son of Apollo, disastrously entrusted with the solar chariot, 3. 76

Phalaris, tyrant of Acragas in Sicily (*c*.570–*c*.550); his legendary cruelty, 3. 82

Pharsalus, battle (48 BC) in Thessaly, Introd. I

Pheneus, town in Arcadia, 3. 56

Philo of Larissa (160–80), head of the Academy, Introd. I, IV, VII; teacher of Cicero, 1. 6; and of Balbus, 1. 17; advises Cotta to attend Zeno the Epicurean's lectures, 1. 59; critical of

Epicureans for rejecting degenerate pleasures, 1. 113

Philodemus, Epicurean philosopher contemporary with Cicero, Introd. IV, V

Phoenician sailors, 2. 106

Phormio, character in Terence's play, 3. 73

Phoronis, parent of Mercury, 3. 56

Phrygian writings, 3. 42

Pierides, set of Muses, 3. 54

Pisistratus, tyrant of Athens 561–527, 3. 82

Piso *see* Pupius

Plaetorius, tribune before 192, introduces bill protecting minors from fraud, 3. 74

Plato (*c*.429–347), Introd. VIII, IX; theology of, 1. 19 f., 68; claims sphere to be most perfect figure, 1. 24; uncle of Speusippus, 1. 32; teacher of Aristotle, 1. 33; school of, 1. 34; teacher of Pamphilus, 1. 72; contradicted by Epicureans, 1. 93; 'the divine philosopher', his views on motion, 2. 32; his account of Socrates' death, 3. 82; also 1. 107
    Laws, 1. 30
    Republic, Introd. II, VIII
    Timaeus, 1. 18, 30

Pleasure (Voluptas), deified, 2. 61

Pleiades (constellation), 2. 112

Ploughman, *see* Arctophylax

Plutarch, Middle Platonist and biographer, Introd. I

Pluto, Greek counterpart of Roman Dis, 2. 66

Poggio Bracciolini (1380–1459), Italian humanist, Introd. IX

Polemarchus, host in Plato's *Republic*, Introd. VIII

Pollux, one of the Dioscuri, a deified human, 2. 62; epiphany at Lake Regillus, 2. 6; temple of, in the Roman forum, 3. 13

Porcius Cato, M., the Censor (234–149), spokesman in the *De senectute*, Introd. II; leading senator in 168 BC, 3. 11; also 2. 165

Porcius Cato Uticensis, M. (95–46), Introd. II

Portunus, divine protector of harbours, 2. 66

Posidonius of Apamea (*c*.135–*c*.50), Stoic philosopher, Introd. I, IV, VI; teacher of Cicero, 1. 6; claims Epicurus to be an atheist, 1. 123; his orrery, 2. 88

Postumius Regillensis, A., dictator at battle of Lake Regillus, 2. 6; 3. 11; dedicates temple to Dioscuri, 3. 13

Poteat, H. M., translator of *The Nature of the Gods*, l

Procyon, star in constellation Canis Minor, 2. 114

Prodicus of Ceos, sophist, argues that gods are benefits personified, 1. 118

Pronoia, the Stoic deity, 1. 18, 20, 22; 2. 58

Proserpina, Roman counterpart of Persephone, married to Dis, 2. 66; daughter of Aether, 3. 53; excites Mercury sexually, 3. 56; mother of Diana, 3. 58; shrine of, at Locri, 3. 83

Protagoras of Abdera (*c*.485–415), noted sophist, Introd. VIII; agnostic about the gods, 1. 2, 29, 63, 117

Pupius Piso, M., Peripatetic friend of Cicero, Introd. I; 1. 16

Pyriphlegethon, stream in Hades, 3. 43

Pyrrho of Elis (*c*.365–275), founder of the Sceptics, Introd. VIII

Pyrrhus of Epirus (319–272), wars with Rome in Italy, 2. 165

Pythagoras/Pythagoreans, unchanging doctrines of, 1. 10; on the world soul and individual souls, 1. 27; deliberate obscurity of utterances, 1. 74; contradicted by Epicurus, 1. 93; music of the spheres, 3. 27; refuses to offer blood-sacrifice, 3. 88; also 1. 107

Quirinus, believed identical with Romulus, 3. 62

Rackham, H., translator of *The Nature of the Gods*, l

Ram (Aries), constellation, 2. 111, 114

Ramus, Peter (1515–72), French humanist, Introd. IX

Reate, Sabine town (modern Rieti), 2. 6

Regillus, Lake, scene of battle of 496, 2. 6; 3. 11

Regulus *see* Atilius

Rhodes, Cicero in, Introd. I; birthplace of the Sun, 3. 54

River (Eridanus), constellation, 2. 114

Romulus, legendary founder of Rome, Introd. IX; as human benefactor deified, 2. 62; 3. 39; founds the state by taking auspices, 3. 5; also 1. 107

Roscius Gallus, Q., handsome Roman actor and friend of Cicero, verses penned in his honour by Catulus, 1. 79

Ross, J. M., contributor to H. C. P. McGregor's translation, l

Rousseau, Jean-Jacques (1712–78), French Deist, Introd. IX

Rutilius Rufus, P., Stoic philosopher and acquaintance of Cicero, Introd. I; exiled to Smyrna, 3. 80; his estate at Formiae, 3. 86

Sabazian festival, instituted to honour Dionysus, 3. 58

Safety (Salus) deified, 2. 61; 3. 61

Sagra *fl.*, river in southern Italy, 2. 6; 3. 11, 13

Sais, city in the Nile Delta, 3. 59

Salaria via, road from area of Ostia to Rome, 3. 11

Salutati Coluccio, Italian humanist, Introd. IX

Samos, residence of Epicurus in his early days, 1. 72

Samothrace, island in north-eastern Aegean, centre of mystery-cult, 1. 119; Diagoras at, 3. 89

Saturn, Roman god; mutilates his father Caelus, 2. 65; 3. 62; this myth as symbolic, 2. 64; equated with Greek Kronos, 2. 64; etymology, 2. 64; 3. 62; greatly revered in West, 3. 44; father of Cretan Jupiter, 3. 53; imprisoned by him, 3. 62

Saturn, planet furthest from earth, 2. 52; and coldest, 2. 119

Satyrs, spirits of rustic life, 3. 43

Scaevola *see* Mucius

Sceptics, Introd. VII

Scipio *see* Cornelius

Scipionic Gardens, 2. 11

Scorpion (Nepa, Scorpio), constellation, 2. 109, 113 f.; accounted a god, 3. 40

Scylla, sea-monster facing Charybdis; non-existent, 1. 108

Scythia, 2. 88

Semele, mother of Liber/Dionysus, 2. 62

Sempronius Gracchus, Ti. (consul 177, 163), father of the Gracchi, 2. 10 f., 165

Sempronius Gracchus, Ti. (tribune 133), revolutionary reformer, 1. 106

Sempronius Tuditanus, C. (consul 129), 2. 14

Serapis, Egyptian deity sometimes identified with Osiris, 3. 47

Seriphus, isolated island in the Cyclades, 1. 88

Serpent (Draco, Anguis), constellation, 2. 106 f.

Serpent-holder (Ophiuchus, Anguitenens), constellation, 2. 108 f.

Servatus Lupus, abbot of Ferrières, Introd. IX

Shaftesbury, Earl of, l

She-goat (Capra), constellation, 3. 40

Sibyl/Sibylline prophecies, 2. 10; 3. 5

Sicilian strait, 3. 24

Sicily, Introd. I, VIII; 3. 55

Sickness (Morbus), deified, 3. 44

Sillis (doubtful name), 1. 93

Silvanus, Italian god of the woodland, identified with Pan, 2. 89

Simonides of Ceos (*c.*556–468), Greek lyric and elegiac poet, at Hiero's court, 1. 60

Smyrna, Introd. I

Socrates (469–399), Introd. II; originator of dialectic, 1. 11; statements about God, 1. 31; teacher of Phaedo, 1. 93; on the source of human intelligence, 2. 18, 3. 27; as 'prince of philosophy' on the fruits of virtue, 2. 167; his death as recorded by Plato, 3. 82

Sosius, O., arsonist, 3. 74

Spain, tides around, 3. 24; Scipios defeated there, 3. 80

Sparta/Spartans, 2. 154, 165; Dioscuri buried there, 3. 11; constitution established by Lycurgus, 3. 91

Speusippus (*c.*407–339), nephew and successor of Plato in the Academy; his idea of God, 1. 32

Spino, *fl.*, stream in neighbourhood of Rome, 3. 52

Stickney, Austin, translator of *The Nature of the Gods*, l

Stoics/Stoicism, Introd. III, VI and *passim*

Strato of Lampsacus, head of Peripatetics *c.*287–269, called the Physicist, 1. 35

Stratonicus of Athens (*fl. c.*410–360), musician and wit, 3. 50

Syracuse, 3. 83

Syria, 3. 59

Syrians, 1. 81; superstitious worship by, 3. 39

Tantalus, father of Pelops and grandfather of Atreus and Thyestes, 3. 90

Teiresias, legendary blind prophet of Thebes, 3. 7

Telamon, hero in drama of Ennius who laments death of his son Ajax, 3. 79

Tellus, deity of the earth, 3. 52

Tenedos, island off the coast of the Troad, 3. 39

Tenes, eponymous hero of Tenedos and son of Apollo, 3. 39

Terence (*c.*190–*c.*159), Latin playwright, Introd. VIII
    Eunuch, 2. 60; 3. 72

Terentius Varro, M. (116–27 BC), wide-ranging scholar and antiquarian, Introd. III, IV, VIII

Tertullian, Christian apologist: *Apology* (197 AD), Introd. IX

Thales, founder of Western science, says water is the first principle, 1. 25; also 1. 91

Thaumas, father of Iris, 3. 51

Thelxinoe, one of the first set of Muses,
3. 54

Theodorus of Cyrene (b. before 340),
notorious atheist, 1. 2, 63, 117

Theophrastus (c.370–288), successor of
Aristotle as head of Peripatetics,
Introd. 1: his inconsistent theology,
1. 35; refuted by Leontium, 1. 93

Theseus, Athenian hero, causes death of
son Hippolytus, 3. 76

Theuth, Egyptian counterpart of
Mercury, 3. 56

Thyestes, son of Pelops and brother of
Atreus whose wife he suborned,
3. 68

Thyone, mother of Dionysus, 3. 58

Tiber, *fl.* 3. 52

Timaeus of Tauromenium (c.356–260),
historian of Sicily, 2. 69

Timocrates, brother of Metrodorus,
attacked by Epicurus, 1. 93; by
Metrodorus, 1. 113

Titan, the sun, 2. 112; Titans, their war
with the Giants, 2. 70

Tmolus, one of the third set of Dioscuri,
3. 53

Toil (Labor) deified, 3. 44

Toulouse, sacked during the Cimbrian
war, 3. 74

Trasimene, Lake, scene of Roman defeat
in 217 by Hannibal, 2. 8

Triton, merman, 1. 78; in Accius' *Medea*,
2. 69

Tritopatreus, one of first set of Dioscuri,
3. 53

Trophonius, Prehellenic chthonic deity,
3. 49; identified with Mercury, 3. 56

Tubulus *see* Hostilius

Tuditanus *see* Sempronius

Tullia, daughter of Cicero, Introd. 11; *see
also* 1. 9

Tullius Cicero, Q. (praetor 62), brother
of Cicero, Introd. 11

Tullus Hostilius, third Roman king, 2. 9

Tusculan Disputations, Introd. 11

Tusculum, provenance of Octavius
Mamilius, 2. 6

Twins (Gemini), constellation, 2. 110,
114

Tyndareus, husband of Leda and
putative father of Dioscuri, 2. 6; 3. 11,
39

Tyre, centre of worship of Hercules,
3. 42

Ulysses, hero in Homer, 2. 166; meets
Hercules in Hades, 3. 41

Upis, father of Diana, 3. 58

Valens, father of Mercury, 3. 56

Valla, Lorenzo, Italian humanist:
De voluptate, (1431), Introd. 1x

Varius Hybrida, Q., (tribune 90), his
iniquities and his painful end, 3. 81

Varro *see* Terentius

Vatinius, P., judiciary prefect at Reate
(168); encounters the Dioscuri, and
transmits their report to the senate,
2. 6; 3. 11, 13

Veiovis, ancient Italian deity, 3. 62

Velleius, C., Epicurean spokesman in
the dialogue, Introd. 1v, v111, and
passim

Venus, Italian goddess identified with
Aphrodite; etymology, 2. 69; 3. 62;
mother of Cupid, 3. 60; various
identities of, 3. 59 f.; statue of, at Cos,
1. 75

Venus, planet, 2.53

Vesta, Roman hearth-goddess,
counterpart of Greek Hestia, 2. 67;
dismissed as deity by Stoic Zeno, 1. 36;
her province, 2. 67; statue of, 3. 80

Victory (Victoria), deified, 2. 61; 3. 61

Virgo, constellation, 2. 110

Virtue (Virtus), deified, 2. 79; 3. 61;
temples of, 2. 61; 3. 88

Vives, Juan Luis (1492–1540), Spanish
humanist, Introd. 1x

Volcanian islands, 3. 55

Voltaire (1694–1778), French writer,
Introd. 1x

Vulcan, Italian fire-god, counterpart of
Greek Hephaestus, representations of,
1. 81; statue by Alcamenes, 1. 83;
different names for, 1. 84; father of
Apollo the Sun, 3. 54, 57; spouse of

Venus, 3. 59; uncertain etymology of,
3. 62; various identities of, 3. 55
Wealth (Ops), deified, 2. 61
wine-bowl (Cratera), constellation,
2. 114

Xenocrates, disciple of Plato and head of
Academy 339–314, 1. 72
The Nature of the Gods, 1. 34
Xenophanes of Colophon (*c.*570–478),
poet and philosopher, deifies the
world, 1. 28
Xenophon (*c.*428–*c.*354), historian and
philosopher, Introd. ix
Memorabilia, 1. 31; 2. 18; 3. 27
Symposium, Introd. viii
Xerxes, king of Persia 486–465, destroys
temples, 1. 115

Yonge, C. D., translator of *The Nature of
the Gods*, l

Zeno of Citium (335–263), founder of
Stoicism, Introd. vi; his theology,
1. 36; teacher of Aristo, 1. 37; of
Persaeus, 1. 38; on sense-data, 1. 70;
syllogisms in, 2. 20 ff.; 3. 18, 22 f., 25;
definition of nature in, 2. 57 f.; 3. 27;
rationalizes mythology, 2. 63; 3. 63;
rejected as religious authority, 3. 5;
also 3. 77
Zeno of Elea (b. *c.*490), pupil of
Parmenides; death under torture, 3. 82
Zeno of Sidon (b. *c.*150), Epicurean
philosopher, Introd. i, iv; his lectures
attended by Cotta, 1. 59; his abuse of
contemporaries, and of Socrates and
Chrysippus, 1. 93

*The
Oxford
World's
Classics
Website*

www.worldsclassics.co.uk

- Browse the full range of Oxford World's Classics online

- Sign up for our monthly e-alert to receive information on new titles

- Read extracts from the Introductions

- Listen to our editors and translators talk about the world's greatest literature with our Oxford World's Classics audio guides

- Join the conversation, follow us on Twitter at OWC_Oxford

- Teachers and lecturers can order inspection copies quickly and simply via our website

www.worldsclassics.co.uk